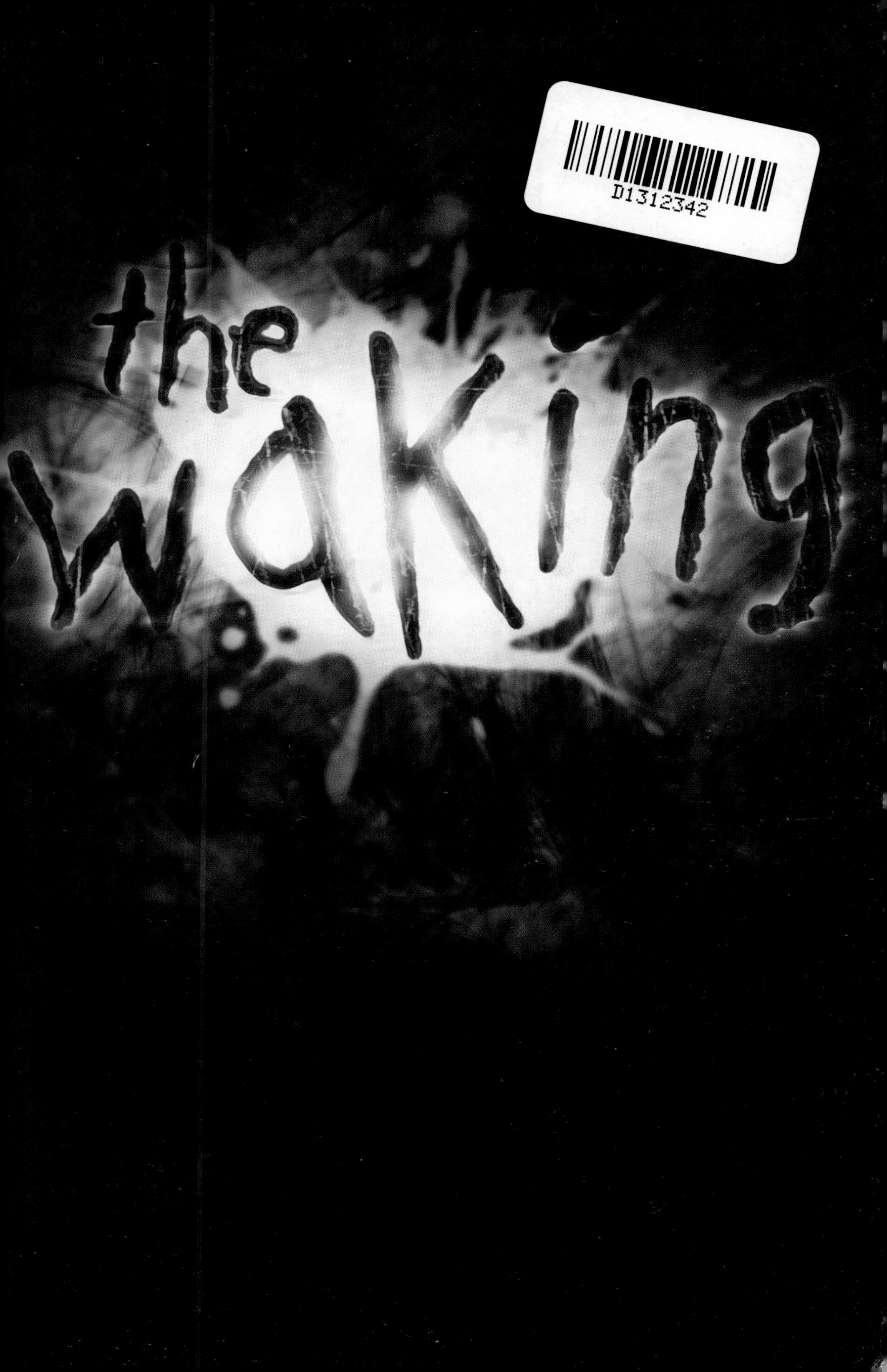
the waking

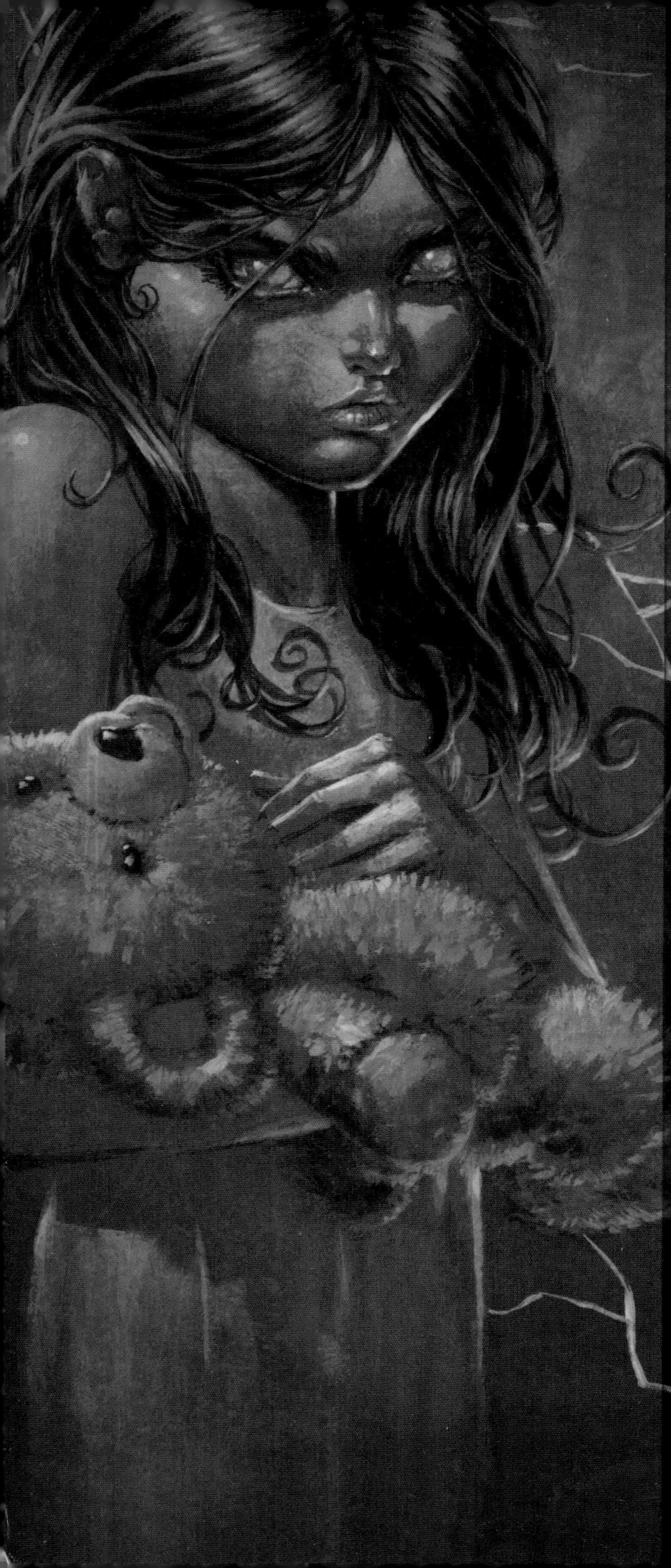

THE WAKING

Created and Written by
Raven Gregory

Pencils by
Vic Drujiniu

Colors by
Mark Roberts

Letters by
Crank!

Layout Assistance by
Marlin Shoop
(Part One pages 1-5, 7, 13-15, 20, 24)
(Part Two pages 1, 2, 4-6, 16, 18, 22)

Trade Design by
Christopher Cote
David Seidman

Trade Edited by
Ralph Tedesco

Consulting Colors Editor
Renae Geerlings

Special Thanks to
Dorian Green

This volume reprints the comic series THE WAKING, issues #1-4 published by Zenescope Entertainment.

www.zenescope.com

First Edition, DECEMBER 2010
ISBN: 978-0-9827507-5-9

The Waking trade paperback, December, 2010. First Printing. Published by Zenescope Entertainment Inc., 501 Office Center Drive, Ste. 8, Fort Washington, Pennsylvania 19034.

the waking

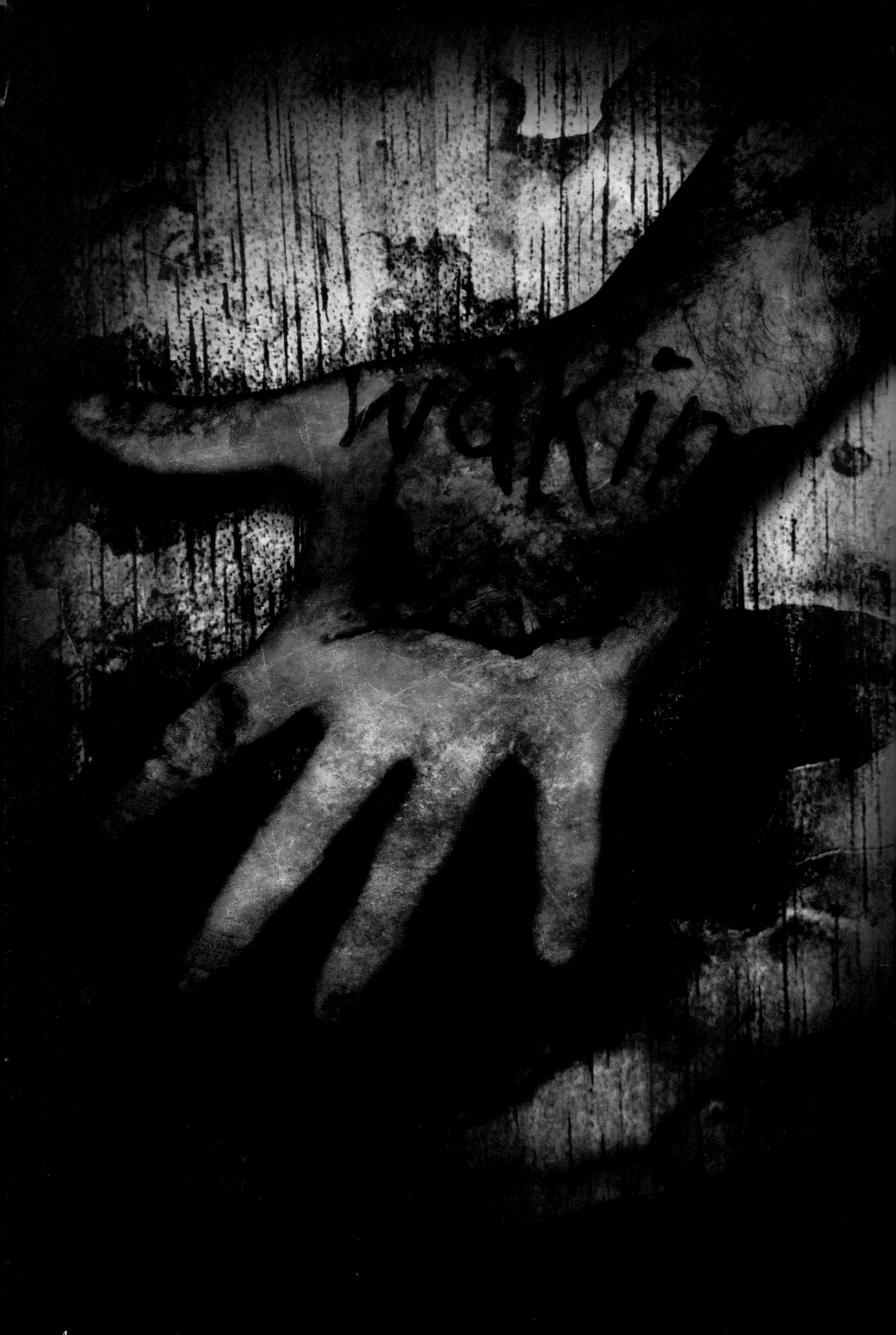
wakin

When Raven Gregory first pitched the idea of *The Waking* to us over here at Zenescope, I'd be lying if I said I wasn't skeptical. I mean another zombie series, are you kidding me? *The Walking Dead* was already in around the 50th issue landmark and was in pre-production as a TV series (an excellent one at that). Max Brooks had *World War Z* on shelves and selling big. We all had seen the dozen or more zombie movies and remakes crop up in the last decade. I mean this craze was sure to end, wasn't it? Well not so much.

When I first read *The Waking*, it was in PDF form on my laptop screen, partially colored and the rest simply in pencils and layouts with lettering crudely layered in there. But it didn't matter because I was immediately hooked within only a few pages. It was so much different than all the other zombie stories I had read or seen. And don't get me wrong, I love *The Walking Dead* and I loved *Dawn of the Dead* and *28 Days Later* and all of those just like them. But Raven's comic wasn't your traditional post-apocalyptic, zombies killing everyone they see, story. This was part *Pet Sematary*, part *Se7en*; it was part comedy, part suspense, part drama. It was a smart, interwoven combination of genres that hadn't been done or even attempted before. And the one thing that really stood out to me, at the center of it all, was the simple yet powerful theme: A father's love for his daughter. Here was a complex and layered story with great characters and twists that managed to put a fresh, new spin on zombie mythology and the main theme at the core of it all was something that almost anyone reading this can relate to in one way or another. And it could only have been told effectively from the point of view of a father; and Raven delivered.

I'm certainly not here to review *The Waking*; that might be deemed just a tad biased. But the important thing to remember when sitting down to read this story is certainly not what I or anyone else thought or thinks of it because frankly that doesn't matter. Read this story because it has a heartbeat unlike any other horror story in comics and in film. And the reason is because it isn't a horror story. It doesn't fall solely into that genre. This is a new genre altogether and Mr. Gregory figured that out before he put pen to paper and delivered a graphic novel so powerful and touching that I knew within five minutes that we would be putting it on shelves and that I'd be damn proud to have *The Waking* be part of the Zenescope label.

Ralph Tedesco
Editor-in-Chief
Zenescope Entertainment

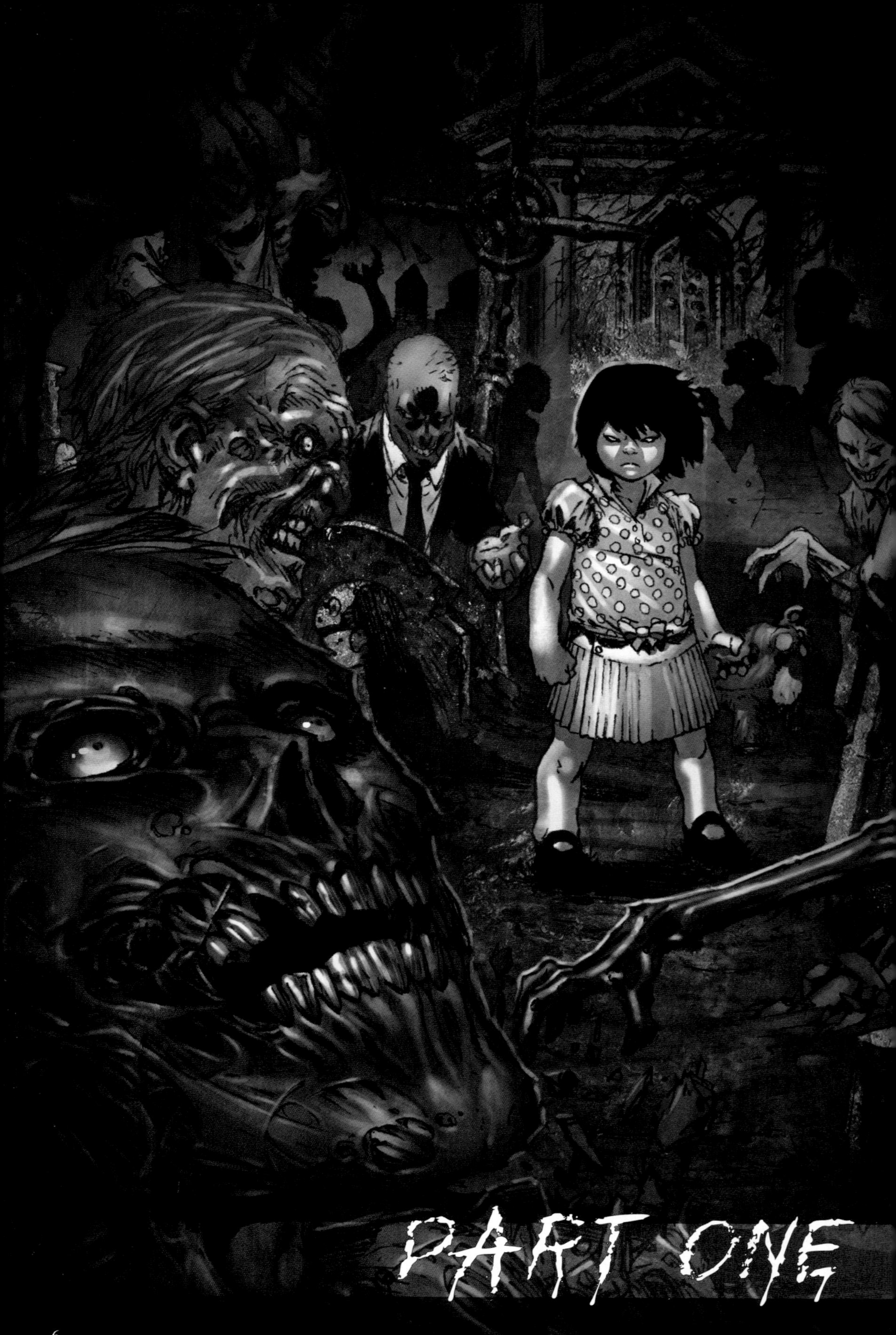
PART ONE

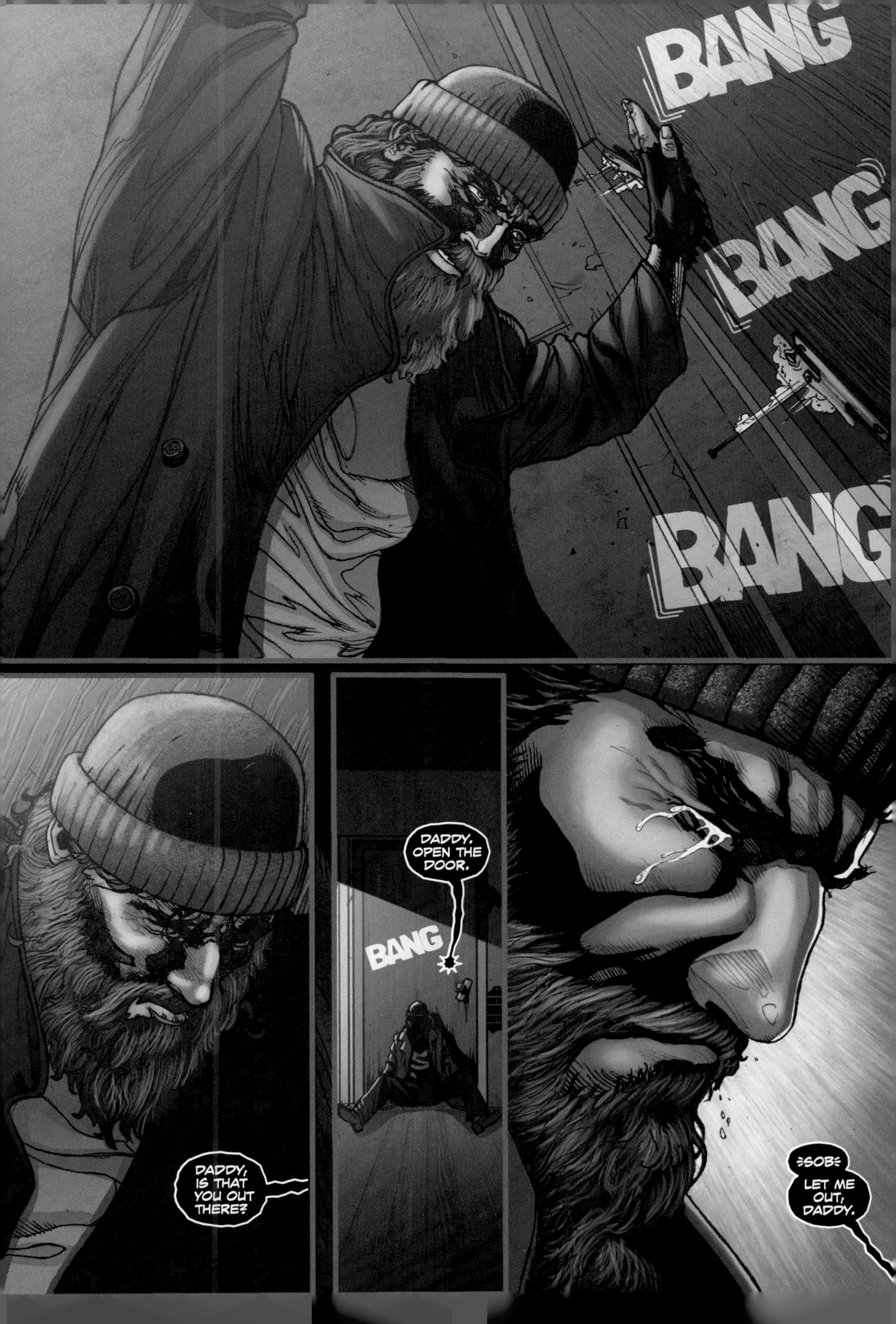
BANG
BANG
BANG
DADDY, IS THAT YOU OUT THERE?
DADDY. OPEN THE DOOR.
BANG
SOB
LET ME OUT, DADDY.

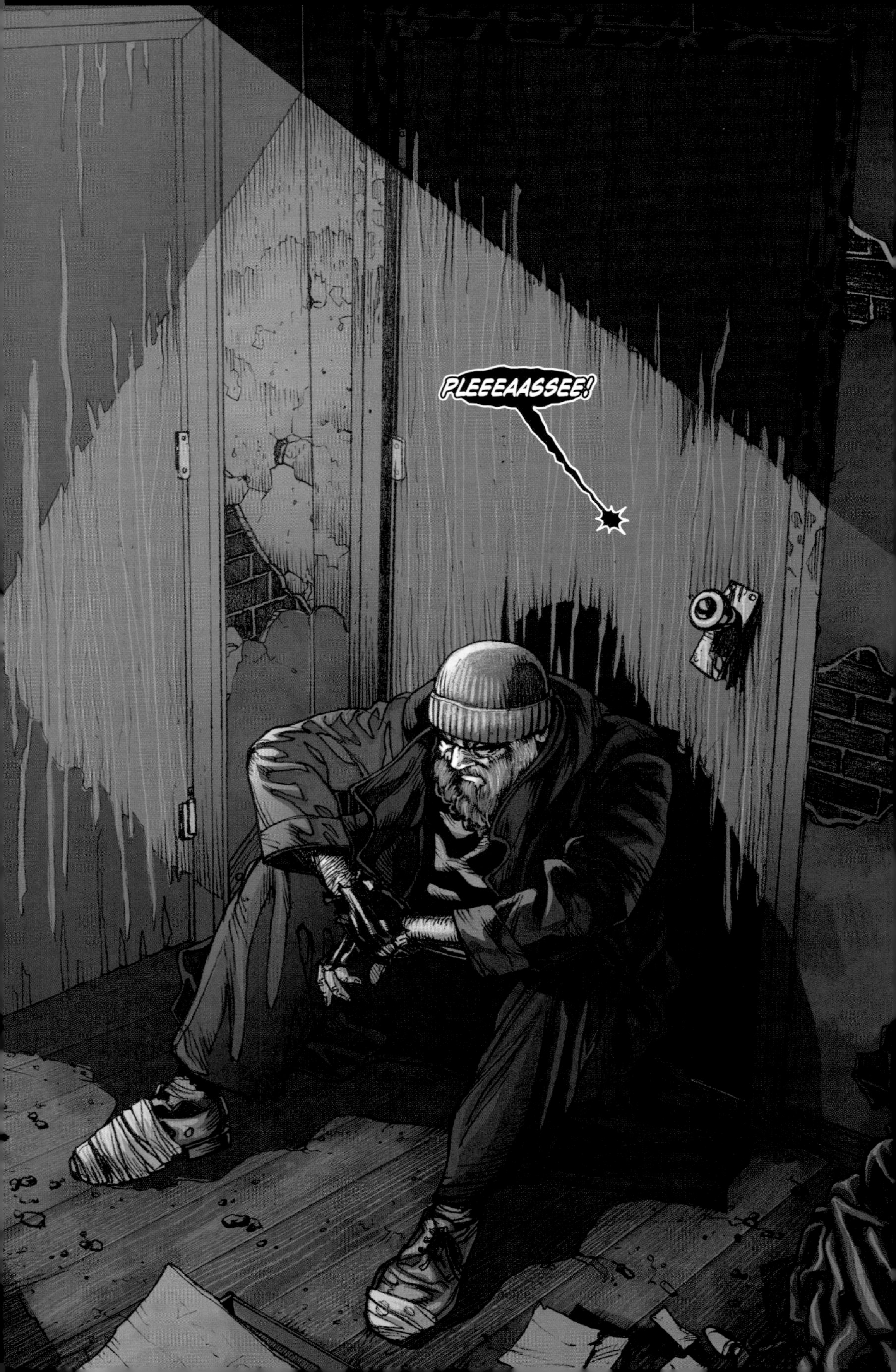
PLEEEAASSEE!

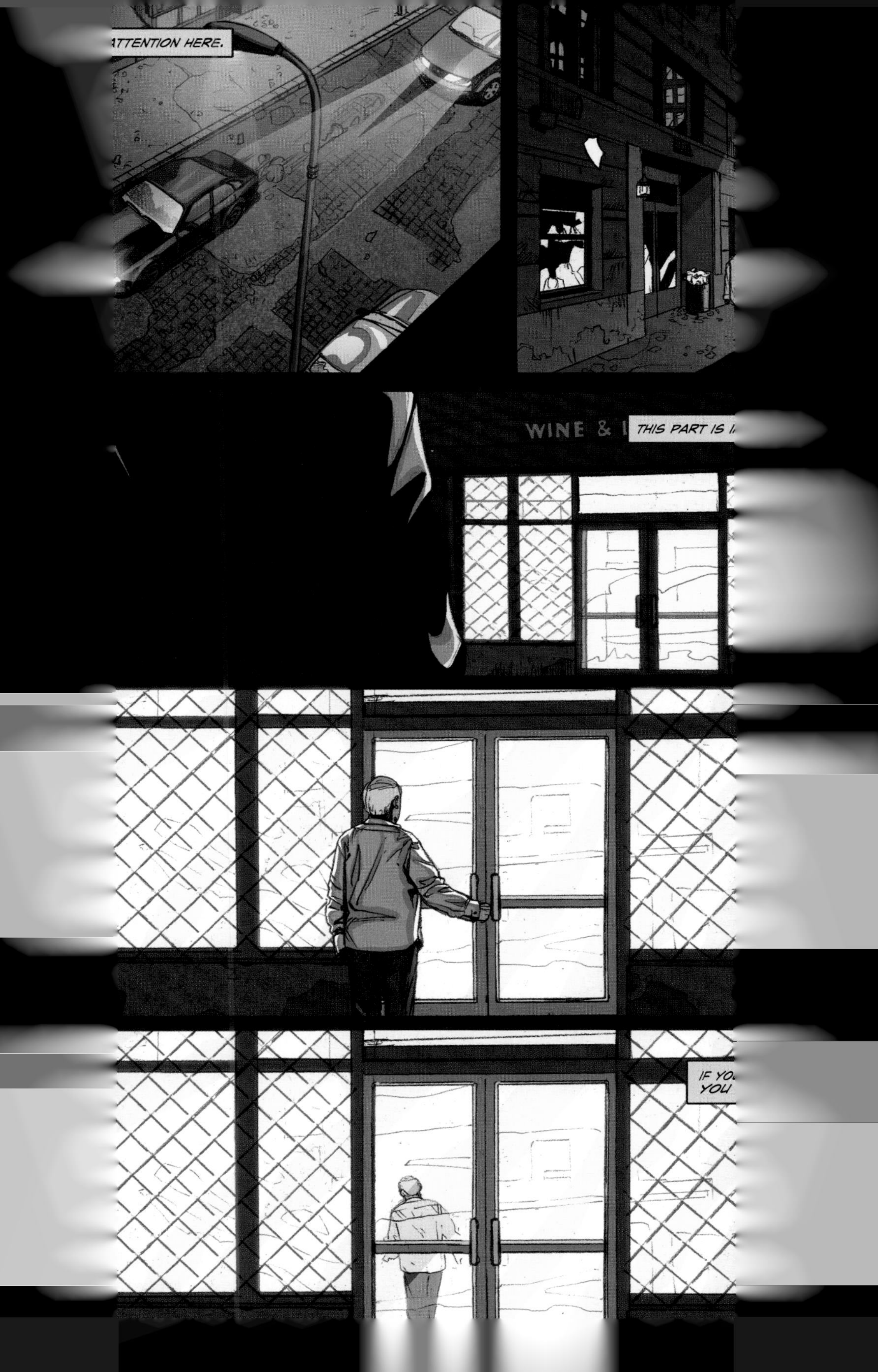
ATTENTION HERE.
WINE & L
THIS PART IS I
IF YO
YOU

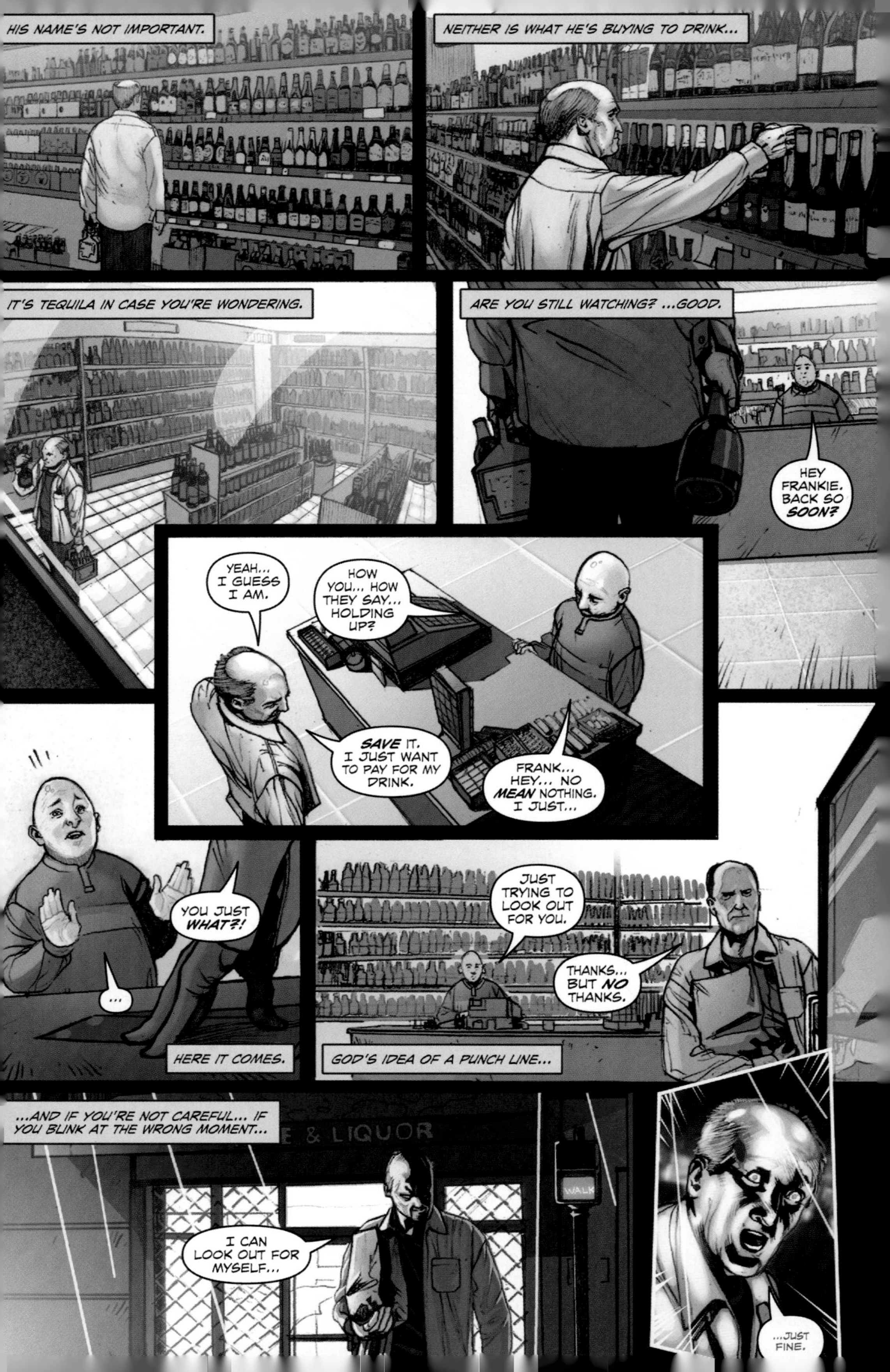
HIS NAME'S NOT IMPORTANT.
NEITHER IS WHAT HE'S BUYING TO DRINK...
IT'S TEQUILA IN CASE YOU'RE WONDERING.
ARE YOU STILL WATCHING? ...GOOD.
HEY FRANKIE. BACK SO SOON?
YEAH... I GUESS I AM.
HOW YOU... HOW THEY SAY... HOLDING UP?
SAVE IT. I JUST WANT TO PAY FOR MY DRINK.
FRANK... HEY... NO MEAN NOTHING. I JUST...
YOU JUST WHAT?!
...
HERE IT COMES.
JUST TRYING TO LOOK OUT FOR YOU.
THANKS... BUT NO THANKS.
GOD'S IDEA OF A PUNCH LINE...
...AND IF YOU'RE NOT CAREFUL... IF YOU BLINK AT THE WRONG MOMENT...
E & LIQUOR
WALK
I CAN LOOK OUT FOR MYSELF...
...JUST FINE.

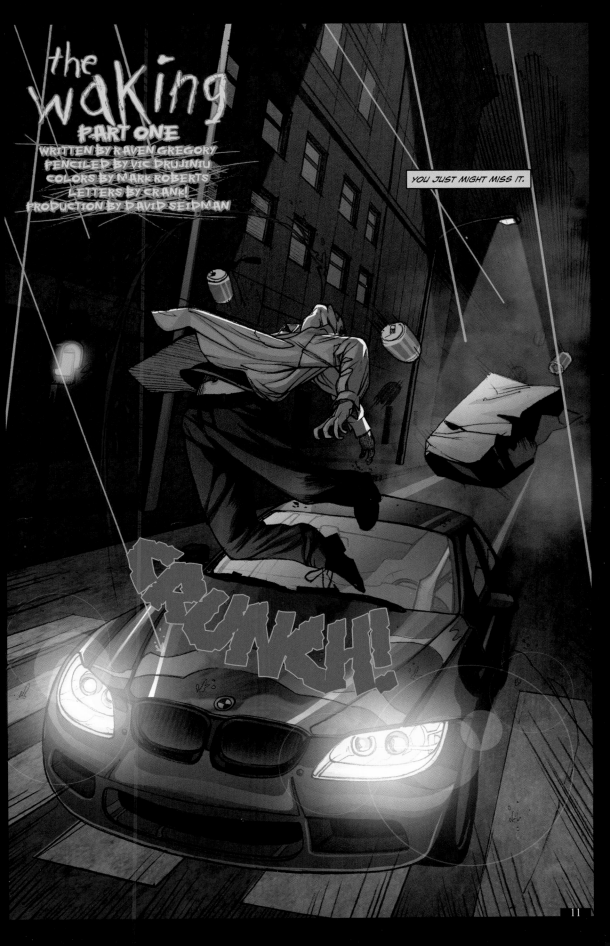

the waking
PART ONE
WRITTEN BY RAVEN GREGORY
PENCILED BY VIC DRUJINIU
COLORS BY MARK ROBERTS
LETTERS BY CRANK!
PRODUCTION BY DAVID SEIDMAN

YOU JUST MIGHT MISS IT.

CRUNCH!

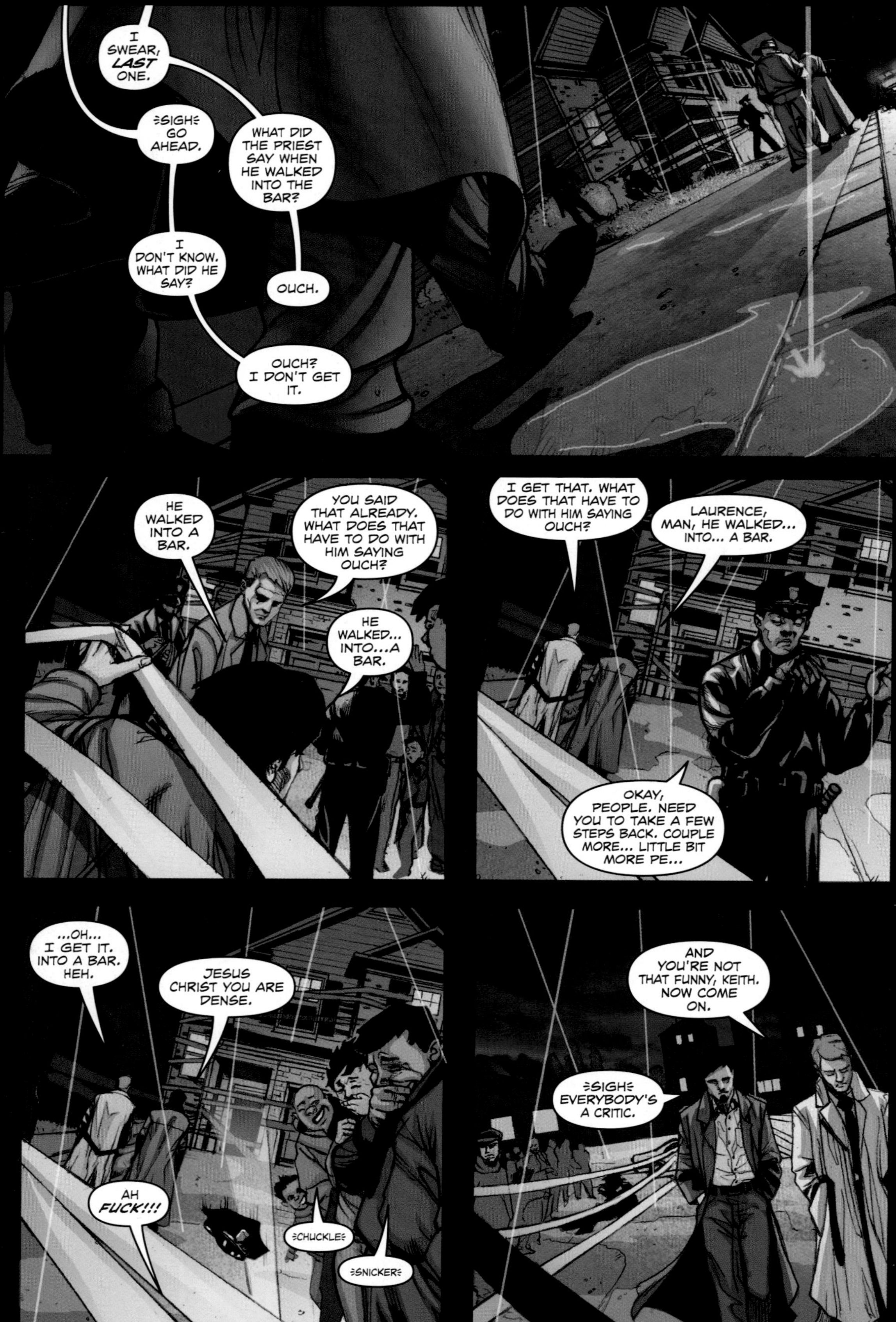
I SWEAR, LAST ONE.
⋮SIGH⋮ GO AHEAD.
WHAT DID THE PRIEST SAY WHEN HE WALKED INTO THE BAR?
I DON'T KNOW. WHAT DID HE SAY?
OUCH.
OUCH? I DON'T GET IT.
HE WALKED INTO A BAR.
YOU SAID THAT ALREADY. WHAT DOES THAT HAVE TO DO WITH HIM SAYING OUCH?
HE WALKED... INTO...A BAR.
I GET THAT. WHAT DOES THAT HAVE TO DO WITH HIM SAYING OUCH?
LAURENCE, MAN, HE WALKED... INTO... A BAR.
OKAY, PEOPLE. NEED YOU TO TAKE A FEW STEPS BACK. COUPLE MORE... LITTLE BIT MORE PE...
...OH... I GET IT. INTO A BAR. HEH.
JESUS CHRIST YOU ARE DENSE.
AH FUCK!!!
⋮CHUCKLE⋮
⋮SNICKER⋮
AND YOU'RE NOT THAT FUNNY, KEITH. NOW COME ON.
⋮SIGH⋮ EVERYBODY'S A CRITIC.

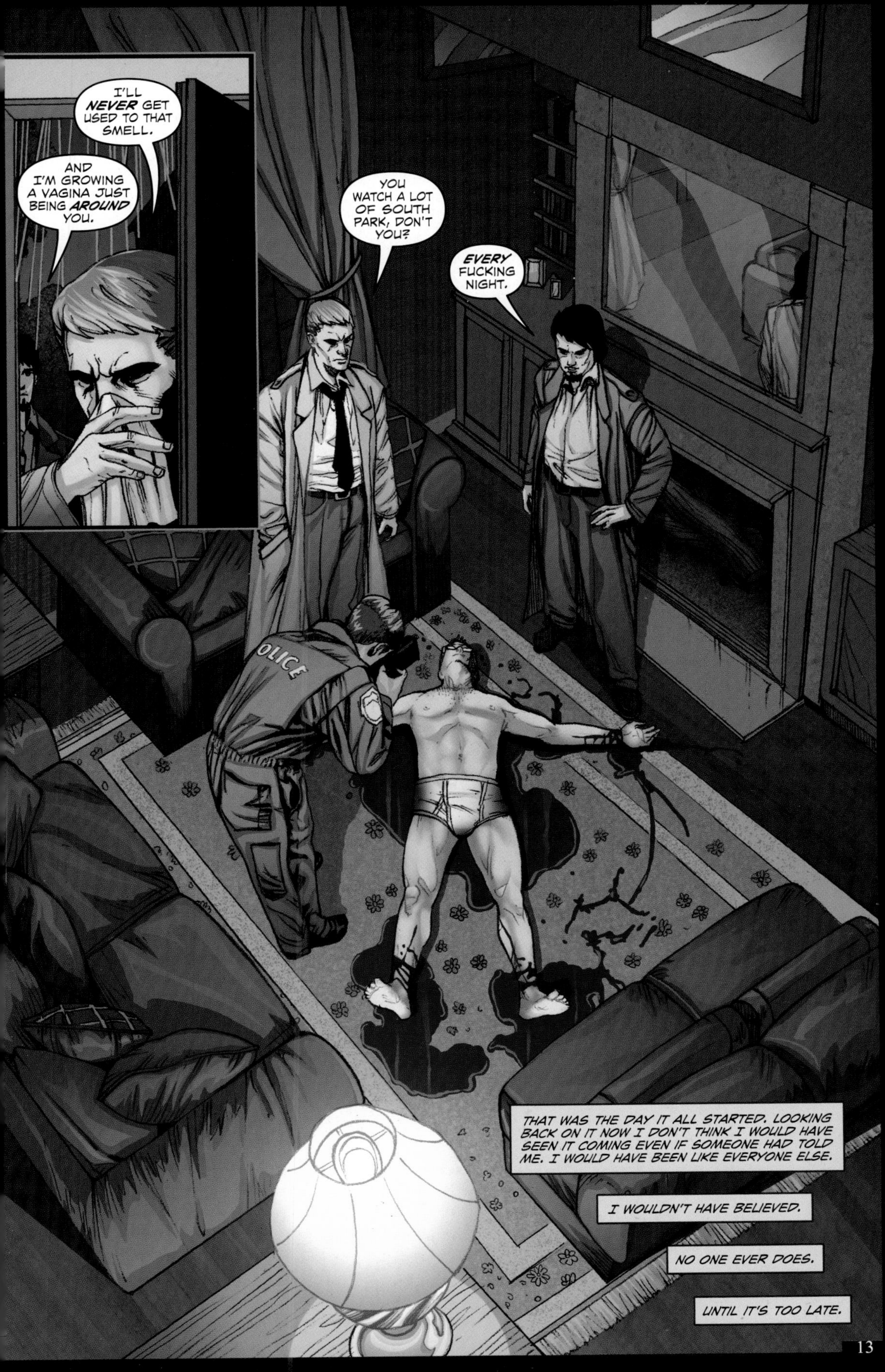
I'LL **NEVER** GET USED TO THAT SMELL.
AND I'M GROWING A VAGINA JUST BEING **AROUND** YOU.
YOU WATCH A LOT OF SOUTH PARK, DON'T YOU?
EVERY FUCKING NIGHT.
OLICE
THAT WAS THE DAY IT ALL STARTED. LOOKING BACK ON IT NOW I DON'T THINK I WOULD HAVE SEEN IT COMING EVEN IF SOMEONE HAD TOLD ME. I WOULD HAVE BEEN LIKE EVERYONE ELSE.
I WOULDN'T HAVE BELIEVED.
NO ONE EVER DOES.
UNTIL IT'S TOO LATE.

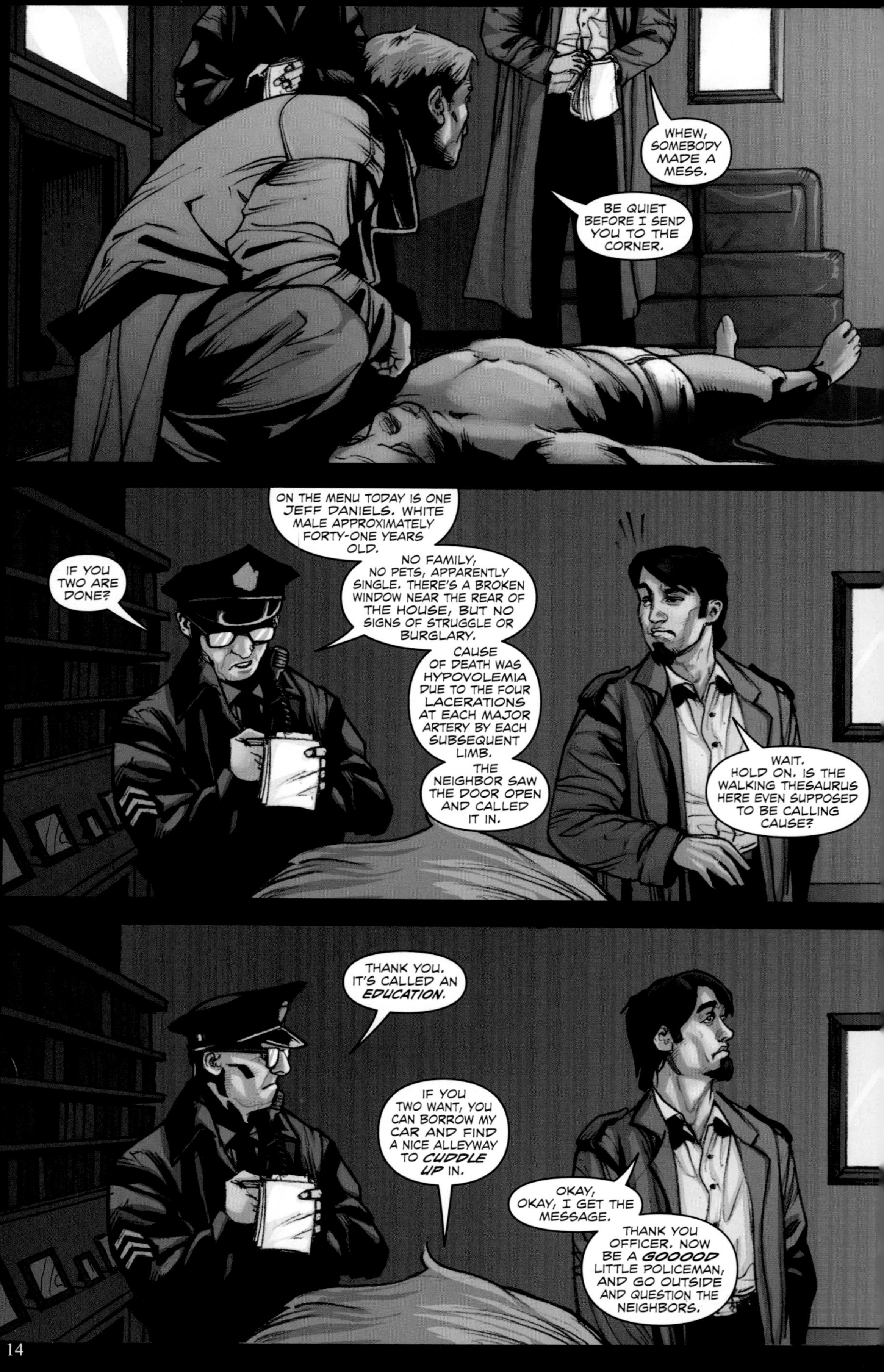
WHEW, SOMEBODY MADE A MESS.
BE QUIET BEFORE I SEND YOU TO THE CORNER.
IF YOU TWO ARE DONE?
ON THE MENU TODAY IS ONE JEFF DANIELS. WHITE MALE APPROXIMATELY FORTY-ONE YEARS OLD.
NO FAMILY, NO PETS, APPARENTLY SINGLE. THERE'S A BROKEN WINDOW NEAR THE REAR OF THE HOUSE, BUT NO SIGNS OF STRUGGLE OR BURGLARY.
CAUSE OF DEATH WAS HYPOVOLEMIA DUE TO THE FOUR LACERATIONS AT EACH MAJOR ARTERY BY EACH SUBSEQUENT LIMB.
THE NEIGHBOR SAW THE DOOR OPEN AND CALLED IT IN.
WAIT. HOLD ON. IS THE WALKING THESAURUS HERE EVEN SUPPOSED TO BE CALLING CAUSE?
THANK YOU. IT'S CALLED AN *EDUCATION*.
IF YOU TWO WANT, YOU CAN BORROW MY CAR AND FIND A NICE ALLEYWAY TO *CUDDLE UP* IN.
OKAY, OKAY, I GET THE MESSAGE.
THANK YOU OFFICER. NOW BE A *GOOOOD* LITTLE POLICEMAN, AND GO OUTSIDE AND QUESTION THE NEIGHBORS.

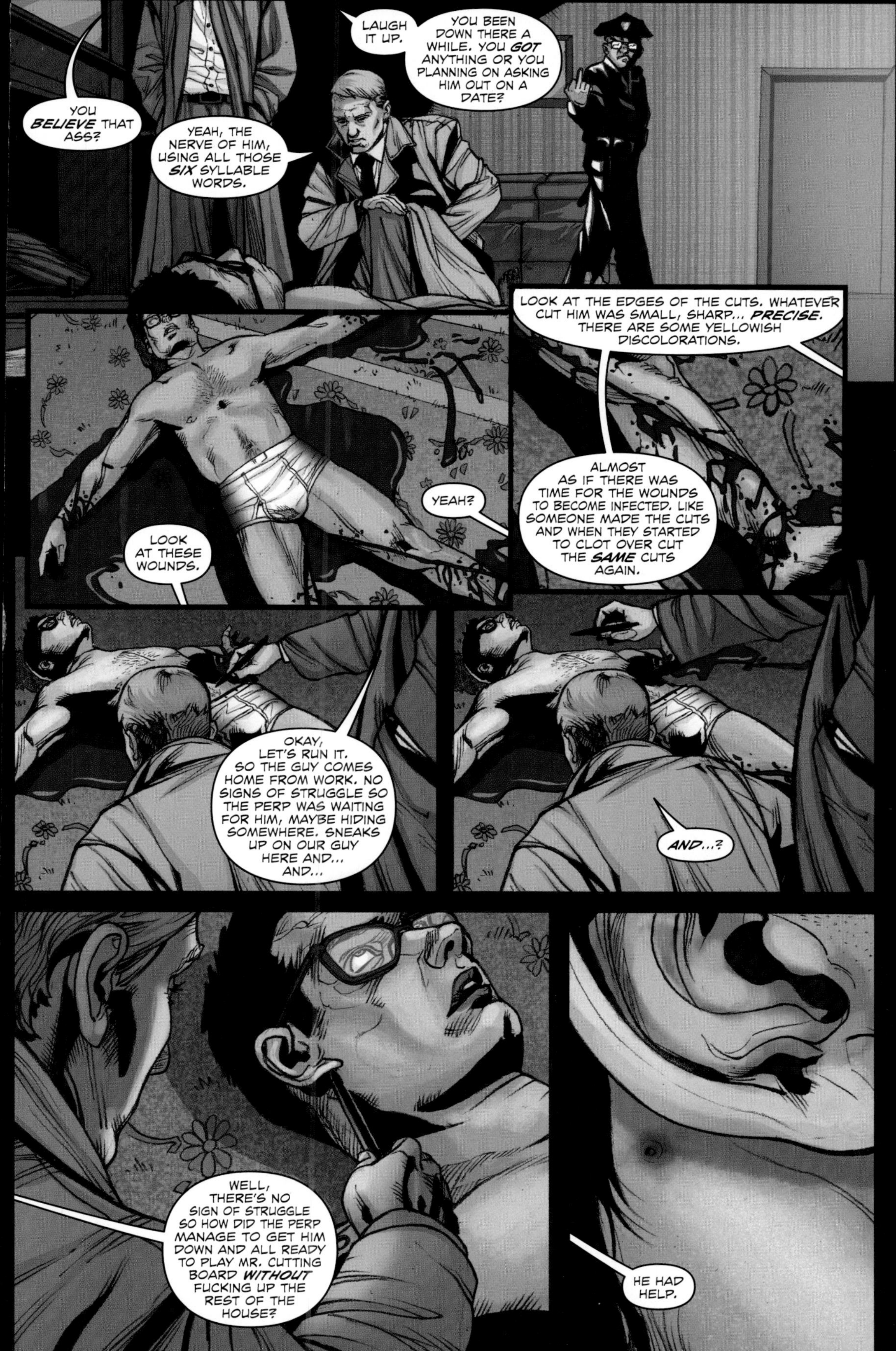

YOU BELIEVE THAT ASS?
YEAH, THE NERVE OF HIM, USING ALL THOSE SIX SYLLABLE WORDS.
LAUGH IT UP.
YOU BEEN DOWN THERE A WHILE. YOU GOT ANYTHING OR YOU PLANNING ON ASKING HIM OUT ON A DATE?
LOOK AT THESE WOUNDS.
YEAH?
LOOK AT THE EDGES OF THE CUTS. WHATEVER CUT HIM WAS SMALL, SHARP... PRECISE. THERE ARE SOME YELLOWISH DISCOLORATIONS.
ALMOST AS IF THERE WAS TIME FOR THE WOUNDS TO BECOME INFECTED. LIKE SOMEONE MADE THE CUTS AND WHEN THEY STARTED TO CLOT OVER CUT THE SAME CUTS AGAIN.
OKAY, LET'S RUN IT. SO THE GUY COMES HOME FROM WORK. NO SIGNS OF STRUGGLE SO THE PERP WAS WAITING FOR HIM, MAYBE HIDING SOMEWHERE. SNEAKS UP ON OUR GUY HERE AND... AND...
AND...?
WELL, THERE'S NO SIGN OF STRUGGLE SO HOW DID THE PERP MANAGE TO GET HIM DOWN AND ALL READY TO PLAY MR. CUTTING BOARD WITHOUT FUCKING UP THE REST OF THE HOUSE?
HE HAD HELP.

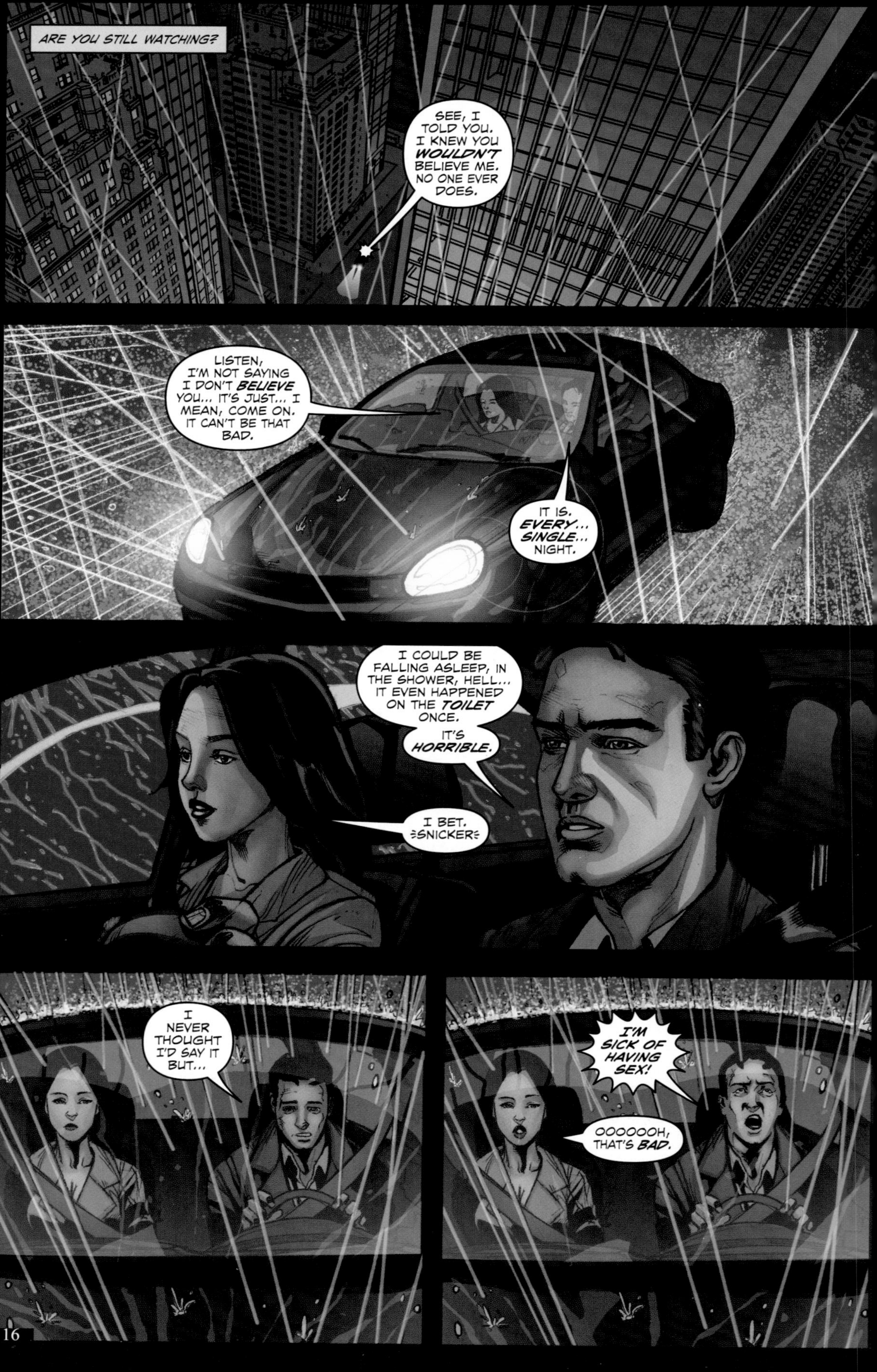
ARE YOU STILL WATCHING?
SEE, I TOLD YOU. I KNEW YOU WOULDN'T BELIEVE ME. NO ONE EVER DOES.
LISTEN, I'M NOT SAYING I DON'T BELIEVE YOU... IT'S JUST... I MEAN, COME ON. IT CAN'T BE THAT BAD.
IT IS. EVERY... SINGLE... NIGHT.
I COULD BE FALLING ASLEEP, IN THE SHOWER, HELL... IT EVEN HAPPENED ON THE TOILET ONCE.
IT'S HORRIBLE.
I BET. SNICKER
I NEVER THOUGHT I'D SAY IT BUT...
I'M SICK OF HAVING SEX!
OOOOOOH, THAT'S BAD.

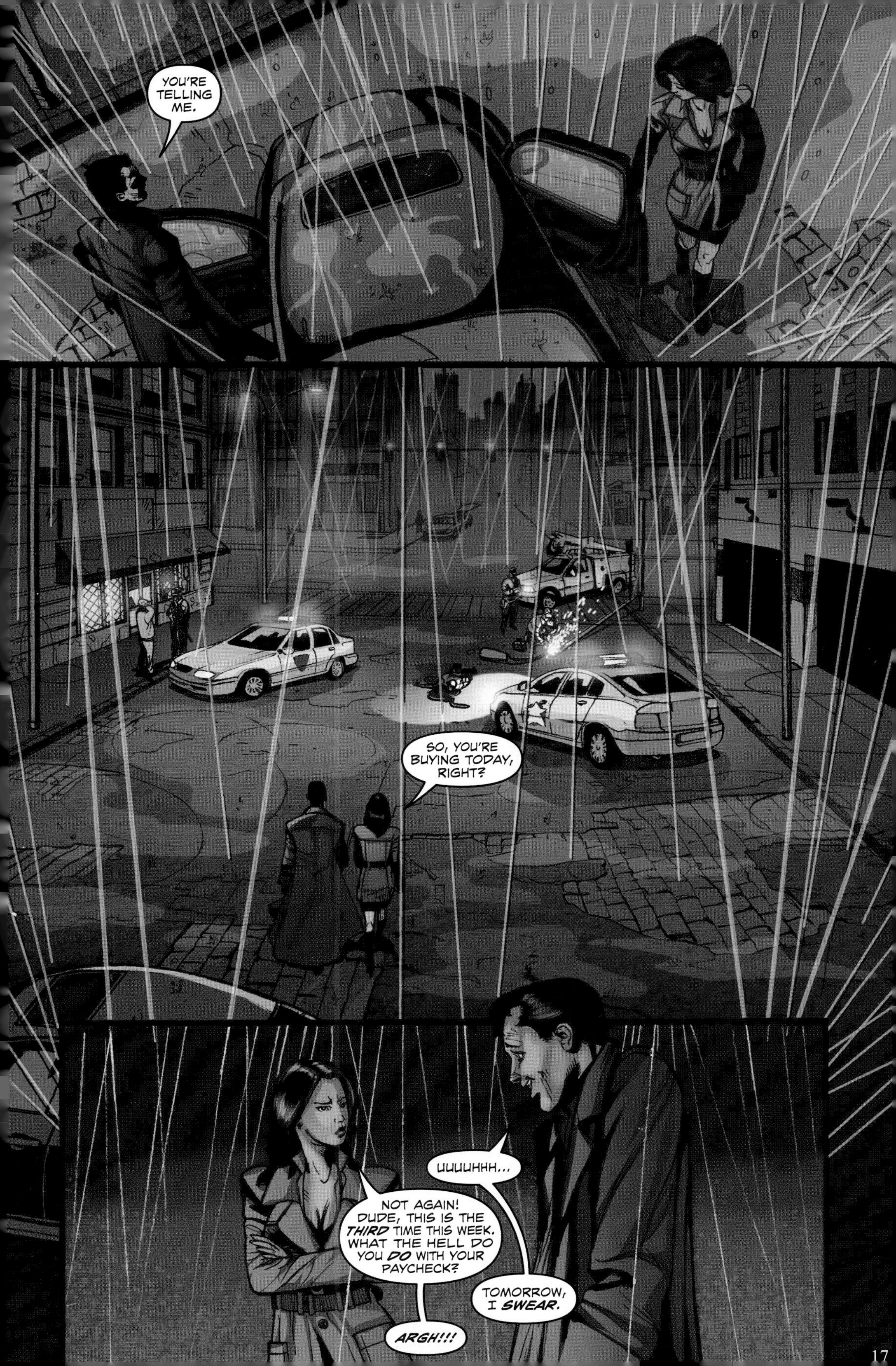
YOU'RE TELLING ME.
SO, YOU'RE BUYING TODAY, RIGHT?
UUUUHHH...
NOT AGAIN! DUDE, THIS IS THE THIRD TIME THIS WEEK. WHAT THE HELL DO YOU DO WITH YOUR PAYCHECK?
TOMORROW, I SWEAR.
ARGH!!!

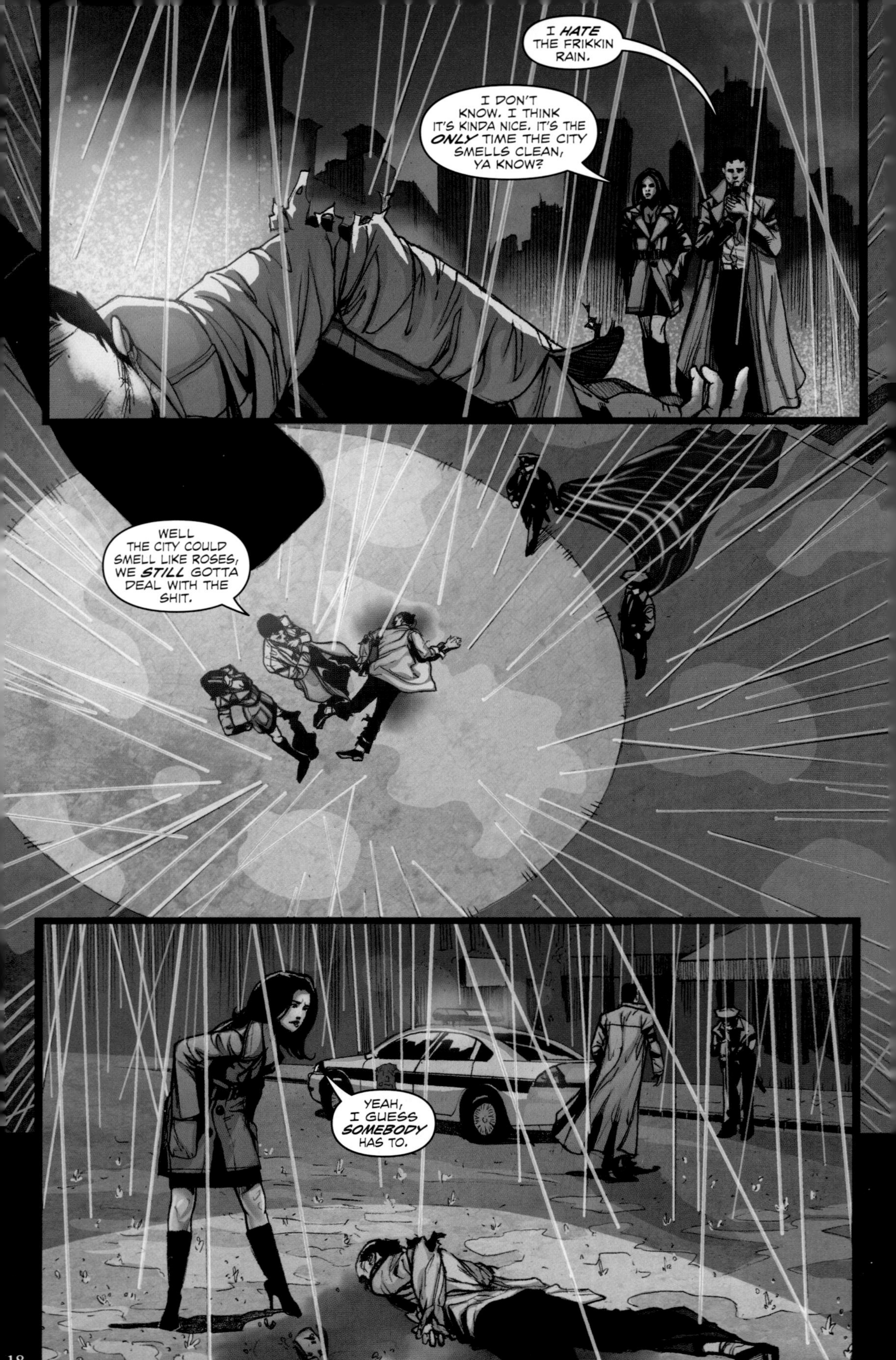
I HATE THE FRIKKIN RAIN.
I DON'T KNOW. I THINK IT'S KINDA NICE. IT'S THE ONLY TIME THE CITY SMELLS CLEAN, YA KNOW?
WELL THE CITY COULD SMELL LIKE ROSES, WE STILL GOTTA DEAL WITH THE SHIT.
YEAH, I GUESS SOMEBODY HAS TO.

HEY GUY, WHAT YA GOT?

A FUCKING *HEADACHE* IS WHAT I'VE GOT. I CAN'T *STAND* THIS RAIN.

SAME HERE. SO WHAT WE GOT?

HIT AND RUN. THE CLERK AT THE STORE CALLED IT IN ABOUT 40 MINUTES AGO.

SAID HE HEARD A LOUD CRASH... WENT TO CHECK AND SAW A CAR HEADING DOWN GEERLINGS STREET.

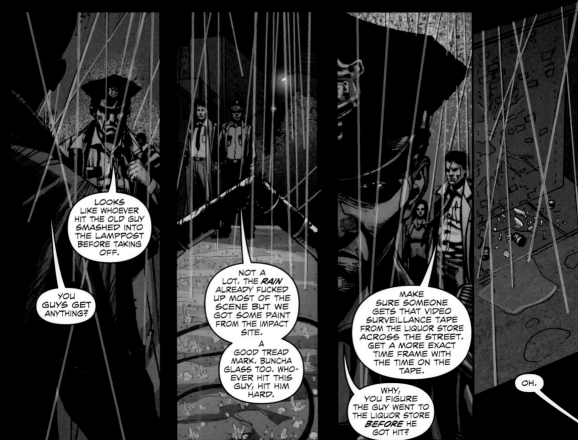

LOOKS LIKE WHOEVER HIT THE OLD GUY SMASHED INTO THE LAMPPOST BEFORE TAKING OFF.

YOU GUYS GET ANYTHING?

NOT A LOT. THE *RAIN* ALREADY FUCKED UP MOST OF THE SCENE BUT WE GOT SOME PAINT FROM THE IMPACT SITE.

A GOOD TREAD MARK. BUNCHA GLASS TOO. WHO-EVER HIT THIS GUY, HIT HIM HARD.

MAKE SURE SOMEONE GETS THAT VIDEO SURVEILLANCE TAPE FROM THE LIQUOR STORE ACROSS THE STREET. GET A MORE EXACT TIME FRAME WITH THE TIME ON THE TAPE.

WHY, YOU FIGURE THE GUY WENT TO THE LIQUOR STORE *BEFORE* HE GOT HIT?

OH.

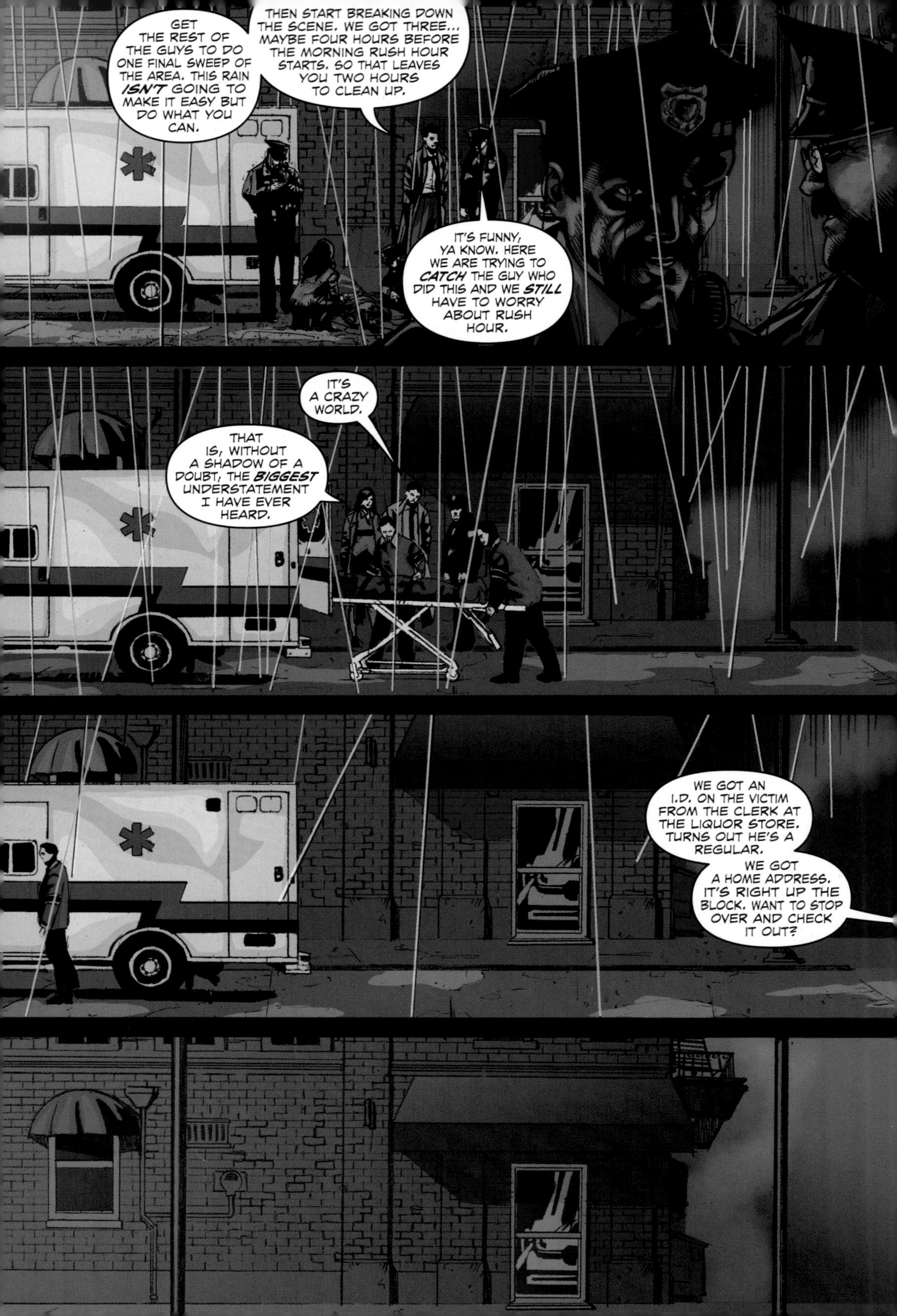
GET THE REST OF THE GUYS TO DO ONE FINAL SWEEP OF THE AREA. THIS RAIN ISN'T GOING TO MAKE IT EASY BUT DO WHAT YOU CAN.
THEN START BREAKING DOWN THE SCENE. WE GOT THREE... MAYBE FOUR HOURS BEFORE THE MORNING RUSH HOUR STARTS. SO THAT LEAVES YOU TWO HOURS TO CLEAN UP.
IT'S FUNNY, YA KNOW. HERE WE ARE TRYING TO CATCH THE GUY WHO DID THIS AND WE STILL HAVE TO WORRY ABOUT RUSH HOUR.
IT'S A CRAZY WORLD.
THAT IS, WITHOUT A SHADOW OF A DOUBT, THE BIGGEST UNDERSTATEMENT I HAVE EVER HEARD.
WE GOT AN I.D. ON THE VICTIM FROM THE CLERK AT THE LIQUOR STORE. TURNS OUT HE'S A REGULAR.
WE GOT A HOME ADDRESS. IT'S RIGHT UP THE BLOCK. WANT TO STOP OVER AND CHECK IT OUT?

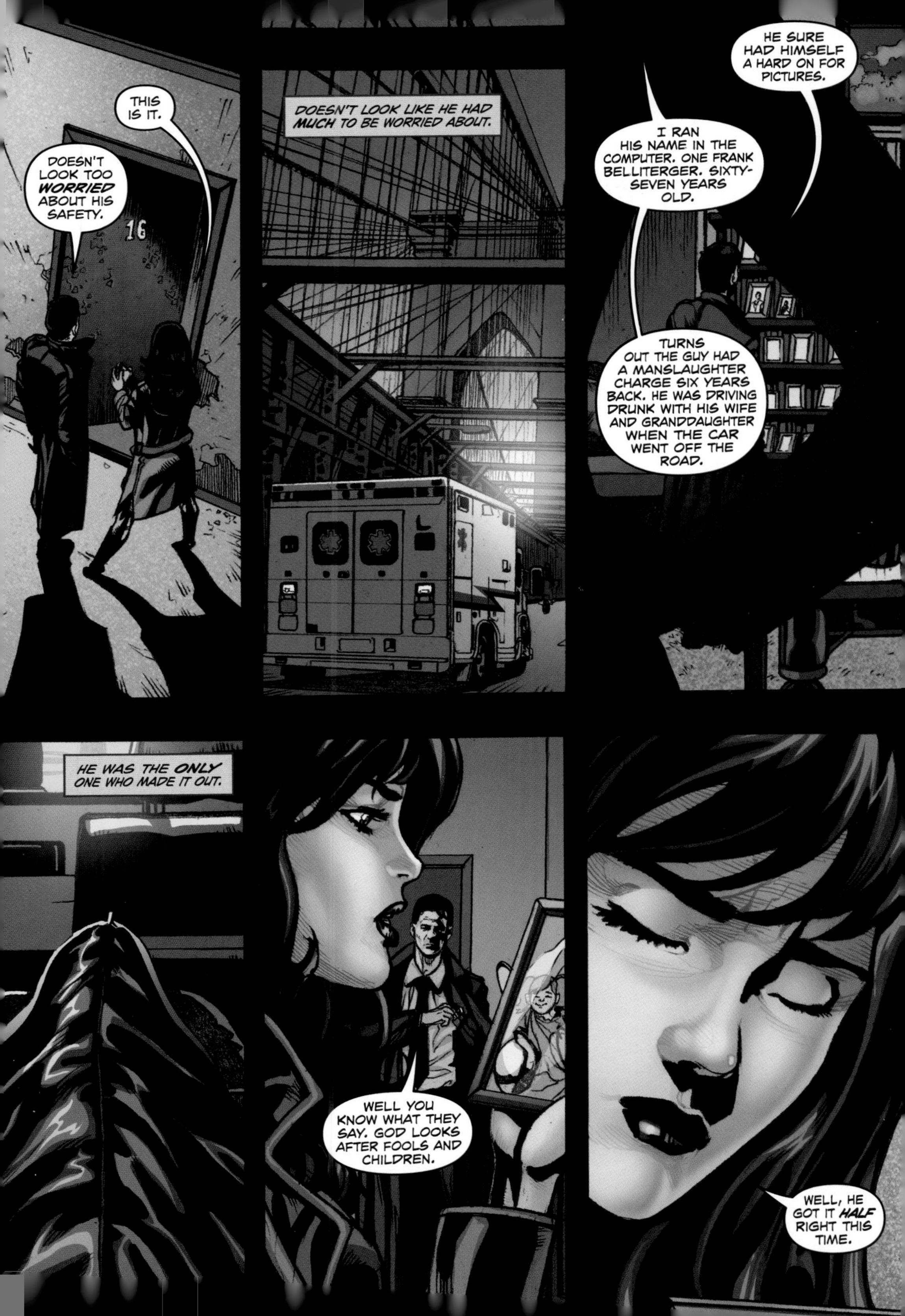
THIS IS IT.
DOESN'T LOOK TOO WORRIED ABOUT HIS SAFETY.
16
DOESN'T LOOK LIKE HE HAD MUCH TO BE WORRIED ABOUT.
I RAN HIS NAME IN THE COMPUTER. ONE FRANK BELLITERGER. SIXTY-SEVEN YEARS OLD.
HE SURE HAD HIMSELF A HARD ON FOR PICTURES.
TURNS OUT THE GUY HAD A MANSLAUGHTER CHARGE SIX YEARS BACK. HE WAS DRIVING DRUNK WITH HIS WIFE AND GRANDDAUGHTER WHEN THE CAR WENT OFF THE ROAD.
HE WAS THE ONLY ONE WHO MADE IT OUT.
WELL YOU KNOW WHAT THEY SAY. GOD LOOKS AFTER FOOLS AND CHILDREN.
WELL, HE GOT IT HALF RIGHT THIS TIME.

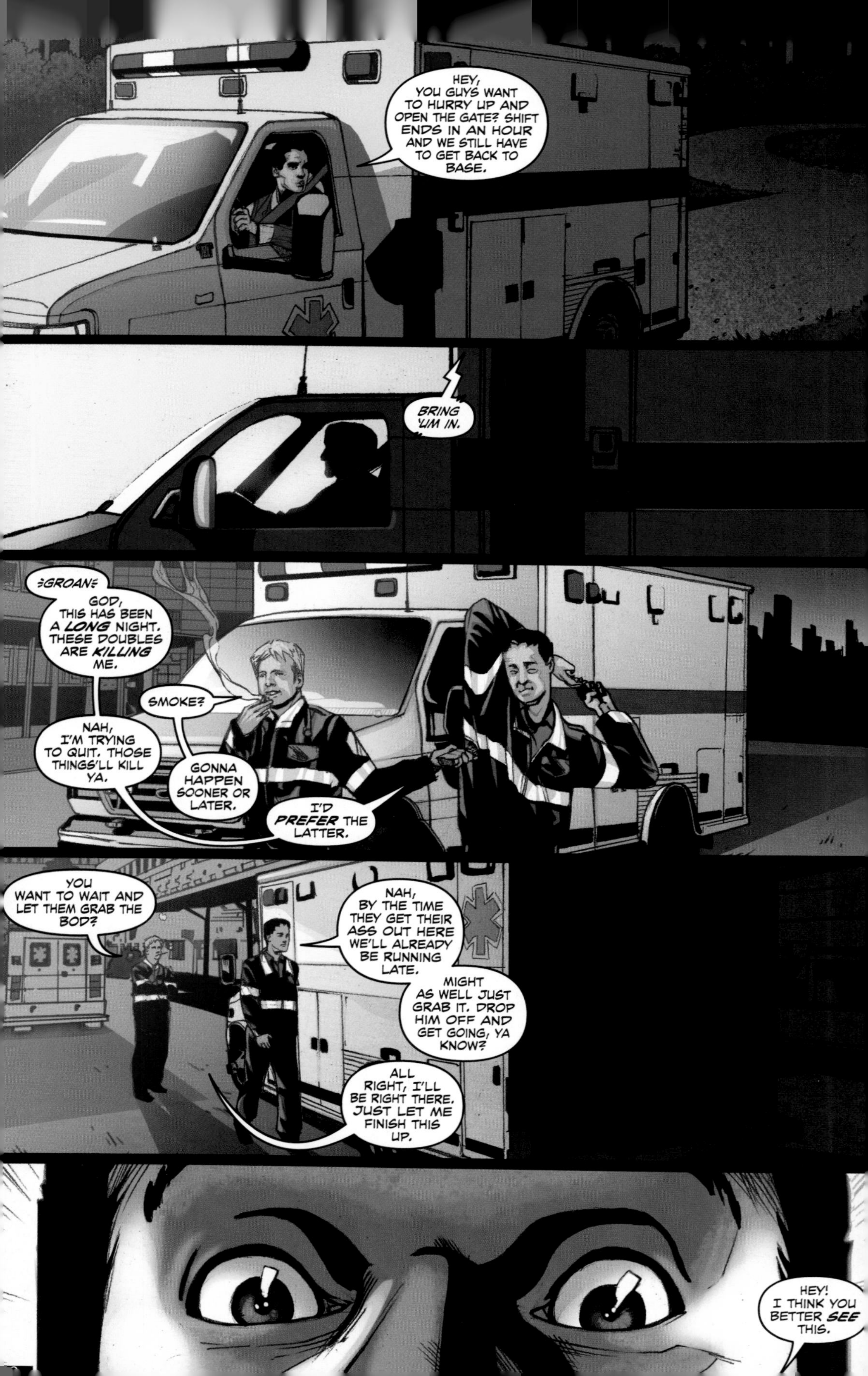
HEY, YOU GUYS WANT TO HURRY UP AND OPEN THE GATE? SHIFT ENDS IN AN HOUR AND WE STILL HAVE TO GET BACK TO BASE.
BRING 'UM IN.
GROAN
GOD, THIS HAS BEEN A LONG NIGHT. THESE DOUBLES ARE KILLING ME.
SMOKE?
NAH, I'M TRYING TO QUIT. THOSE THINGS'LL KILL YA.
GONNA HAPPEN SOONER OR LATER.
I'D PREFER THE LATTER.
YOU WANT TO WAIT AND LET THEM GRAB THE BOD?
NAH, BY THE TIME THEY GET THEIR ASS OUT HERE WE'LL ALREADY BE RUNNING LATE.
MIGHT AS WELL JUST GRAB IT. DROP HIM OFF AND GET GOING, YA KNOW?
ALL RIGHT, I'LL BE RIGHT THERE. JUST LET ME FINISH THIS UP.
HEY! I THINK YOU BETTER SEE THIS.

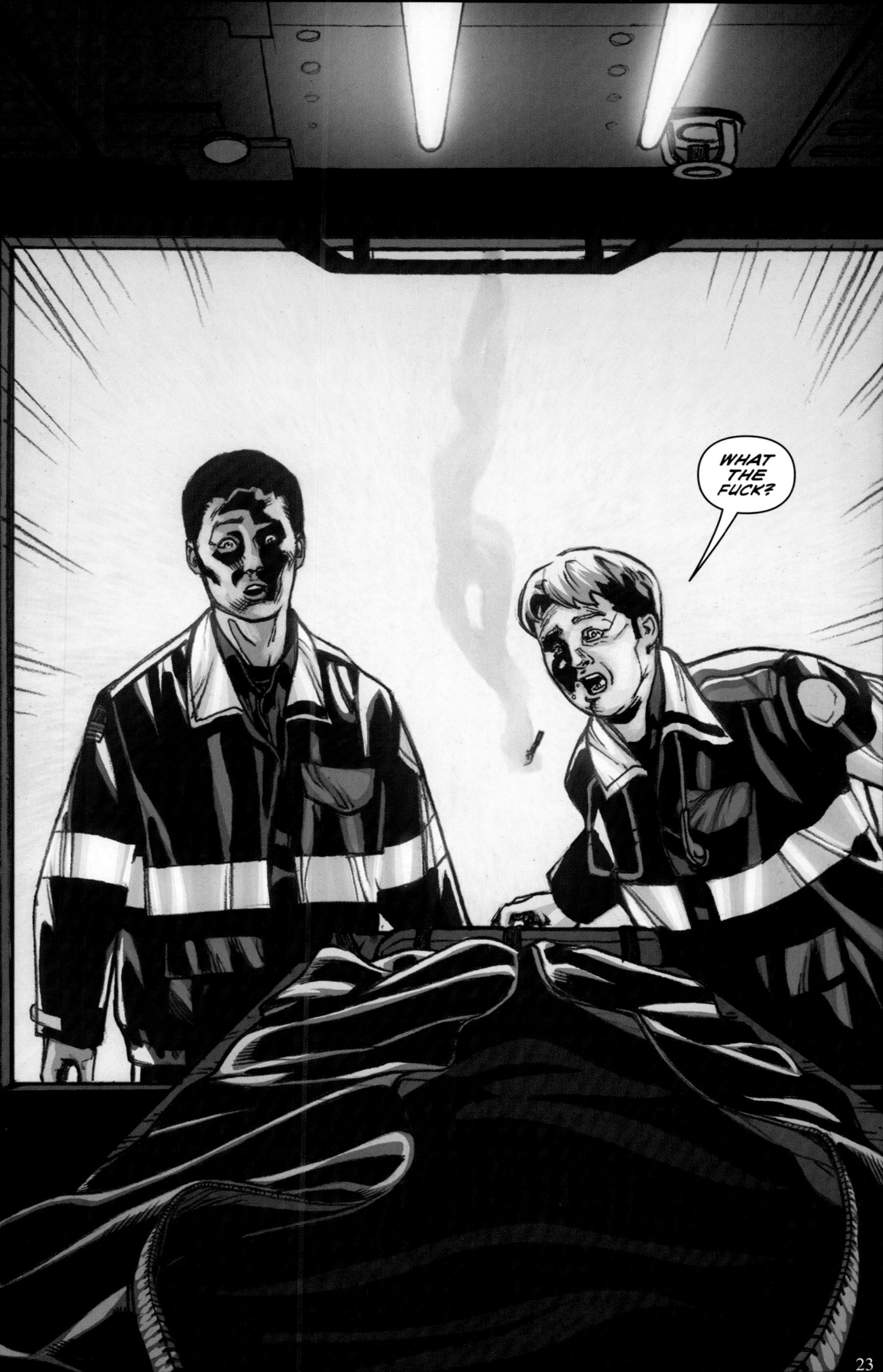
WHAT THE FUCK?

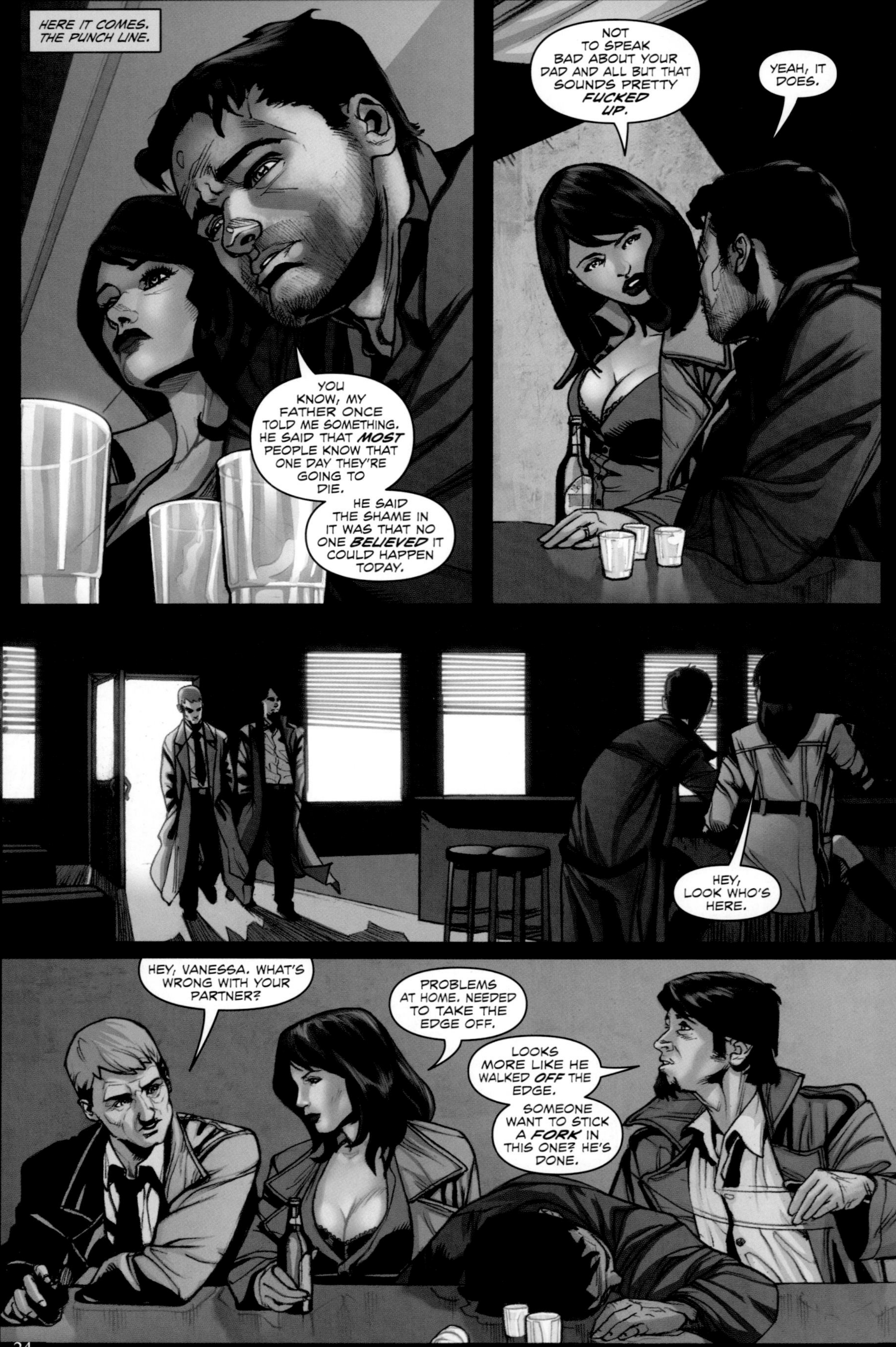
HERE IT COMES. THE PUNCH LINE.
YOU KNOW, MY FATHER ONCE TOLD ME SOMETHING. HE SAID THAT MOST PEOPLE KNOW THAT ONE DAY THEY'RE GOING TO DIE.
HE SAID THE SHAME IN IT WAS THAT NO ONE BELIEVED IT COULD HAPPEN TODAY.
NOT TO SPEAK BAD ABOUT YOUR DAD AND ALL BUT THAT SOUNDS PRETTY FUCKED UP.
YEAH, IT DOES.
HEY, LOOK WHO'S HERE.
HEY, VANESSA. WHAT'S WRONG WITH YOUR PARTNER?
PROBLEMS AT HOME. NEEDED TO TAKE THE EDGE OFF.
LOOKS MORE LIKE HE WALKED OFF THE EDGE.
SOMEONE WANT TO STICK A FORK IN THIS ONE? HE'S DONE.

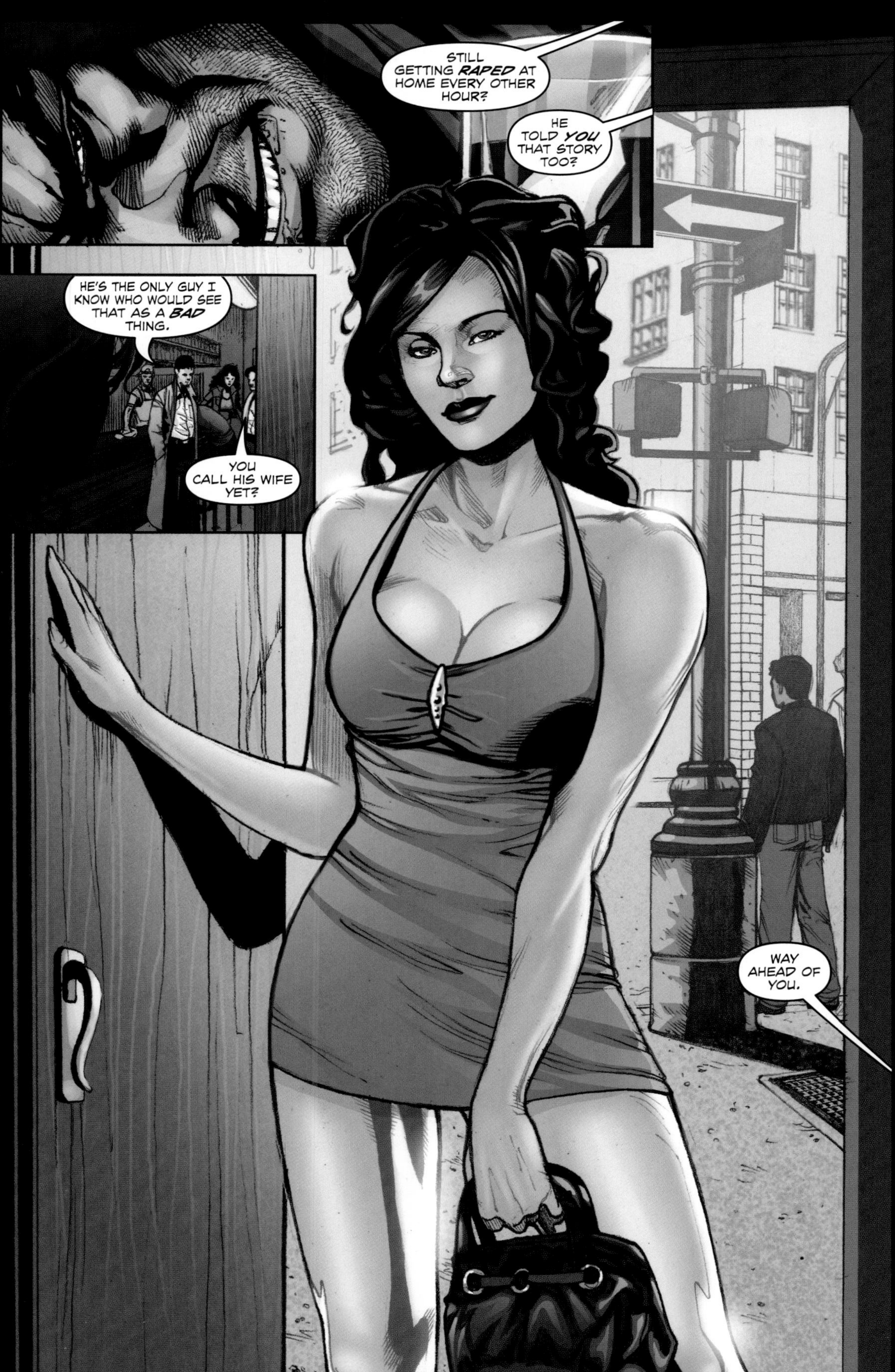
STILL GETTING RAPED AT HOME EVERY OTHER HOUR?
HE TOLD YOU THAT STORY TOO?
HE'S THE ONLY GUY I KNOW WHO WOULD SEE THAT AS A BAD THING.
YOU CALL HIS WIFE YET?
WAY AHEAD OF YOU.

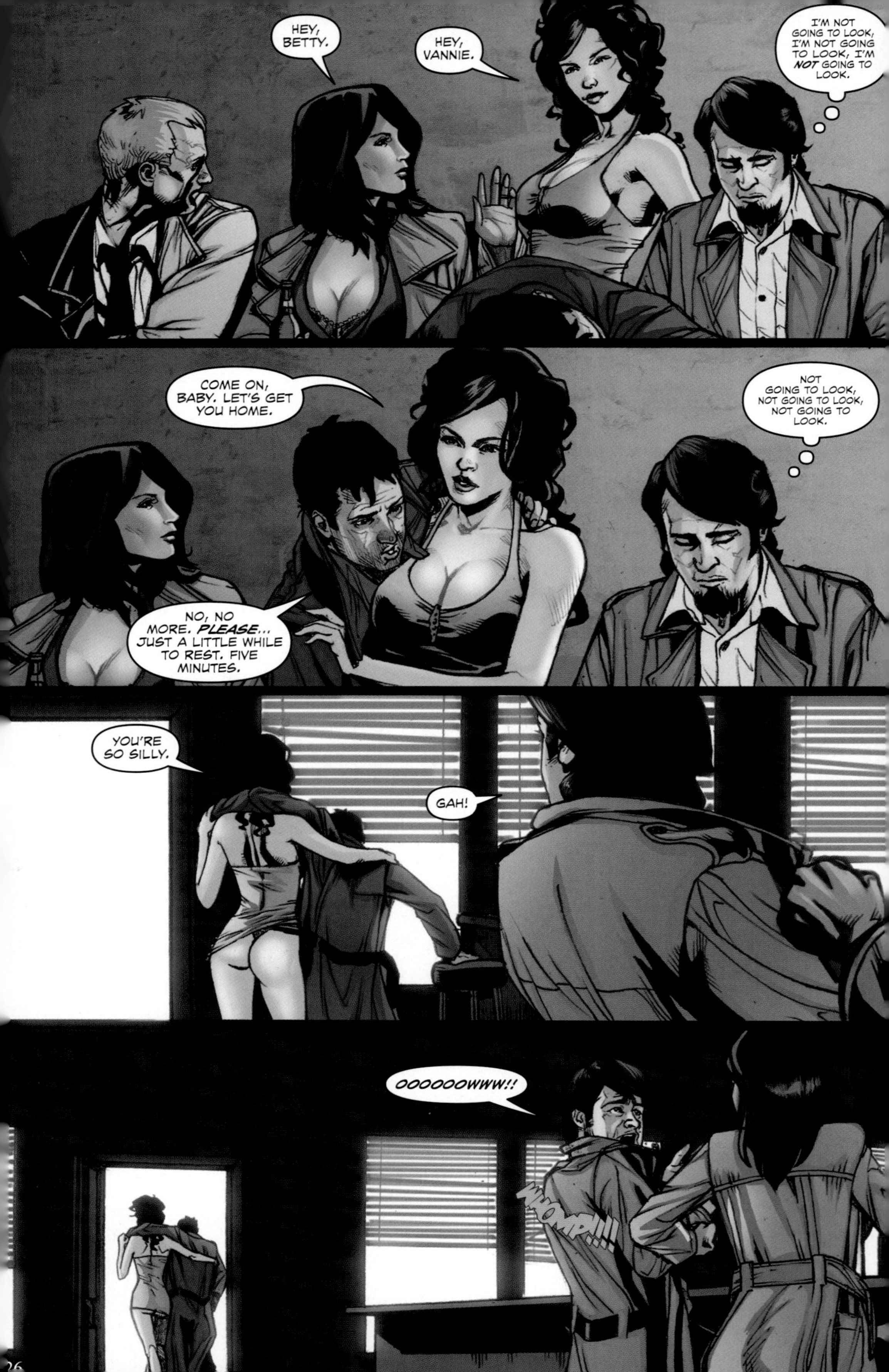
HEY, BETTY.
HEY, VANNIE.
I'M NOT GOING TO LOOK, I'M NOT GOING TO LOOK, I'M NOT GOING TO LOOK.
COME ON, BABY. LET'S GET YOU HOME.
NOT GOING TO LOOK, NOT GOING TO LOOK, NOT GOING TO LOOK.
NO, NO MORE. PLEASE... JUST A LITTLE WHILE TO REST. FIVE MINUTES.
YOU'RE SO SILLY.
GAH!
OOOOOOWWW!!
WHOMP!!!

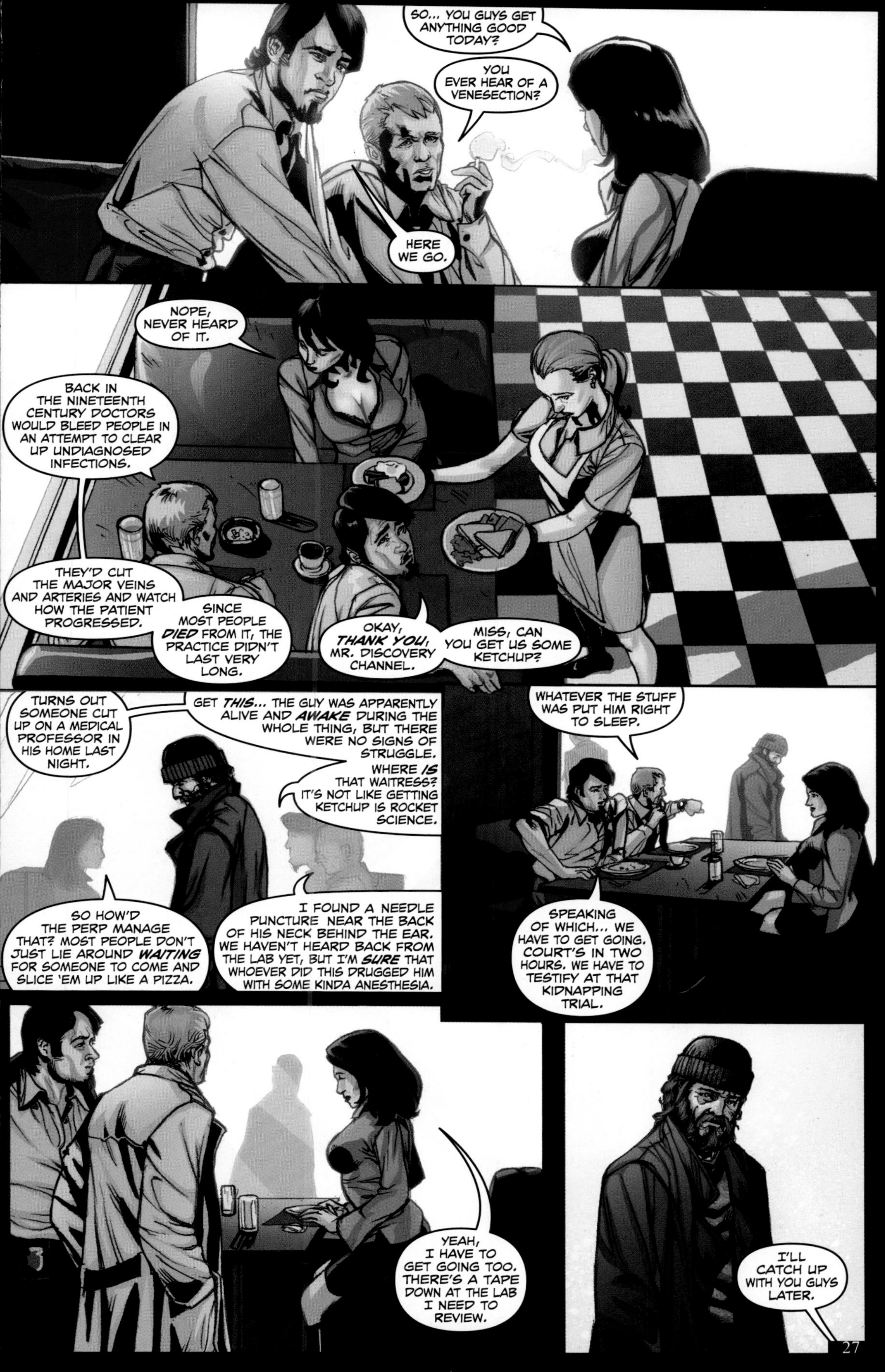
SO... YOU GUYS GET ANYTHING GOOD TODAY?
YOU EVER HEAR OF A VENESECTION?
HERE WE GO.
NOPE, NEVER HEARD OF IT.
BACK IN THE NINETEENTH CENTURY DOCTORS WOULD BLEED PEOPLE IN AN ATTEMPT TO CLEAR UP UNDIAGNOSED INFECTIONS.
THEY'D CUT THE MAJOR VEINS AND ARTERIES AND WATCH HOW THE PATIENT PROGRESSED.
SINCE MOST PEOPLE *DIED* FROM IT, THE PRACTICE DIDN'T LAST VERY LONG.
OKAY, *THANK YOU*, MR. DISCOVERY CHANNEL.
MISS, CAN YOU GET US SOME KETCHUP?
TURNS OUT SOMEONE CUT UP ON A MEDICAL PROFESSOR IN HIS HOME LAST NIGHT.
GET *THIS*... THE GUY WAS APPARENTLY ALIVE AND *AWAKE* DURING THE WHOLE THING, BUT THERE WERE NO SIGNS OF STRUGGLE.
WHERE *IS* THAT WAITRESS? IT'S NOT LIKE GETTING KETCHUP IS ROCKET SCIENCE.
SO HOW'D THE PERP MANAGE THAT? MOST PEOPLE DON'T JUST LIE AROUND *WAITING* FOR SOMEONE TO COME AND SLICE 'EM UP LIKE A PIZZA.
I FOUND A NEEDLE PUNCTURE NEAR THE BACK OF HIS NECK BEHIND THE EAR. WE HAVEN'T HEARD BACK FROM THE LAB YET, BUT I'M *SURE* THAT WHOEVER DID THIS DRUGGED HIM WITH SOME KINDA ANESTHESIA.
WHATEVER THE STUFF WAS PUT HIM RIGHT TO SLEEP.
SPEAKING OF WHICH... WE HAVE TO GET GOING. COURT'S IN TWO HOURS. WE HAVE TO TESTIFY AT THAT KIDNAPPING TRIAL.
YEAH, I HAVE TO GET GOING TOO. THERE'S A TAPE DOWN AT THE LAB I NEED TO REVIEW.
I'LL CATCH UP WITH YOU GUYS LATER.

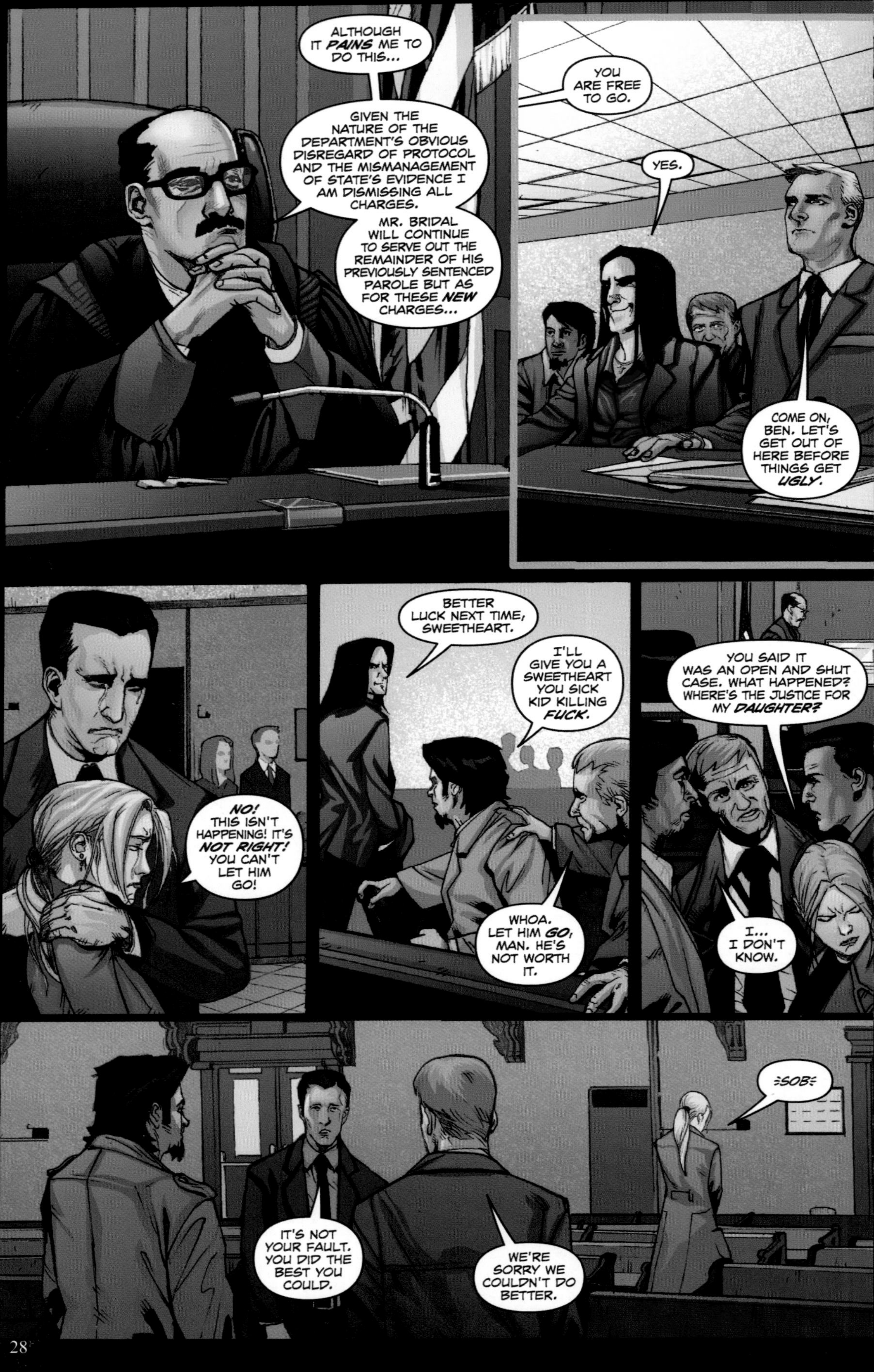
ALTHOUGH IT PAINS ME TO DO THIS...
GIVEN THE NATURE OF THE DEPARTMENT'S OBVIOUS DISREGARD OF PROTOCOL AND THE MISMANAGEMENT OF STATE'S EVIDENCE I AM DISMISSING ALL CHARGES.
MR. BRIDAL WILL CONTINUE TO SERVE OUT THE REMAINDER OF HIS PREVIOUSLY SENTENCED PAROLE BUT AS FOR THESE NEW CHARGES...
YOU ARE FREE TO GO.
YES.
COME ON, BEN. LET'S GET OUT OF HERE BEFORE THINGS GET UGLY.
NO! THIS ISN'T HAPPENING! IT'S NOT RIGHT! YOU CAN'T LET HIM GO!
BETTER LUCK NEXT TIME, SWEETHEART.
I'LL GIVE YOU A SWEETHEART YOU SICK KID KILLING FUCK.
WHOA. LET HIM GO, MAN. HE'S NOT WORTH IT.
YOU SAID IT WAS AN OPEN AND SHUT CASE. WHAT HAPPENED? WHERE'S THE JUSTICE FOR MY DAUGHTER?
I... I DON'T KNOW.
SOB
IT'S NOT YOUR FAULT. YOU DID THE BEST YOU COULD.
WE'RE SORRY WE COULDN'T DO BETTER.

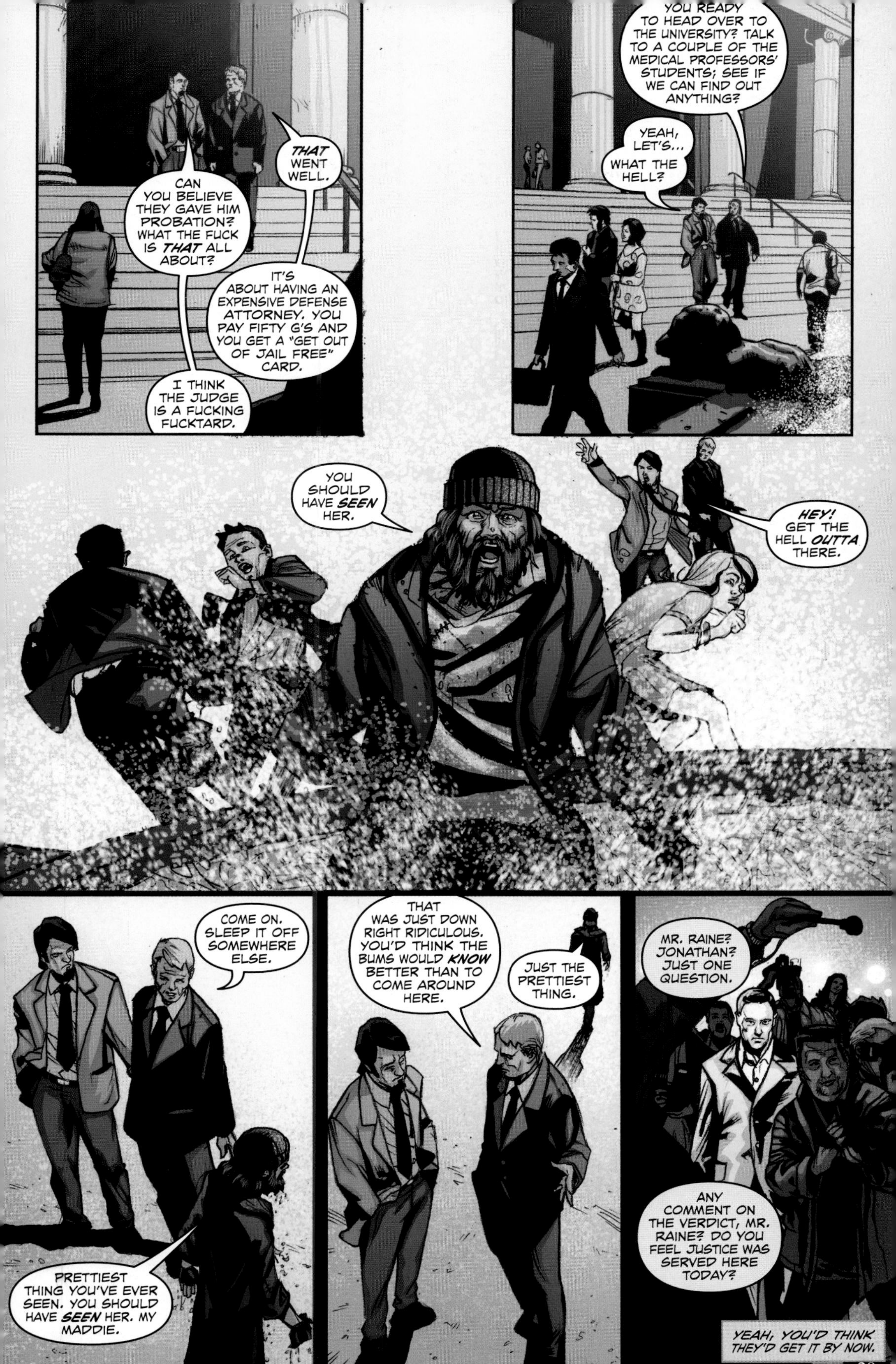
CAN YOU BELIEVE THEY GAVE HIM PROBATION? WHAT THE FUCK IS THAT ALL ABOUT?
THAT WENT WELL.
IT'S ABOUT HAVING AN EXPENSIVE DEFENSE ATTORNEY. YOU PAY FIFTY G'S AND YOU GET A "GET OUT OF JAIL FREE" CARD.
I THINK THE JUDGE IS A FUCKING FUCKTARD.
YOU READY TO HEAD OVER TO THE UNIVERSITY? TALK TO A COUPLE OF THE MEDICAL PROFESSORS' STUDENTS; SEE IF WE CAN FIND OUT ANYTHING?
YEAH, LET'S... WHAT THE HELL?
YOU SHOULD HAVE SEEN HER.
HEY! GET THE HELL OUTTA THERE.
COME ON. SLEEP IT OFF SOMEWHERE ELSE.
PRETTIEST THING YOU'VE EVER SEEN. YOU SHOULD HAVE SEEN HER. MY MADDIE.
THAT WAS JUST DOWN RIGHT RIDICULOUS. YOU'D THINK THE BUMS WOULD KNOW BETTER THAN TO COME AROUND HERE.
JUST THE PRETTIEST THING.
MR. RAINE? JONATHAN? JUST ONE QUESTION.
ANY COMMENT ON THE VERDICT, MR. RAINE? DO YOU FEEL JUSTICE WAS SERVED HERE TODAY?
YEAH, YOU'D THINK THEY'D GET IT BY NOW.

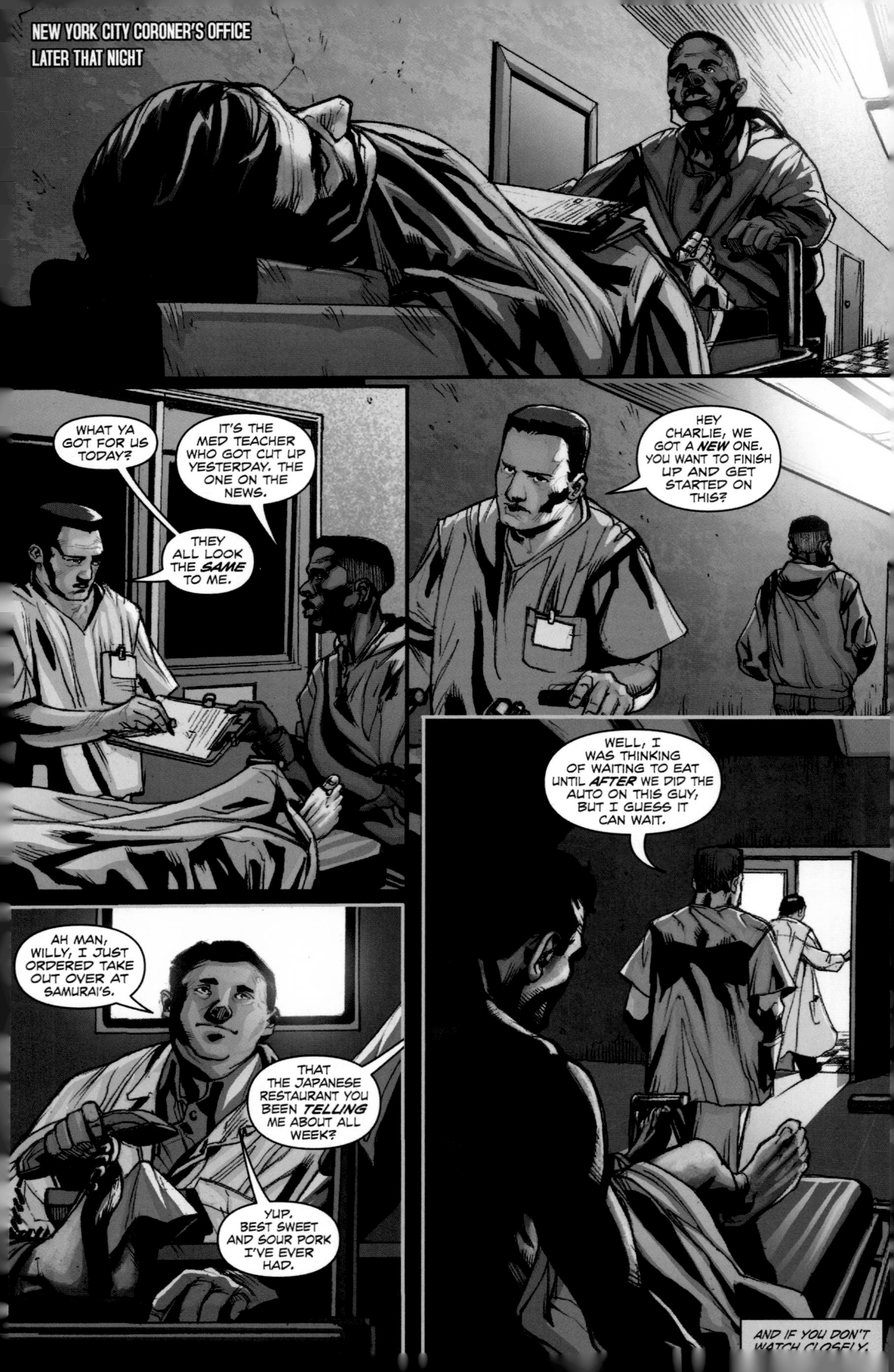
NEW YORK CITY CORONER'S OFFICE
LATER THAT NIGHT
WHAT YA GOT FOR US TODAY?
IT'S THE MED TEACHER WHO GOT CUT UP YESTERDAY. THE ONE ON THE NEWS.
THEY ALL LOOK THE SAME TO ME.
HEY CHARLIE, WE GOT A NEW ONE. YOU WANT TO FINISH UP AND GET STARTED ON THIS?
AH MAN, WILLY, I JUST ORDERED TAKE OUT OVER AT SAMURAI'S.
THAT THE JAPANESE RESTAURANT YOU BEEN TELLING ME ABOUT ALL WEEK?
YUP. BEST SWEET AND SOUR PORK I'VE EVER HAD.
WELL, I WAS THINKING OF WAITING TO EAT UNTIL AFTER WE DID THE AUTO ON THIS GUY, BUT I GUESS IT CAN WAIT.
AND IF YOU DON'T WATCH CLOSELY.

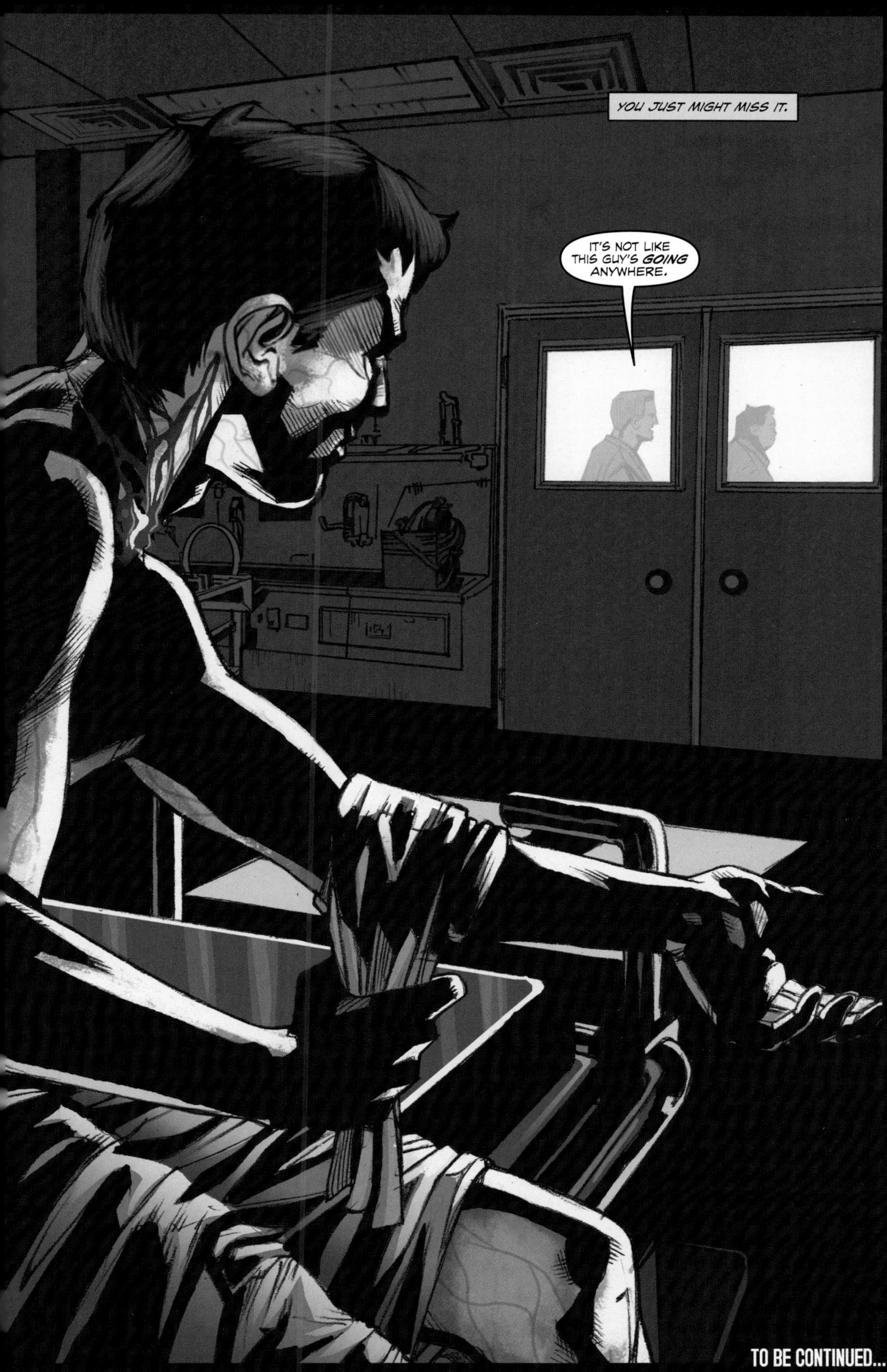
YOU JUST MIGHT MISS IT.
IT'S NOT LIKE THIS GUY'S GOING ANYWHERE.
TO BE CONTINUED...

CAST OF CHARACTERS

DETECTIVE LAURENCE WILLIAMS

Williams is highly intelligent and even headed with eight years on the force. Five of those years he has been partnered with Keith O'brien. Williams is the guy you go to for answers. The Velma of the group. He knows the tricks of the trade and no one can break a case faster than this guy.

DETECTIVE KEITH O'BRIEN

O'Brien is a smart-ass and bit of a hot head. He's six years on the force and is always the first one at the bar after his shift. He's known as a loose cannon but when the shit hits the fan he'll be the first one to have your back... and the first one to crack a beer afterward.

OFFICER VANESSA PELAGRENO

Pelagreno is sexy, confidant and smart but still pretty green and naive at times. She's in her first year on the force after graduating at the top of her class. Her outlook has always been that people are essentially good at heart and she generally sees things as black and white and right or wrong. But she's in for a wake up call.

NARRATOR

Casual but dedicated although he's sometimes too laid back. Been on the force for eleven years and is thinking about calling it quits. He's not a cynic like Keith but he's having problems believing that the world is worth fighting for. He has been partners with Vanessa for six months.

BETTY

The narrator's wife. She likes to have sex.

JONATHAN RAINE

Man with a deep dark secret.

FRANK BELLITERGER

Alcoholic killed in a hit and run outside of a liquor store.

MADISON RAINE

The secret.

JEFF DANIELS

Medical proffesor found murdered at his home.

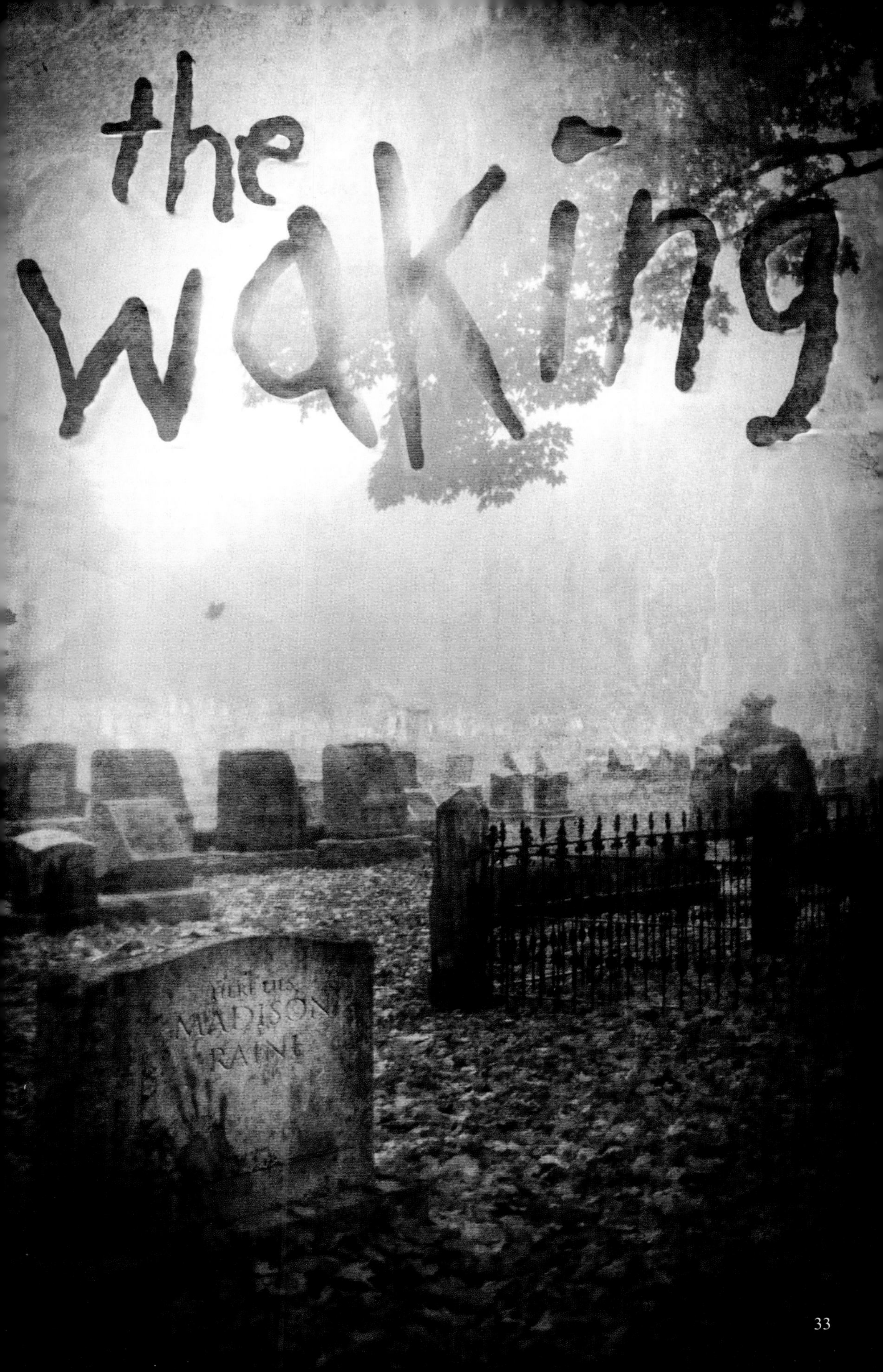
the waking
MADISON
RAINE

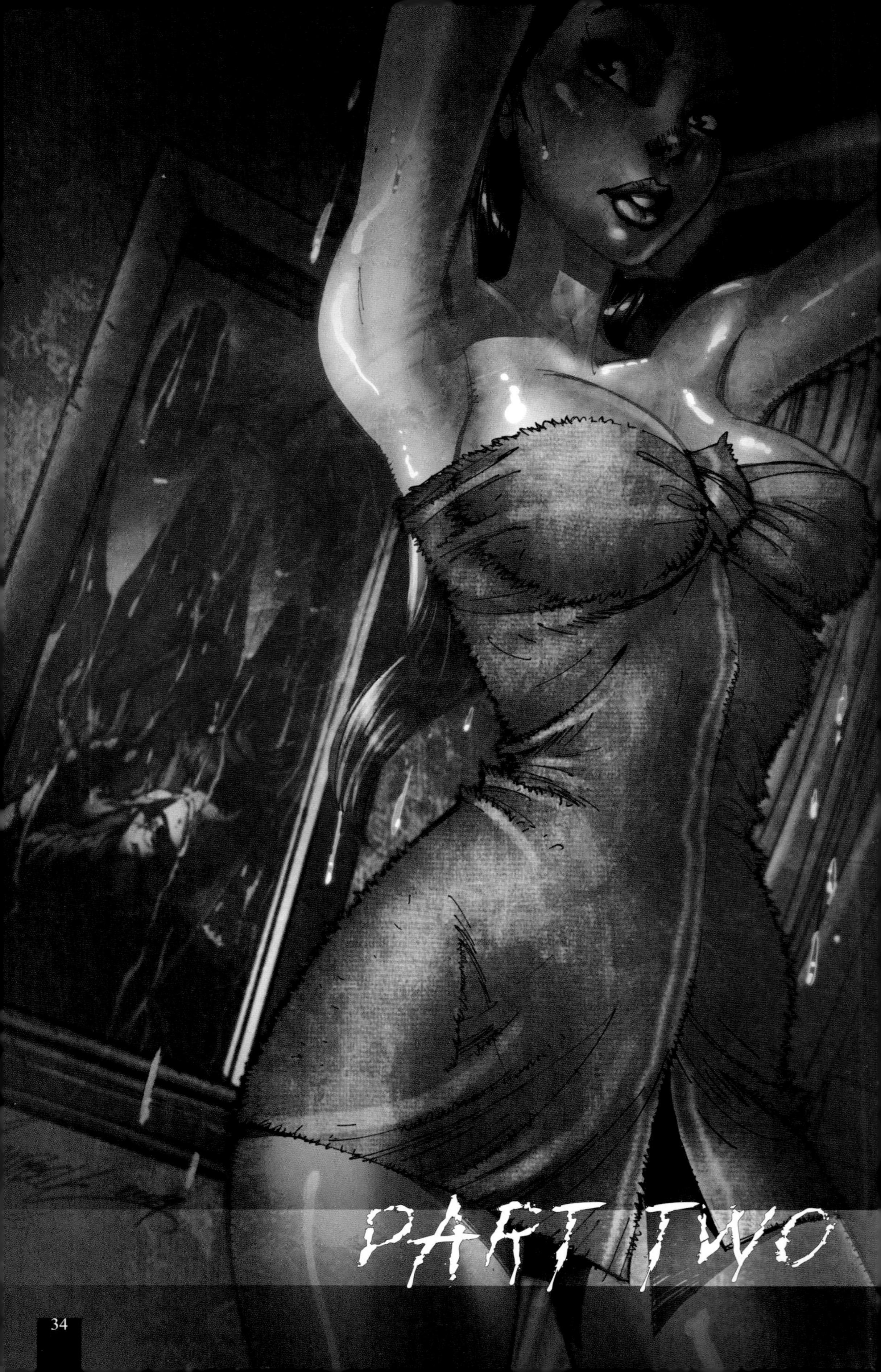
PART TWO

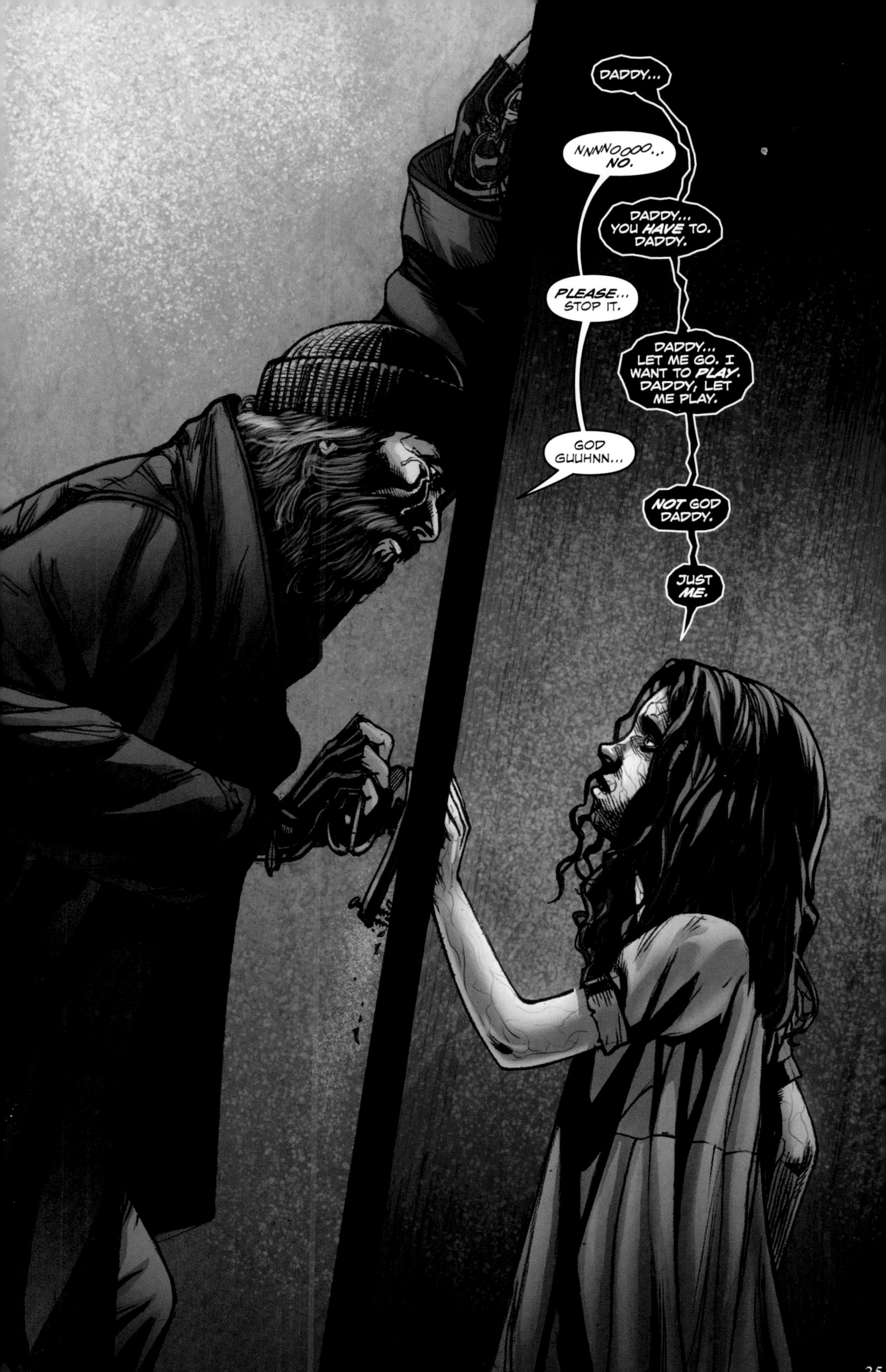
DADDY...
NNNNOOOO... NO.
DADDY... YOU HAVE TO. DADDY.
PLEASE... STOP IT.
DADDY... LET ME GO. I WANT TO PLAY. DADDY, LET ME PLAY.
GOD GUUHNN...
NOT GOD DADDY.
JUST ME.

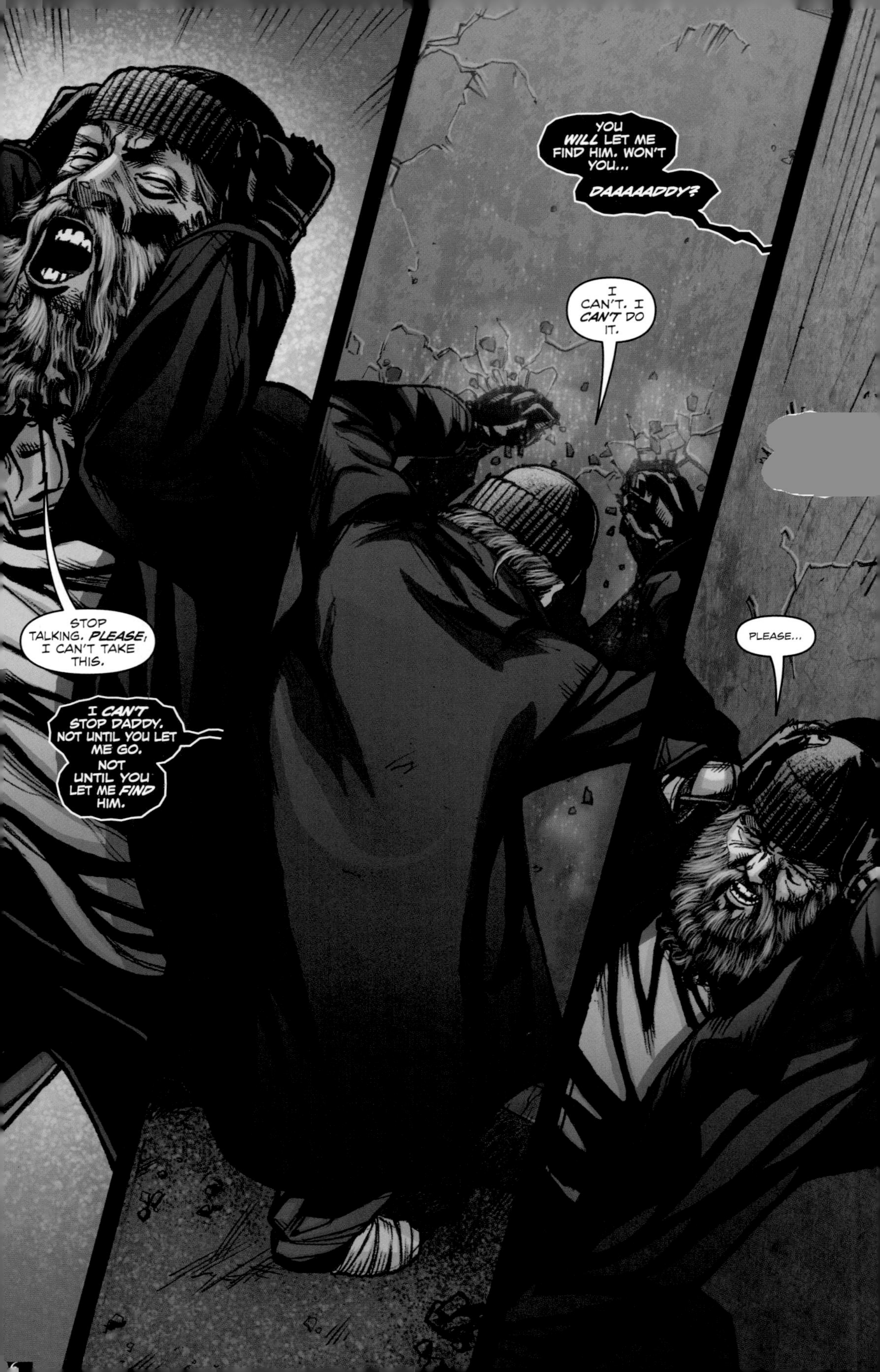
YOU WILL LET ME FIND HIM. WON'T YOU...
DAAAAADDY?
I CAN'T. I CAN'T DO IT.
STOP TALKING. PLEASE, I CAN'T TAKE THIS.
I CAN'T STOP DADDY. NOT UNTIL YOU LET ME GO.
NOT UNTIL YOU LET ME FIND HIM.
PLEASE...

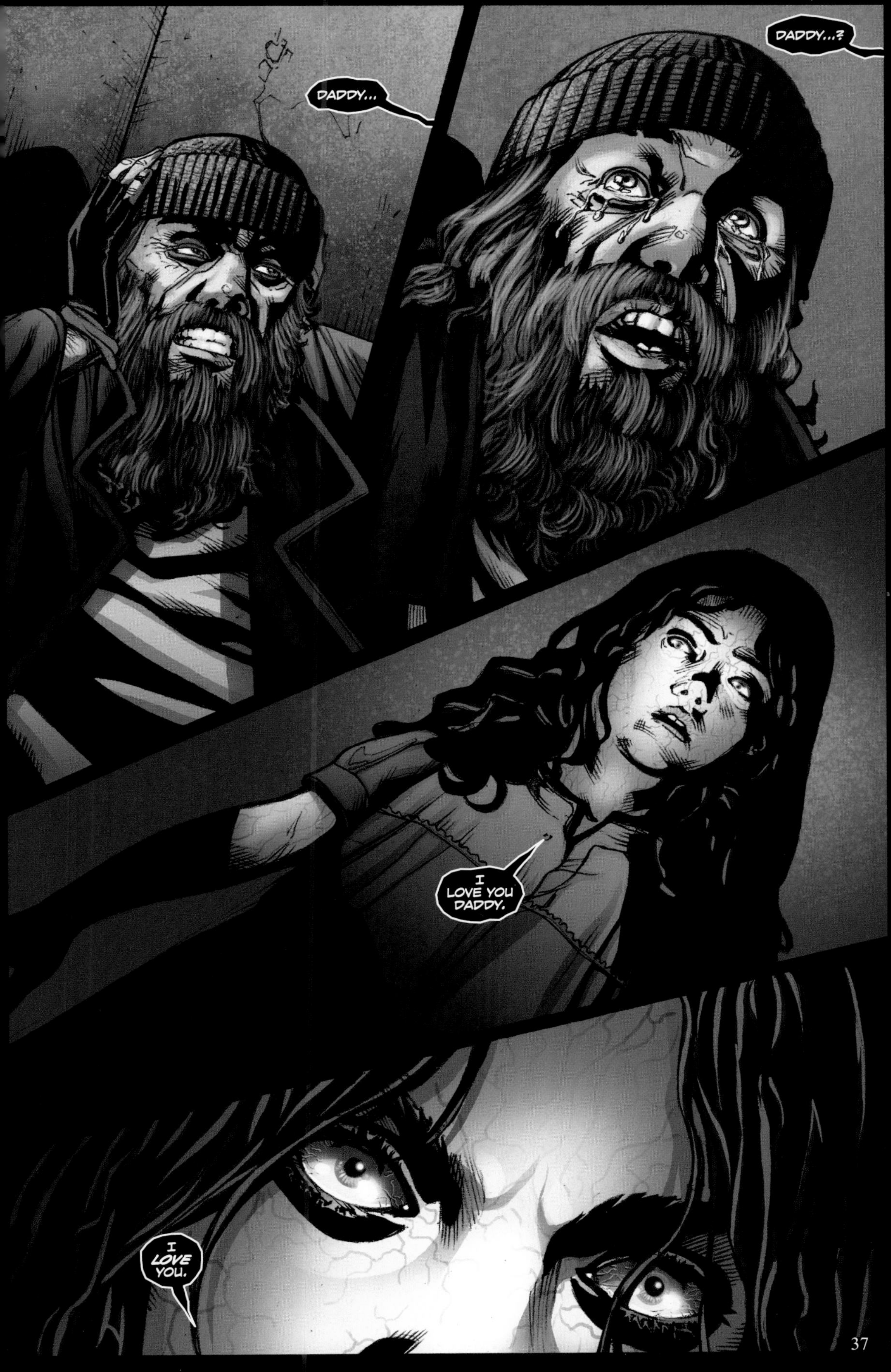
DADDY...
DADDY...?
I LOVE YOU DADDY.
I LOVE YOU.

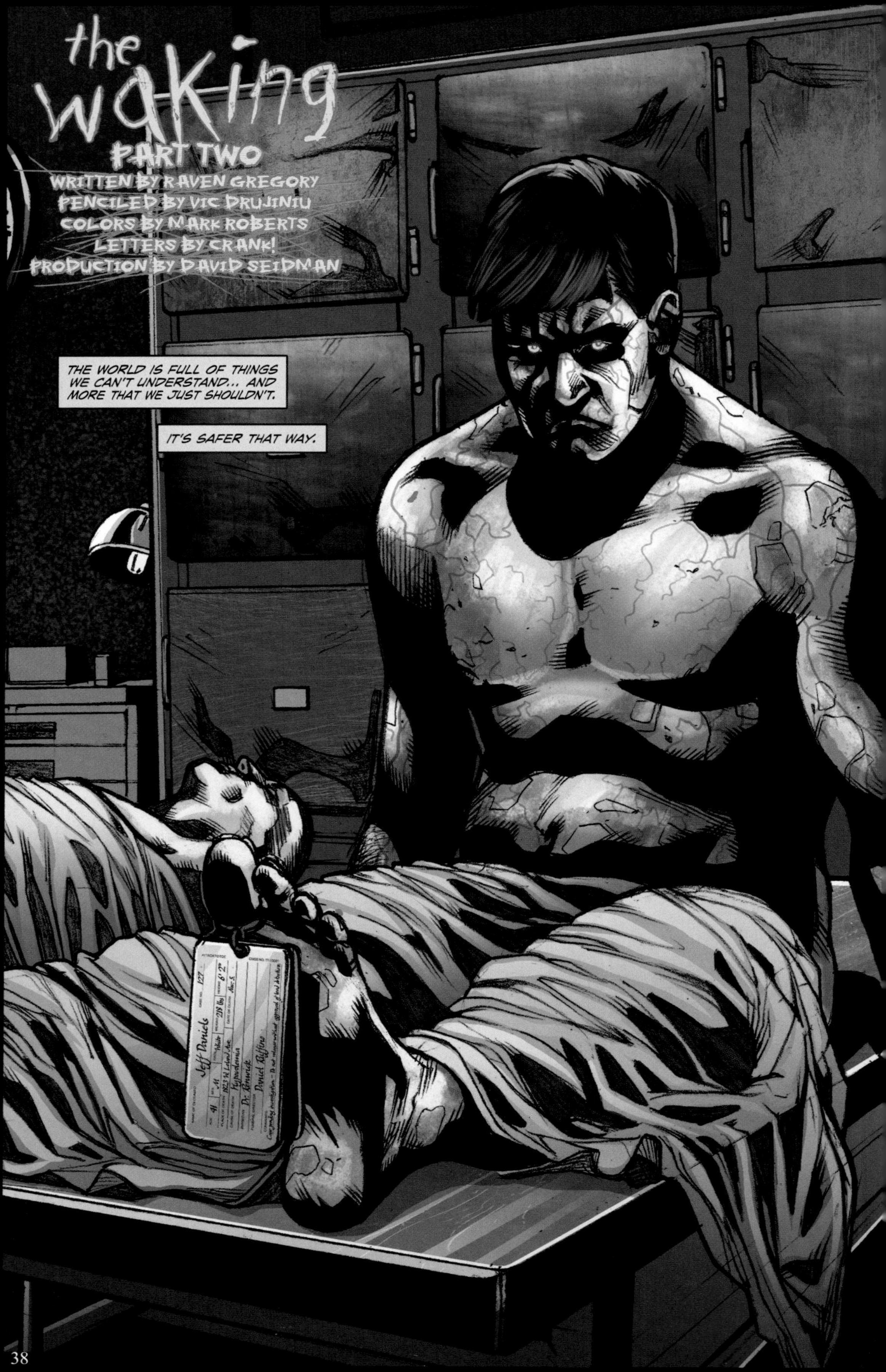
the waking
PART TWO
WRITTEN BY RAVEN GREGORY
PENCILED BY VIC DRUJINIU
COLORS BY MARK ROBERTS
LETTERS BY CRANK!
PRODUCTION BY DAVID SEIDMAN
THE WORLD IS FULL OF THINGS WE CAN'T UNDERSTAND... AND MORE THAT WE JUST SHOULDN'T.
IT'S SAFER THAT WAY.
Jeff Daniels

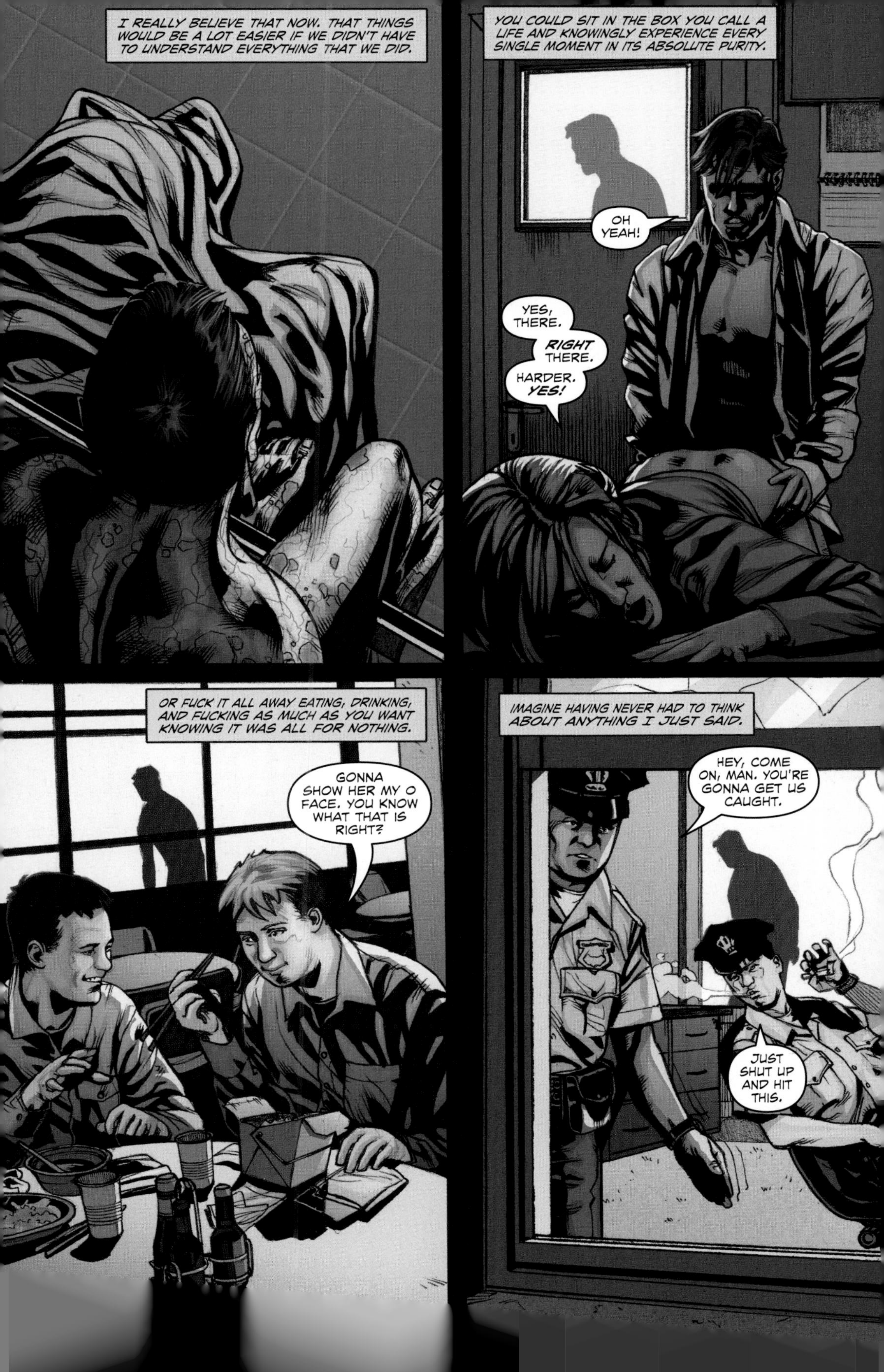
I REALLY BELIEVE THAT NOW. THAT THINGS WOULD BE A LOT EASIER IF WE DIDN'T HAVE TO UNDERSTAND EVERYTHING THAT WE DID.
YOU COULD SIT IN THE BOX YOU CALL A LIFE AND KNOWINGLY EXPERIENCE EVERY SINGLE MOMENT IN ITS ABSOLUTE PURITY.
OH YEAH!
YES, THERE. RIGHT THERE. HARDER. YES!
OR FUCK IT ALL AWAY EATING, DRINKING, AND FUCKING AS MUCH AS YOU WANT KNOWING IT WAS ALL FOR NOTHING.
GONNA SHOW HER MY O FACE. YOU KNOW WHAT THAT IS RIGHT?
IMAGINE HAVING NEVER HAD TO THINK ABOUT ANYTHING I JUST SAID.
HEY, COME ON, MAN. YOU'RE GONNA GET US CAUGHT.
JUST SHUT UP AND HIT THIS.

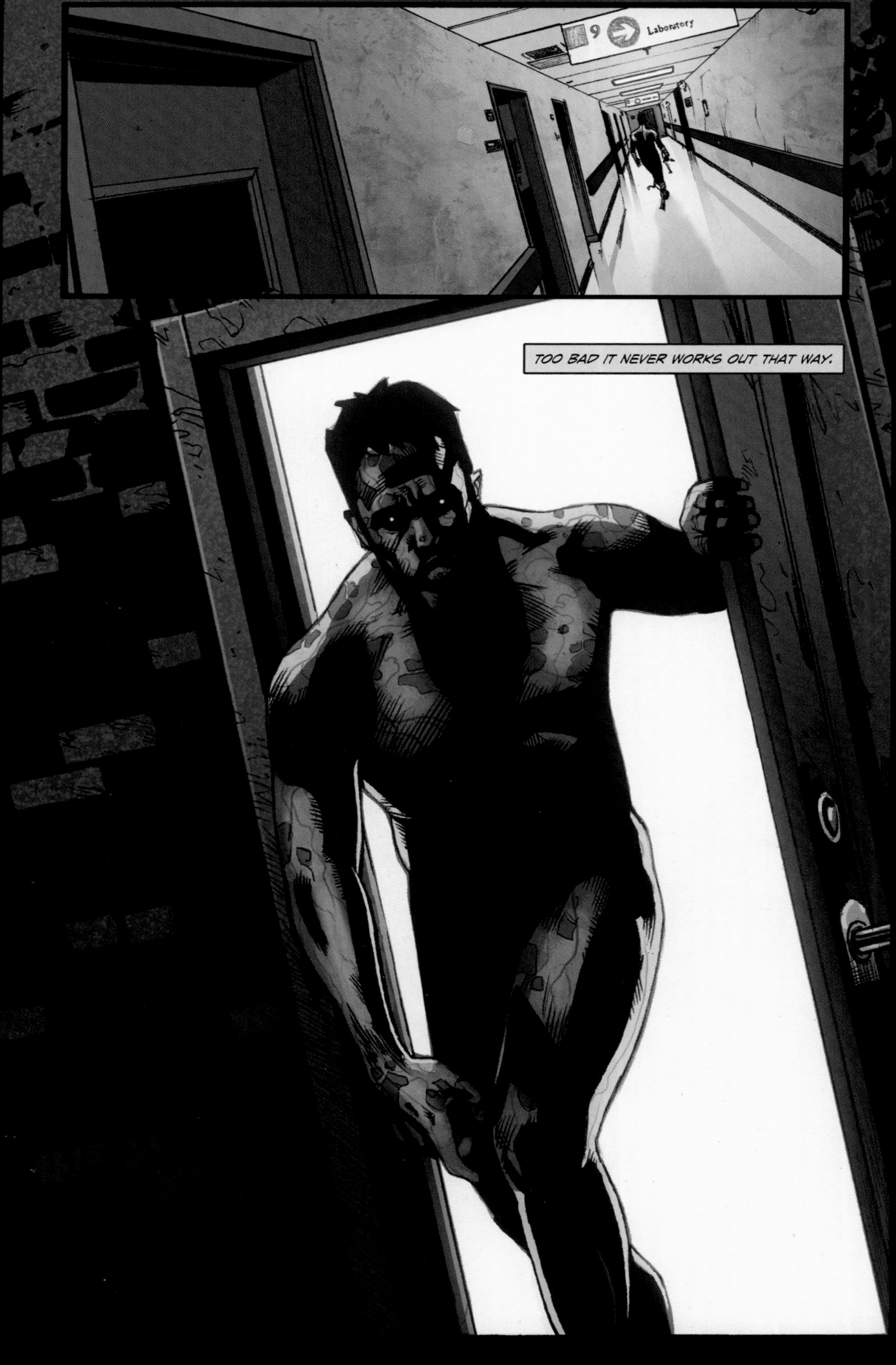
Laboratory
TOO BAD IT NEVER WORKS OUT THAT WAY.

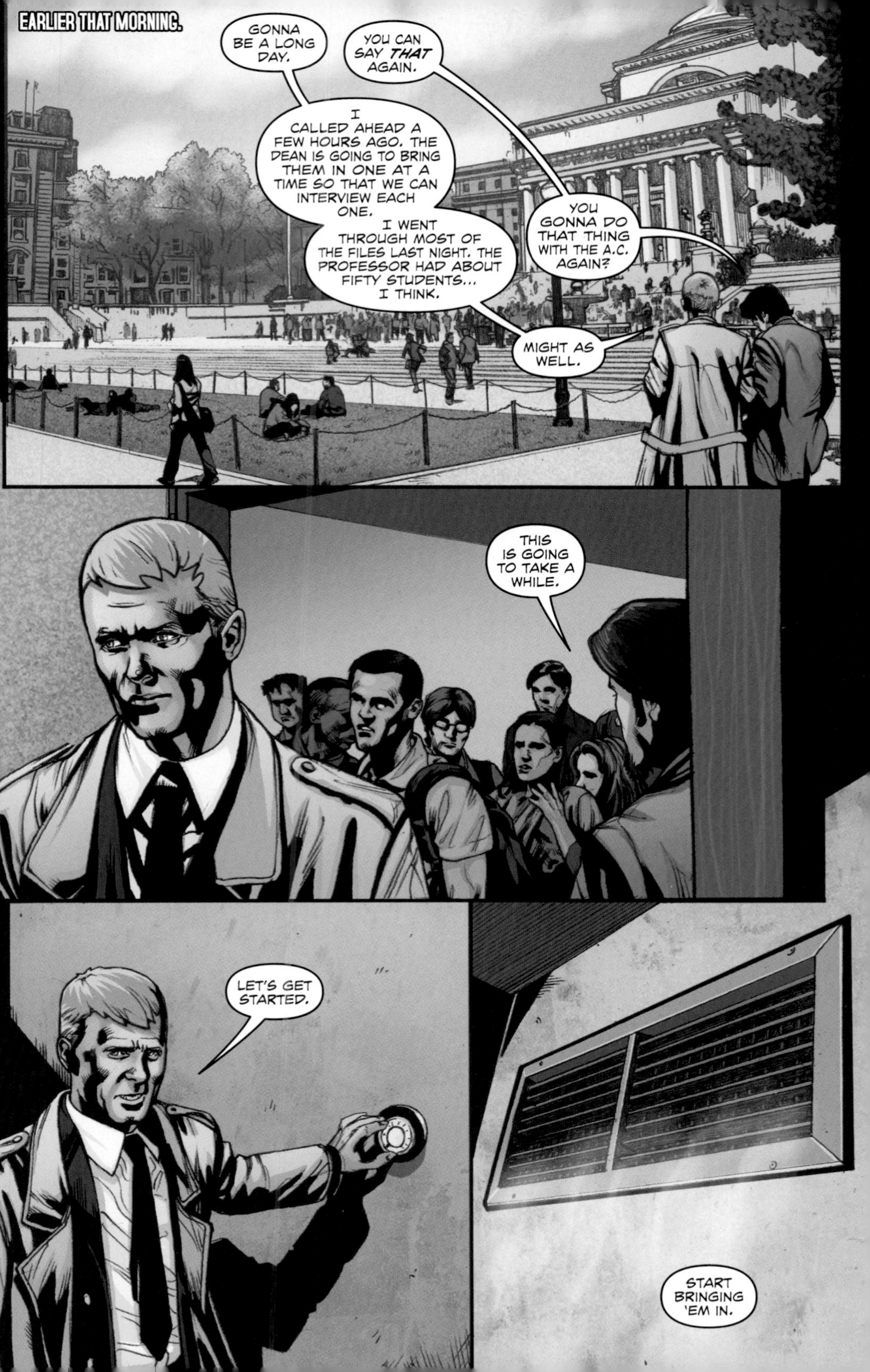
EARLIER THAT MORNING.
GONNA BE A LONG DAY.
YOU CAN SAY THAT AGAIN.
I CALLED AHEAD A FEW HOURS AGO. THE DEAN IS GOING TO BRING THEM IN ONE AT A TIME SO THAT WE CAN INTERVIEW EACH ONE.
I WENT THROUGH MOST OF THE FILES LAST NIGHT. THE PROFESSOR HAD ABOUT FIFTY STUDENTS... I THINK.
YOU GONNA DO THAT THING WITH THE A.C. AGAIN?
MIGHT AS WELL.
THIS IS GOING TO TAKE A WHILE.
LET'S GET STARTED.
START BRINGING 'EM IN.

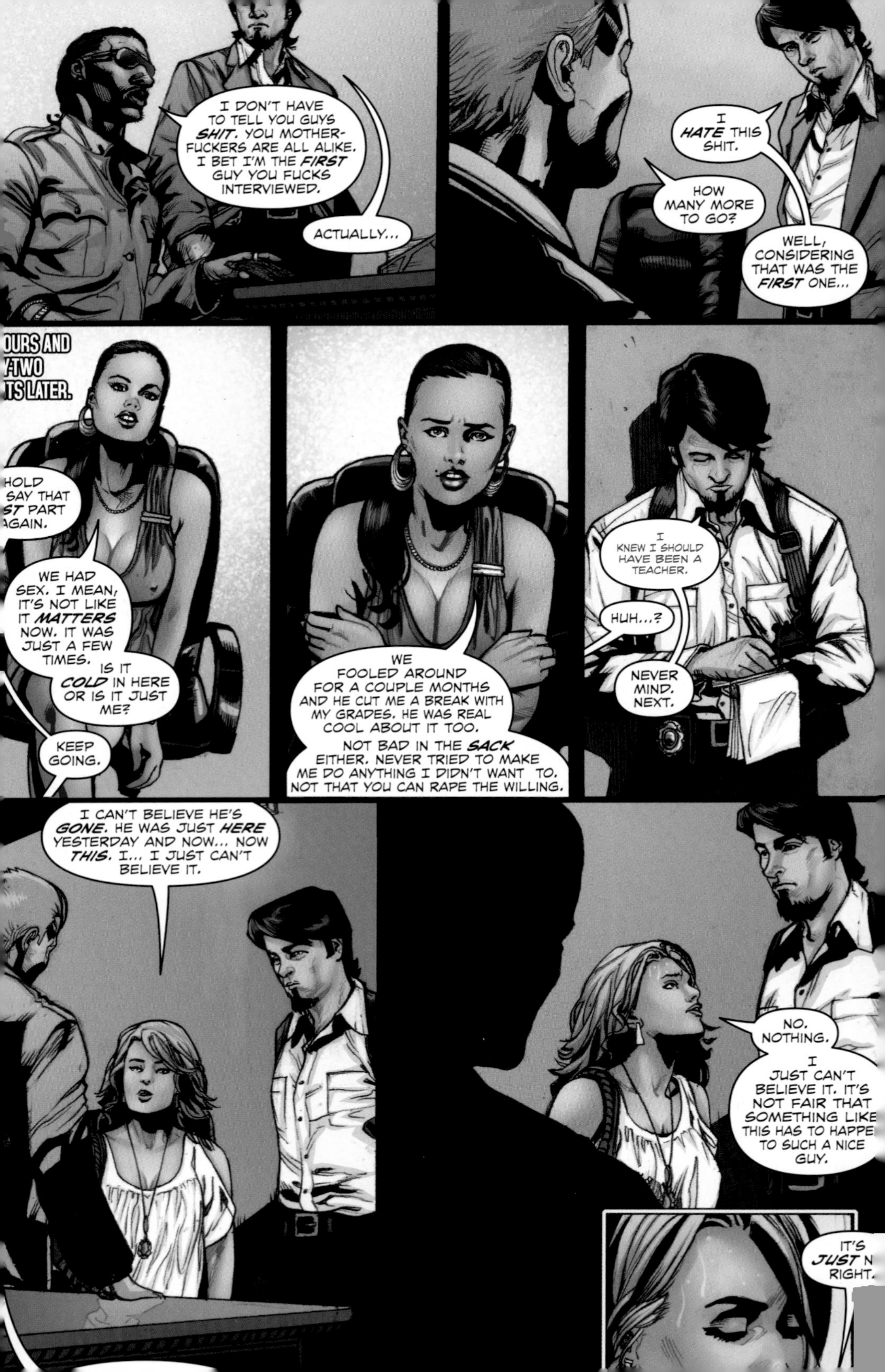
I DON'T HAVE TO TELL YOU GUYS SHIT. YOU MOTHER-FUCKERS ARE ALL ALIKE. I BET I'M THE FIRST GUY YOU FUCKS INTERVIEWED.
ACTUALLY...
I HATE THIS SHIT.
HOW MANY MORE TO GO?
WELL, CONSIDERING THAT WAS THE FIRST ONE...
OURS AND
-TWO
TS LATER.
HOLD
SAY THAT
ST PART
AGAIN.
WE HAD SEX. I MEAN, IT'S NOT LIKE IT MATTERS NOW. IT WAS JUST A FEW TIMES.
IS IT COLD IN HERE OR IS IT JUST ME?
KEEP GOING.
WE FOOLED AROUND FOR A COUPLE MONTHS AND HE CUT ME A BREAK WITH MY GRADES. HE WAS REAL COOL ABOUT IT TOO.
NOT BAD IN THE SACK EITHER. NEVER TRIED TO MAKE ME DO ANYTHING I DIDN'T WANT TO. NOT THAT YOU CAN RAPE THE WILLING.
I KNEW I SHOULD HAVE BEEN A TEACHER.
HUH...?
NEVER MIND. NEXT.
I CAN'T BELIEVE HE'S GONE. HE WAS JUST HERE YESTERDAY AND NOW... NOW THIS. I... I JUST CAN'T BELIEVE IT.
NO. NOTHING.
I JUST CAN'T BELIEVE IT. IT'S NOT FAIR THAT SOMETHING LIKE THIS HAS TO HAPPE TO SUCH A NICE GUY.
IT'S JUST N RIGHT.

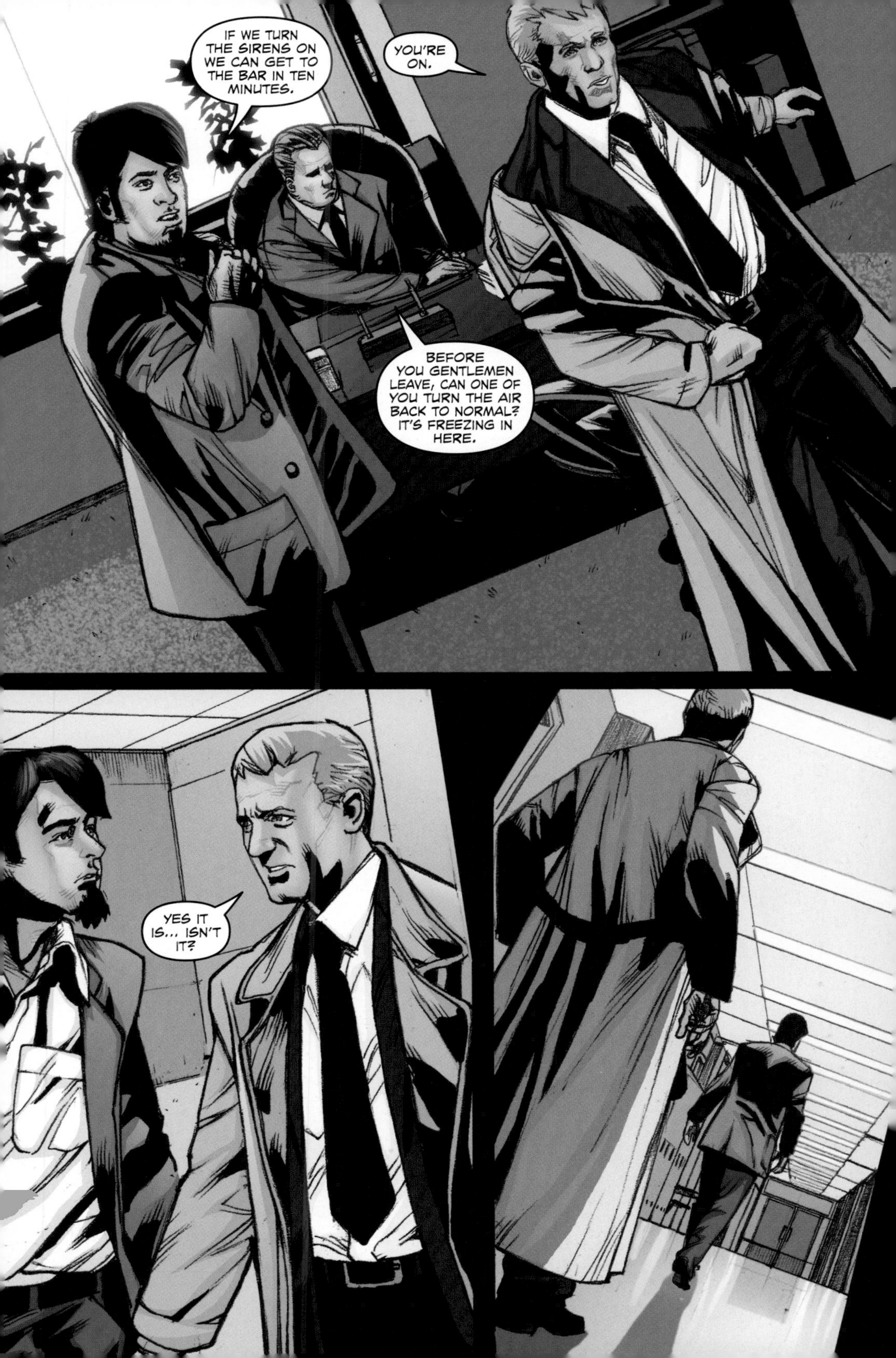
IF WE TURN THE SIRENS ON WE CAN GET TO THE BAR IN TEN MINUTES.
YOU'RE ON.
BEFORE YOU GENTLEMEN LEAVE, CAN ONE OF YOU TURN THE AIR BACK TO NORMAL? IT'S FREEZING IN HERE.
YES IT IS... ISN'T IT?

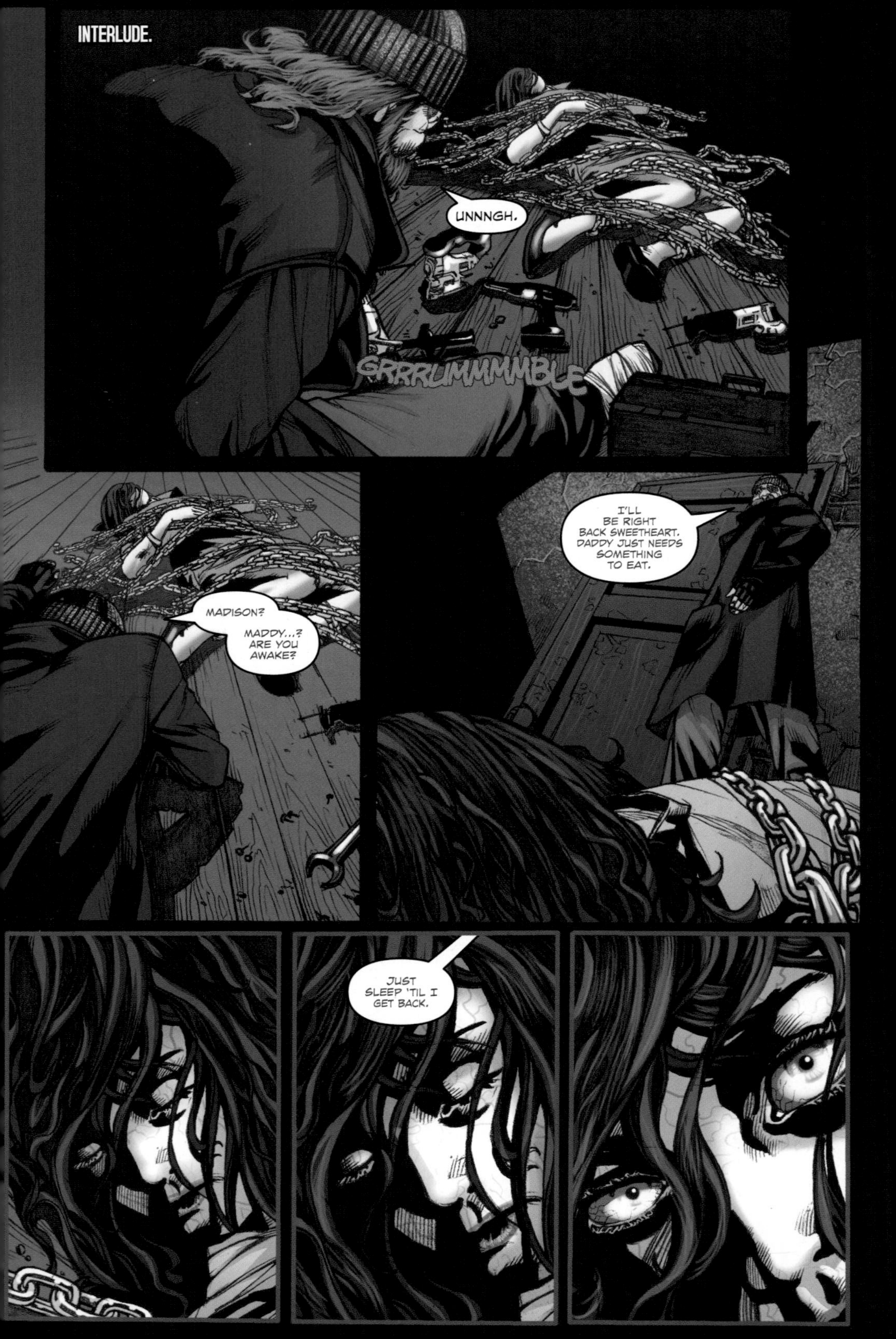
INTERLUDE.
UNNNGH.
GRRRUMMMMBLE
MADISON?
MADDY...? ARE YOU AWAKE?
I'LL BE RIGHT BACK SWEETHEART. DADDY JUST NEEDS SOMETHING TO EAT.
JUST SLEEP 'TIL I GET BACK.

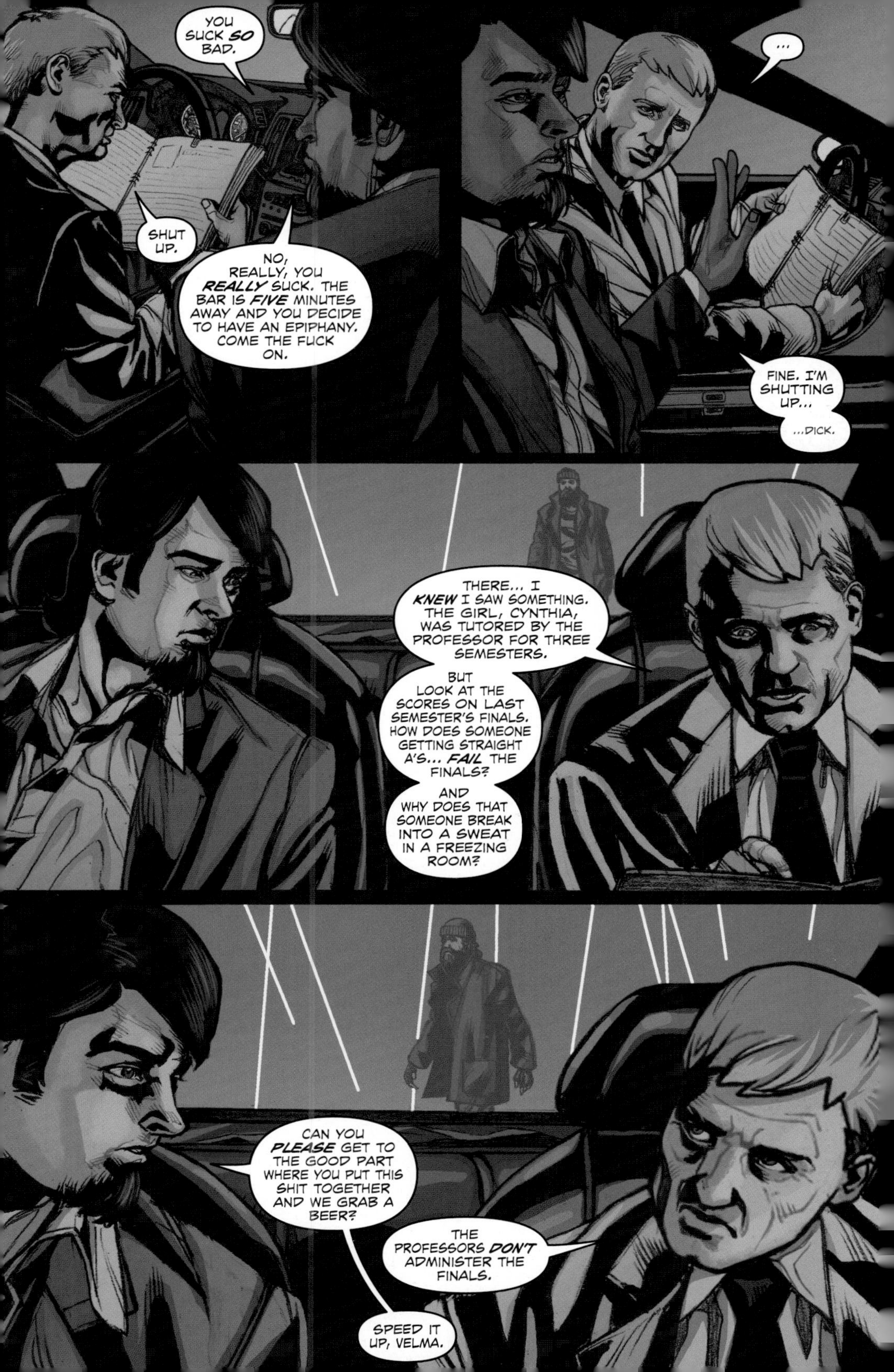

YOU SUCK SO BAD.
SHUT UP.
NO, REALLY, YOU REALLY SUCK. THE BAR IS FIVE MINUTES AWAY AND YOU DECIDE TO HAVE AN EPIPHANY. COME THE FUCK ON.
...
FINE. I'M SHUTTING UP...
...DICK.
THERE... I KNEW I SAW SOMETHING. THE GIRL, CYNTHIA, WAS TUTORED BY THE PROFESSOR FOR THREE SEMESTERS.
BUT LOOK AT THE SCORES ON LAST SEMESTER'S FINALS. HOW DOES SOMEONE GETTING STRAIGHT A'S... FAIL THE FINALS?
AND WHY DOES THAT SOMEONE BREAK INTO A SWEAT IN A FREEZING ROOM?
CAN YOU PLEASE GET TO THE GOOD PART WHERE YOU PUT THIS SHIT TOGETHER AND WE GRAB A BEER?
SPEED IT UP, VELMA.
THE PROFESSORS DON'T ADMINISTER THE FINALS.

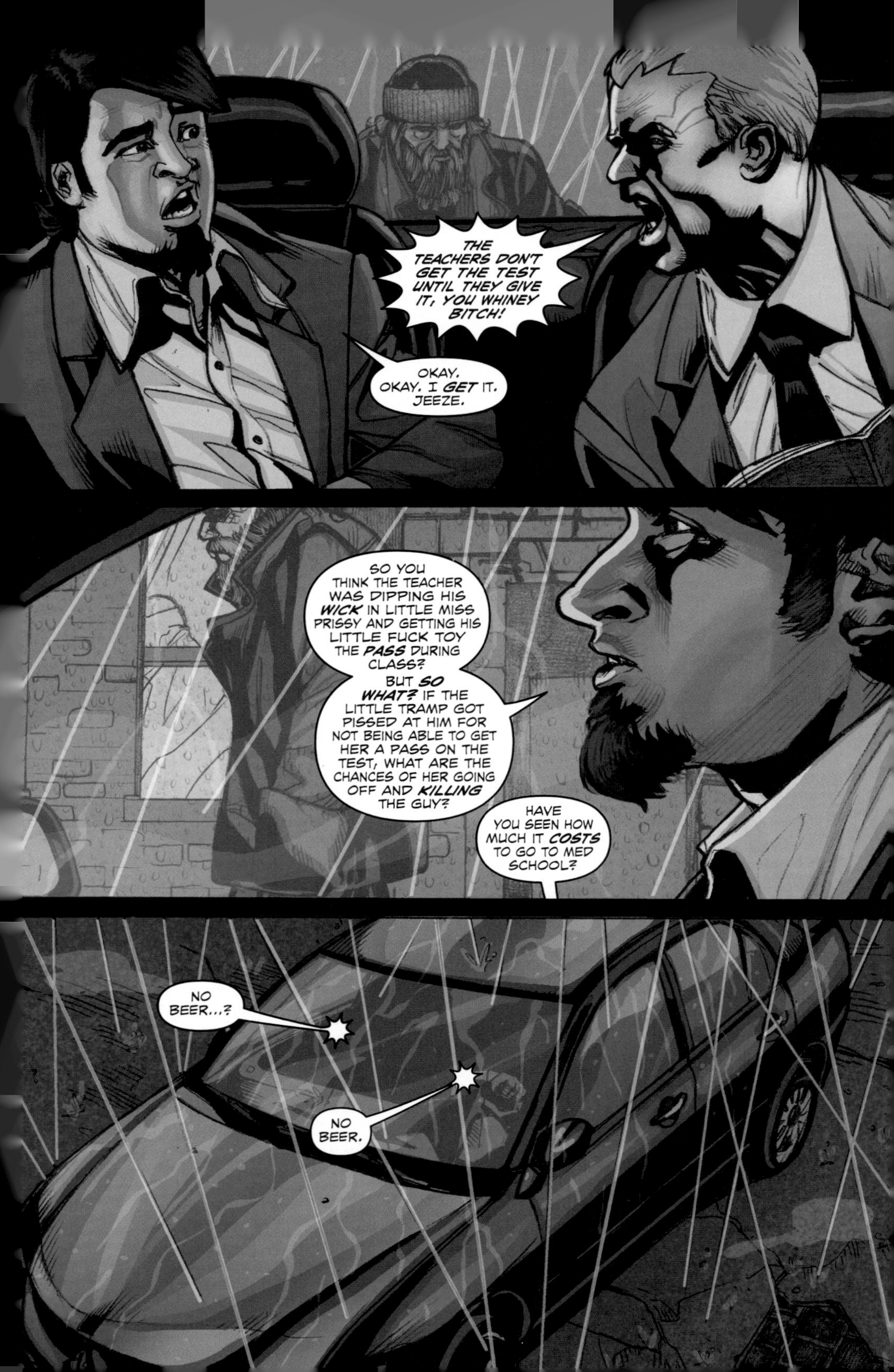
THE TEACHERS DON'T GET THE TEST UNTIL THEY GIVE IT, YOU WHINEY BITCH!
OKAY. OKAY. I GET IT. JEEZE.
SO YOU THINK THE TEACHER WAS DIPPING HIS WICK IN LITTLE MISS PRISSY AND GETTING HIS LITTLE FUCK TOY THE PASS DURING CLASS?
BUT SO WHAT? IF THE LITTLE TRAMP GOT PISSED AT HIM FOR NOT BEING ABLE TO GET HER A PASS ON THE TEST, WHAT ARE THE CHANCES OF HER GOING OFF AND KILLING THE GUY?
HAVE YOU SEEN HOW MUCH IT COSTS TO GO TO MED SCHOOL?
NO BEER...?
NO BEER.

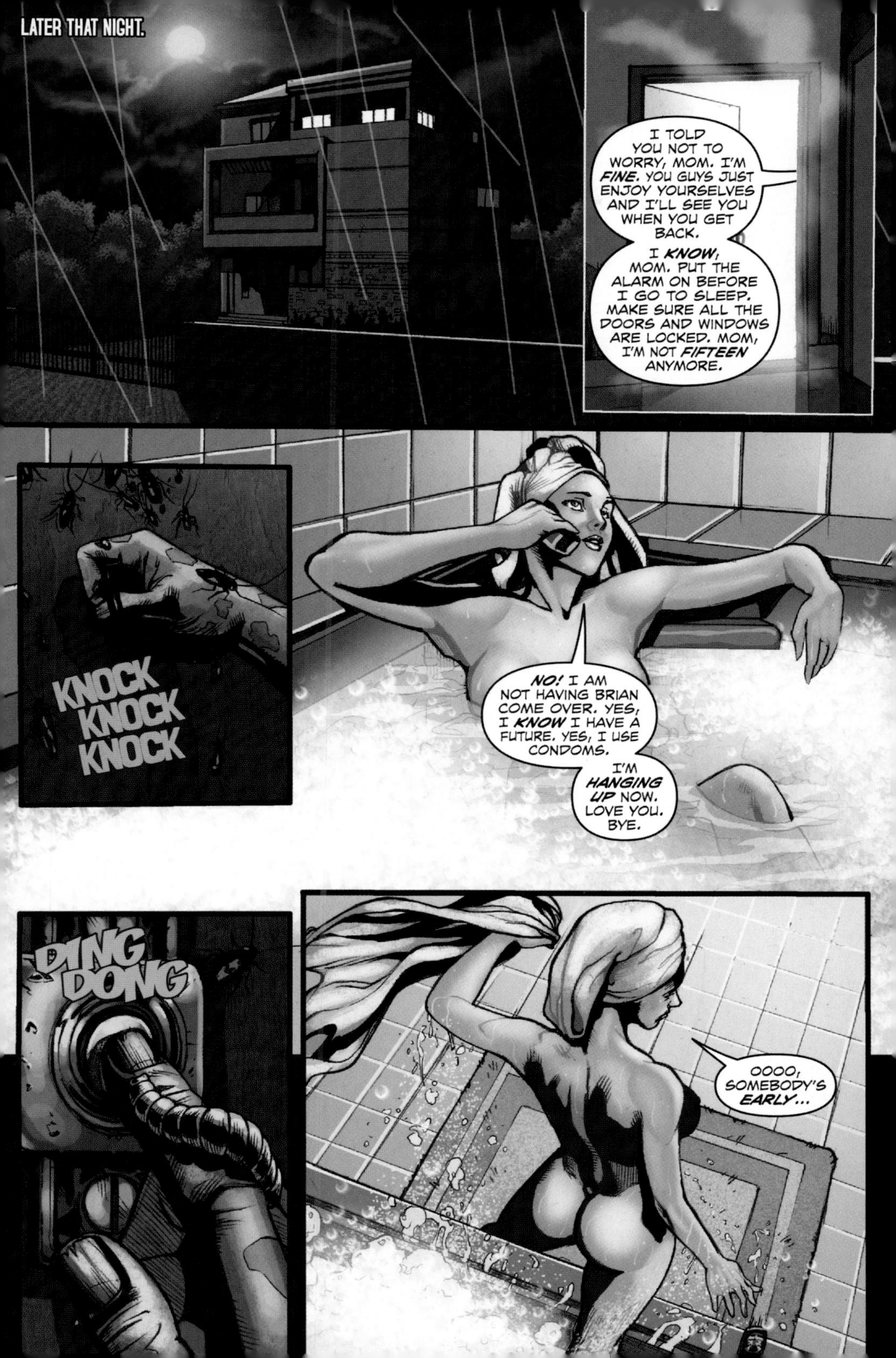
LATER THAT NIGHT.
I TOLD YOU NOT TO WORRY, MOM. I'M FINE. YOU GUYS JUST ENJOY YOURSELVES AND I'LL SEE YOU WHEN YOU GET BACK.
I KNOW, MOM. PUT THE ALARM ON BEFORE I GO TO SLEEP. MAKE SURE ALL THE DOORS AND WINDOWS ARE LOCKED. MOM, I'M NOT FIFTEEN ANYMORE.
KNOCK KNOCK KNOCK
NO! I AM NOT HAVING BRIAN COME OVER. YES, I KNOW I HAVE A FUTURE. YES, I USE CONDOMS.
I'M HANGING UP NOW. LOVE YOU. BYE.
DING DONG
OOOO, SOMEBODY'S EARLY...

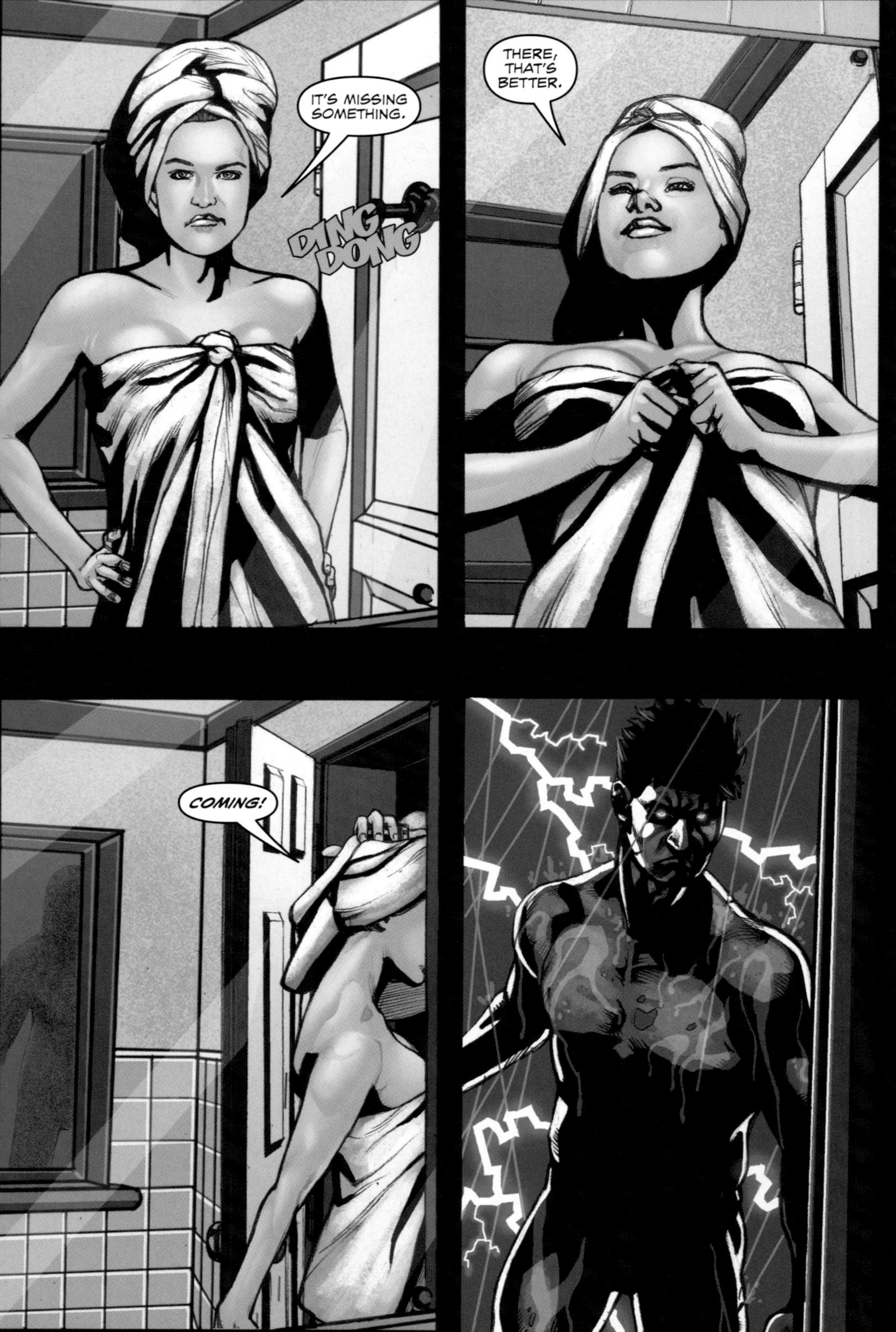
IT'S MISSING SOMETHING.
DING DONG
THERE, THAT'S BETTER.
COMING!

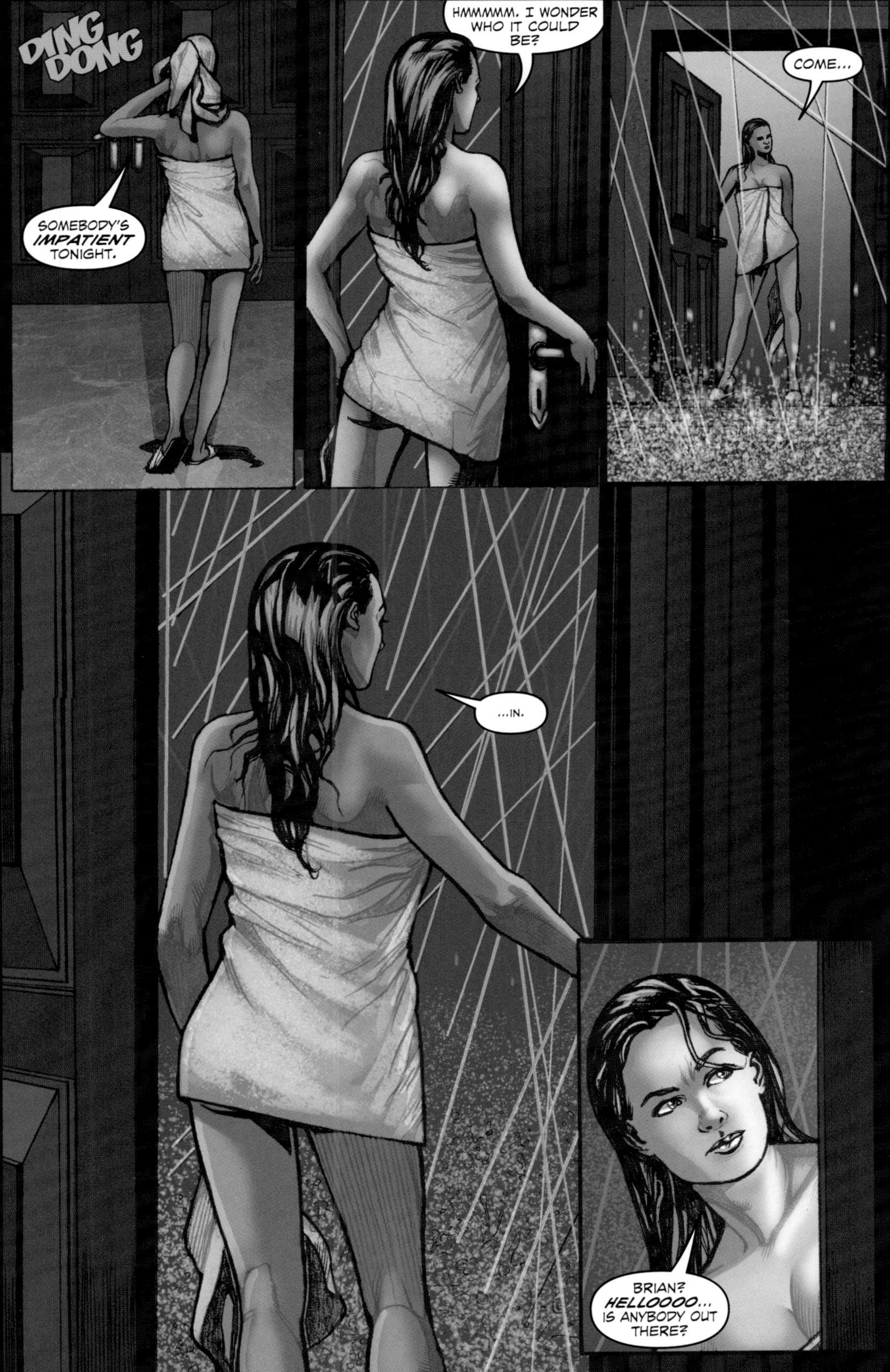
DING DONG
SOMEBODY'S *IMPATIENT* TONIGHT.
HMMMMM. I WONDER WHO IT COULD BE?
COME...
...IN.
BRIAN? *HELLOOOO...* IS ANYBODY OUT THERE?

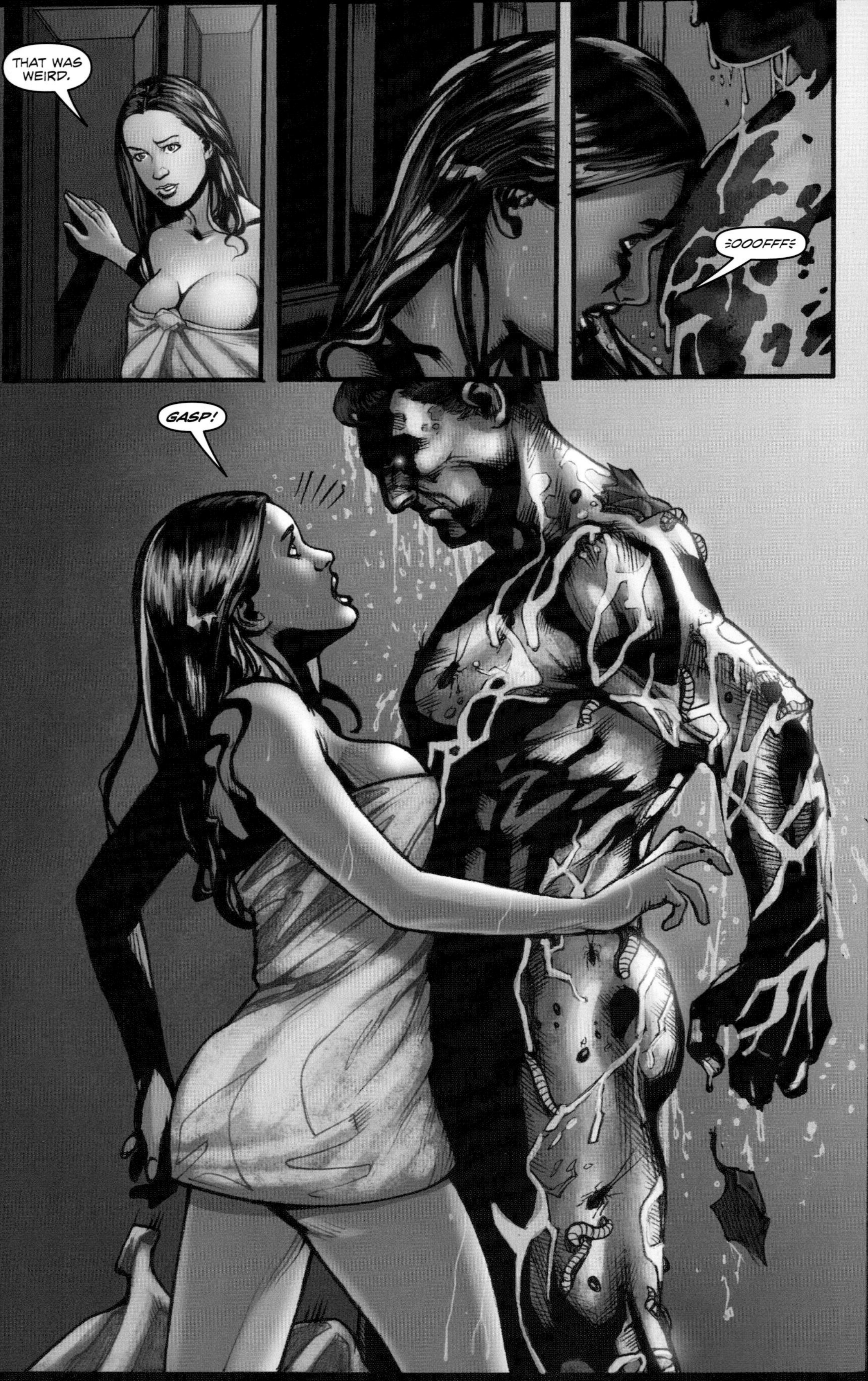
THAT WAS WEIRD.
OOOFFF
GASP!

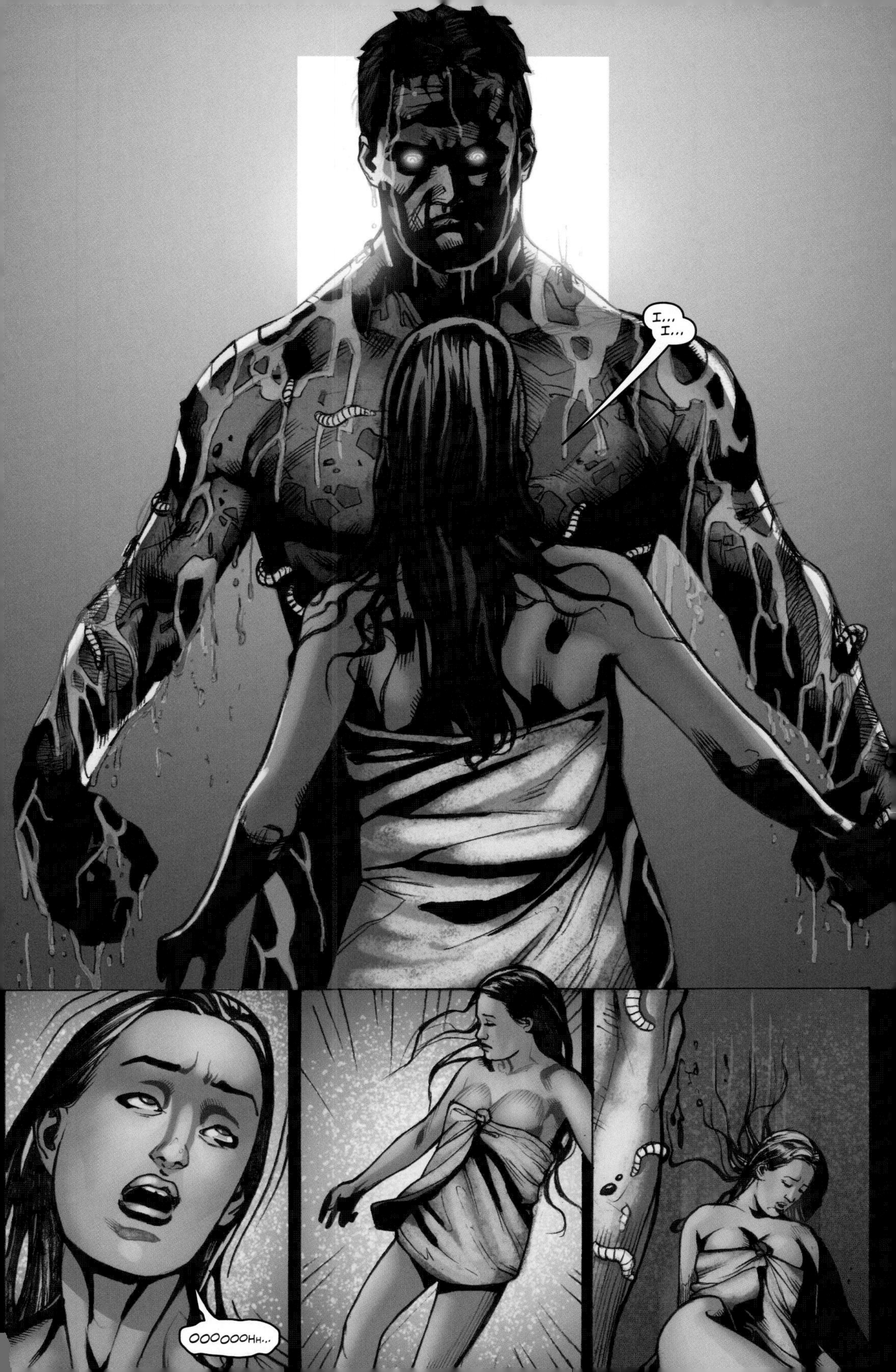
I...
I...
OOOOOOHH...

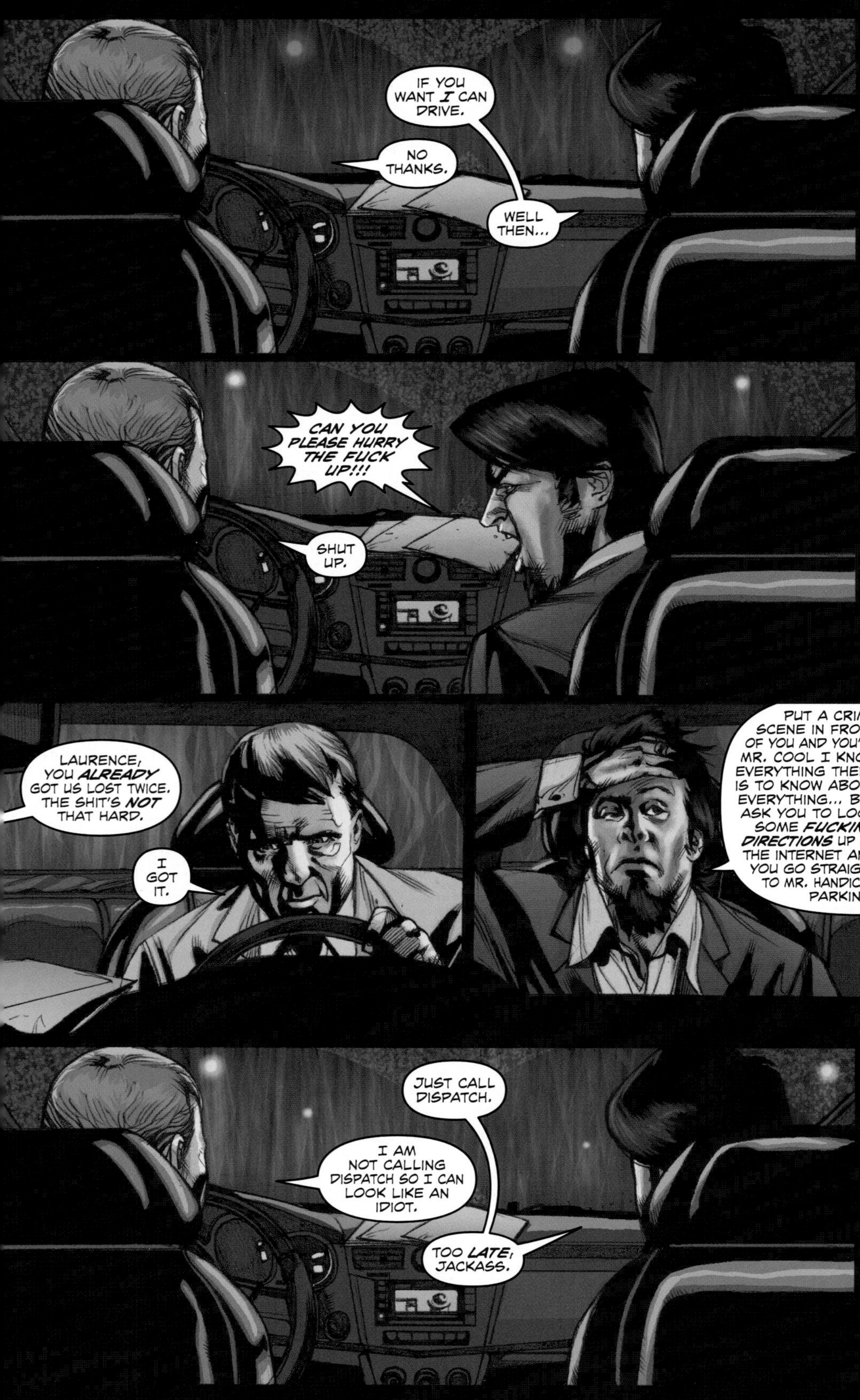
IF YOU WANT I CAN DRIVE.
NO THANKS.
WELL THEN...
CAN YOU PLEASE HURRY THE FUCK UP!!!
SHUT UP.
LAURENCE, YOU ALREADY GOT US LOST TWICE. THE SHIT'S NOT THAT HARD.
I GOT IT.
PUT A CRIME SCENE IN FRONT OF YOU AND YOU'RE MR. COOL I KNOW EVERYTHING THERE IS TO KNOW ABOUT EVERYTHING... BUT ASK YOU TO LOOK SOME FUCKING DIRECTIONS UP ON THE INTERNET AND YOU GO STRAIGHT TO MR. HANDICAP PARKING.
JUST CALL DISPATCH.
I AM NOT CALLING DISPATCH SO I CAN LOOK LIKE AN IDIOT.
TOO LATE, JACKASS.

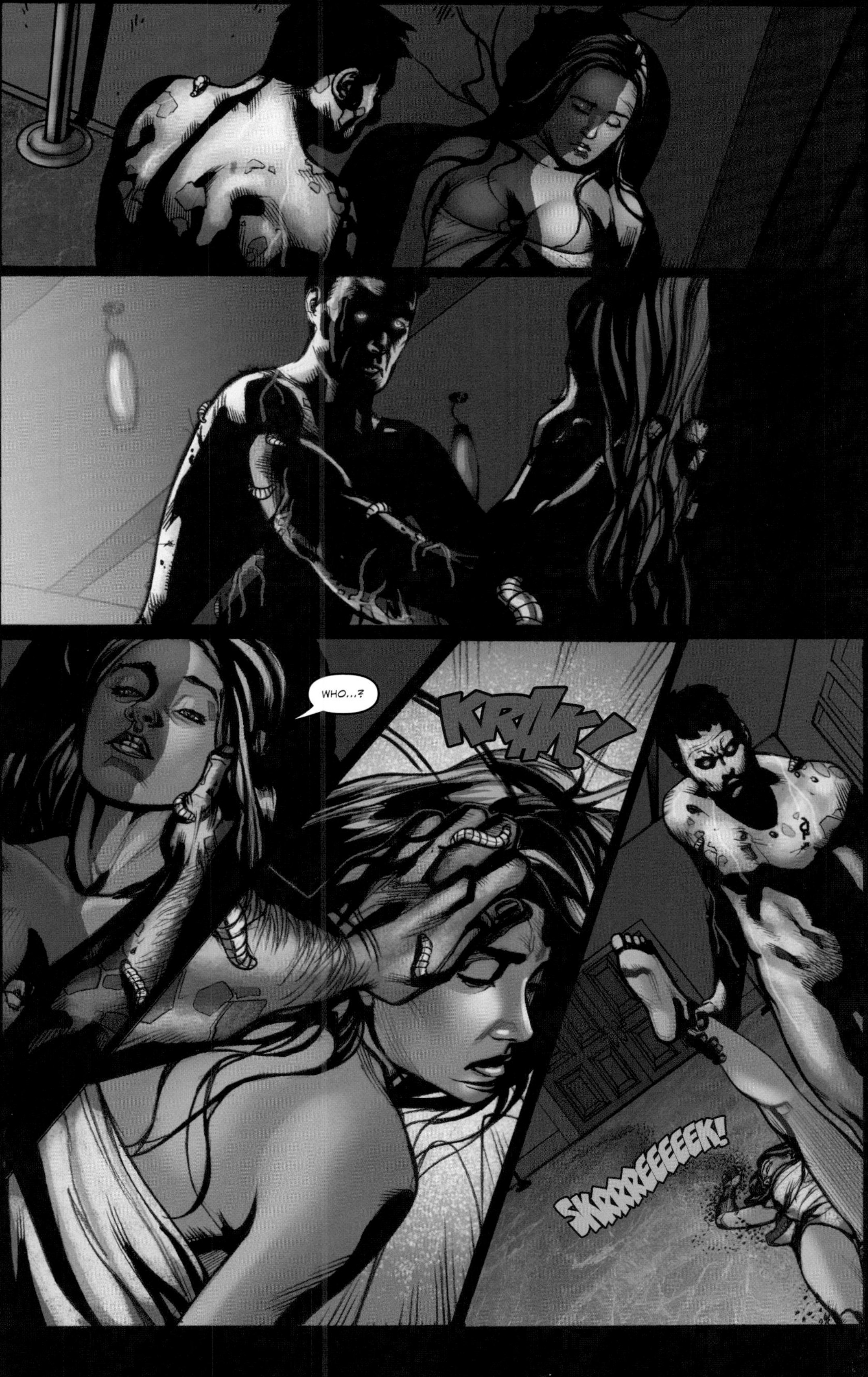
WHO...?
KRAK!
SKRRREEEEEK!

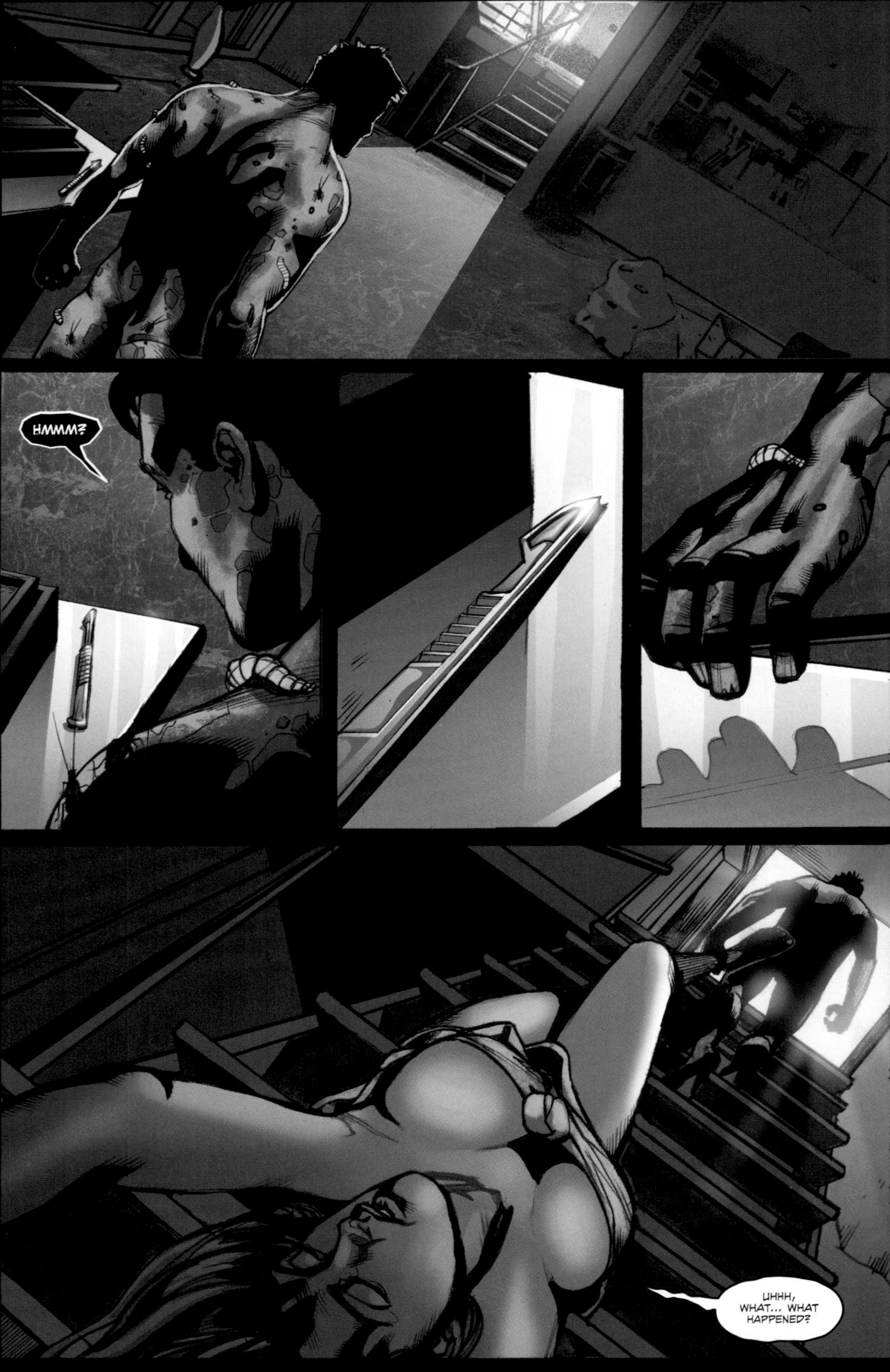
HMMM?
UHHH, WHAT... WHAT HAPPENED?

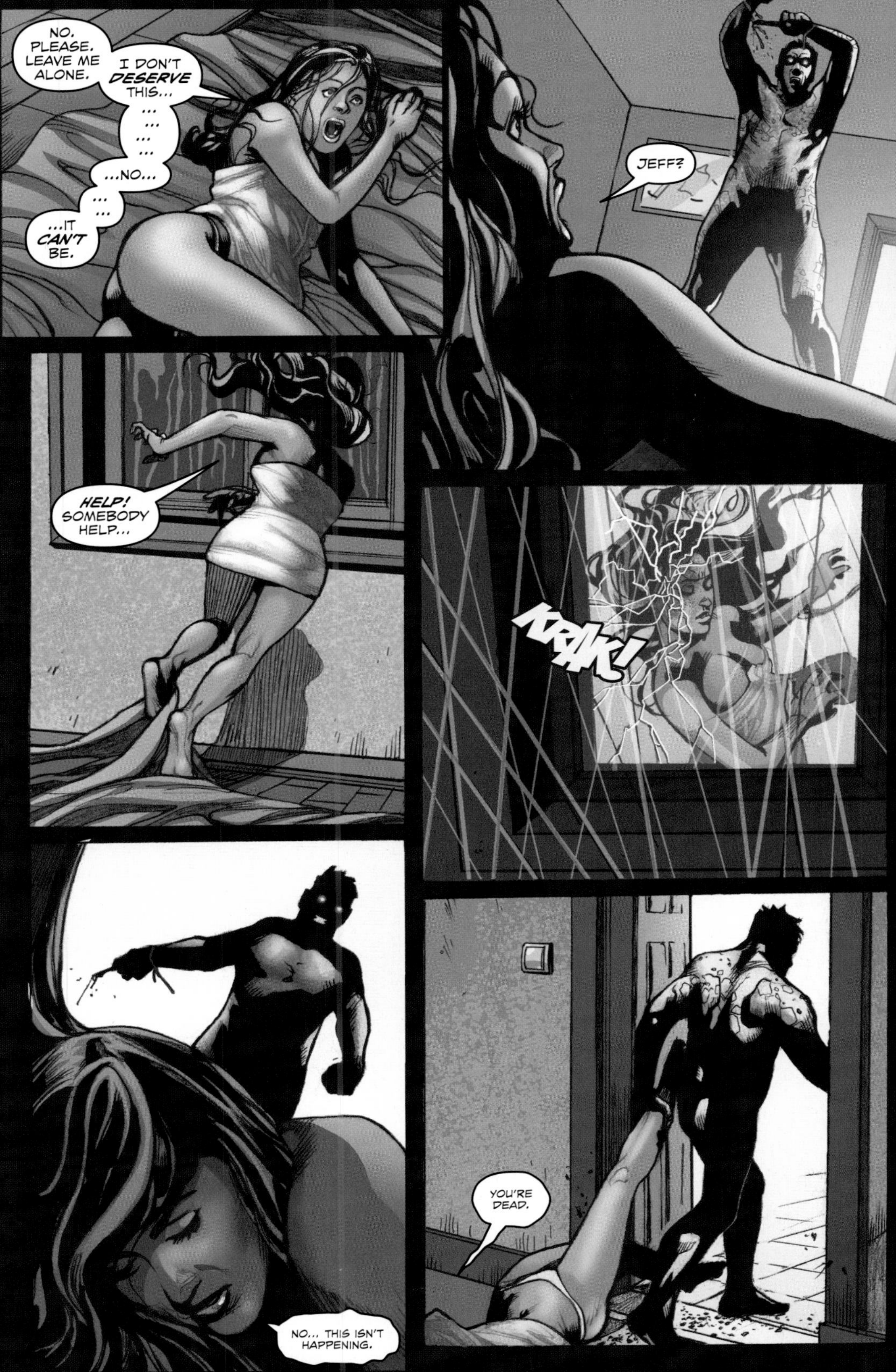
NO. PLEASE. LEAVE ME ALONE.
I DON'T *DESERVE* THIS...
...
...
...
...
...NO...
...
...
...IT *CAN'T* BE.
JEFF?
HELP! SOMEBODY HELP...
KRAK!
YOU'RE DEAD.
NO... THIS ISN'T HAPPENING.

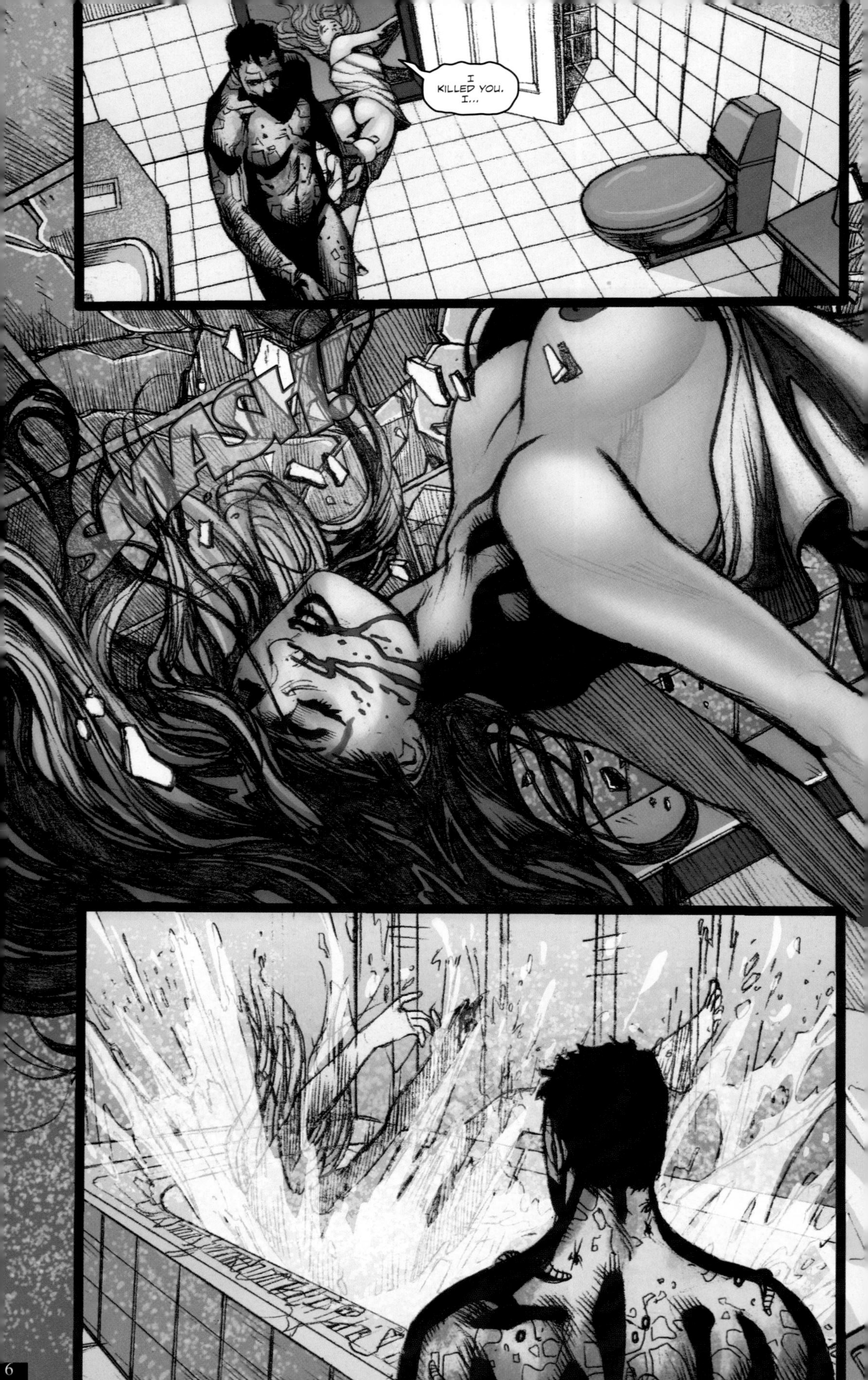
I KILLED YOU. I...
SMASH!

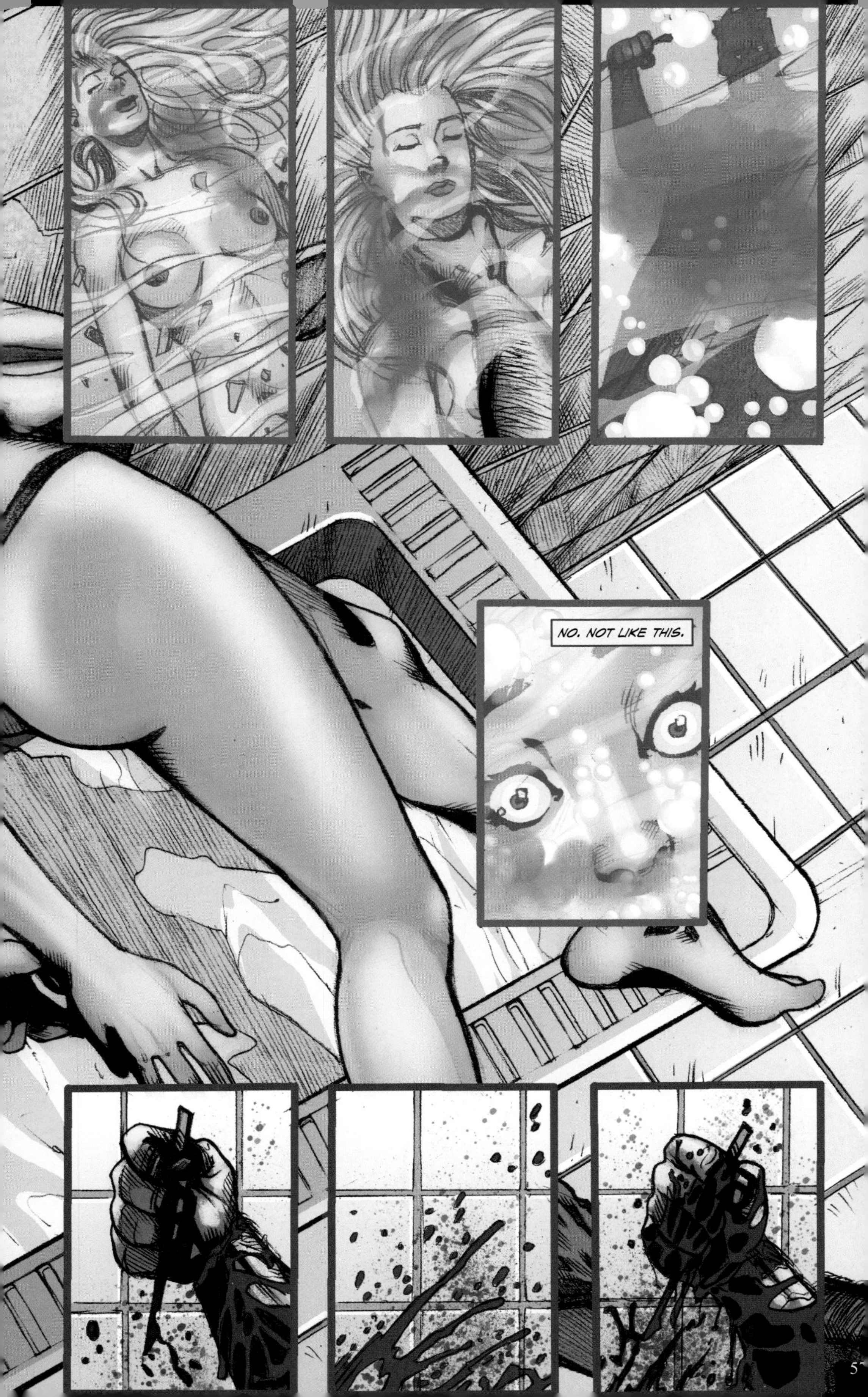
NO. NOT LIKE THIS.

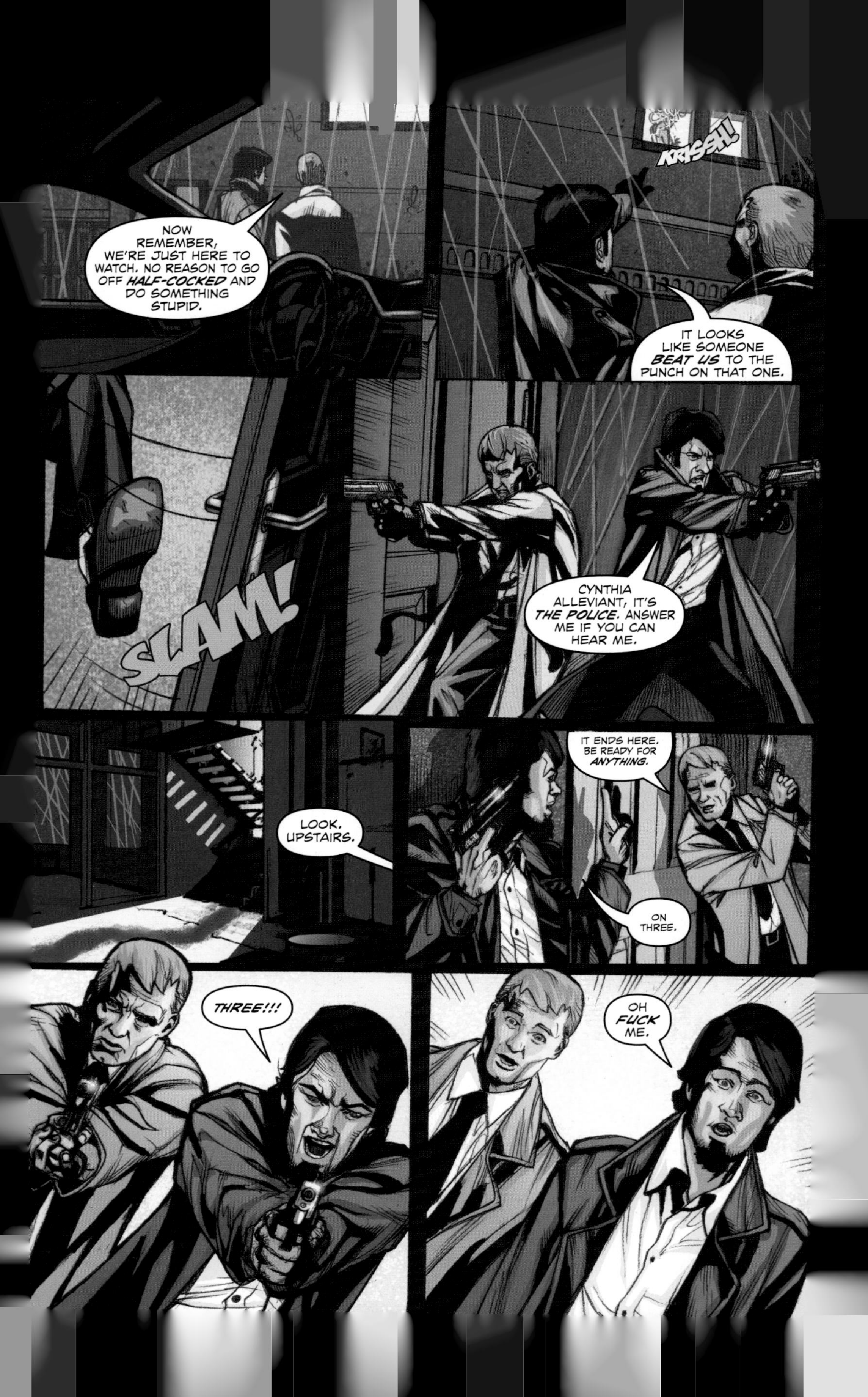
NOW REMEMBER, WE'RE JUST HERE TO WATCH. NO REASON TO GO OFF *HALF-COCKED* AND DO SOMETHING STUPID.
KRISSH!
IT LOOKS LIKE SOMEONE *BEAT US* TO THE PUNCH ON THAT ONE.
SLAM!
CYNTHIA ALLEVIANT, IT'S *THE POLICE.* ANSWER ME IF YOU CAN HEAR ME.
LOOK. UPSTAIRS.
IT ENDS HERE. BE READY FOR *ANYTHING.*
ON THREE.
THREE!!!
OH *FUCK* ME.

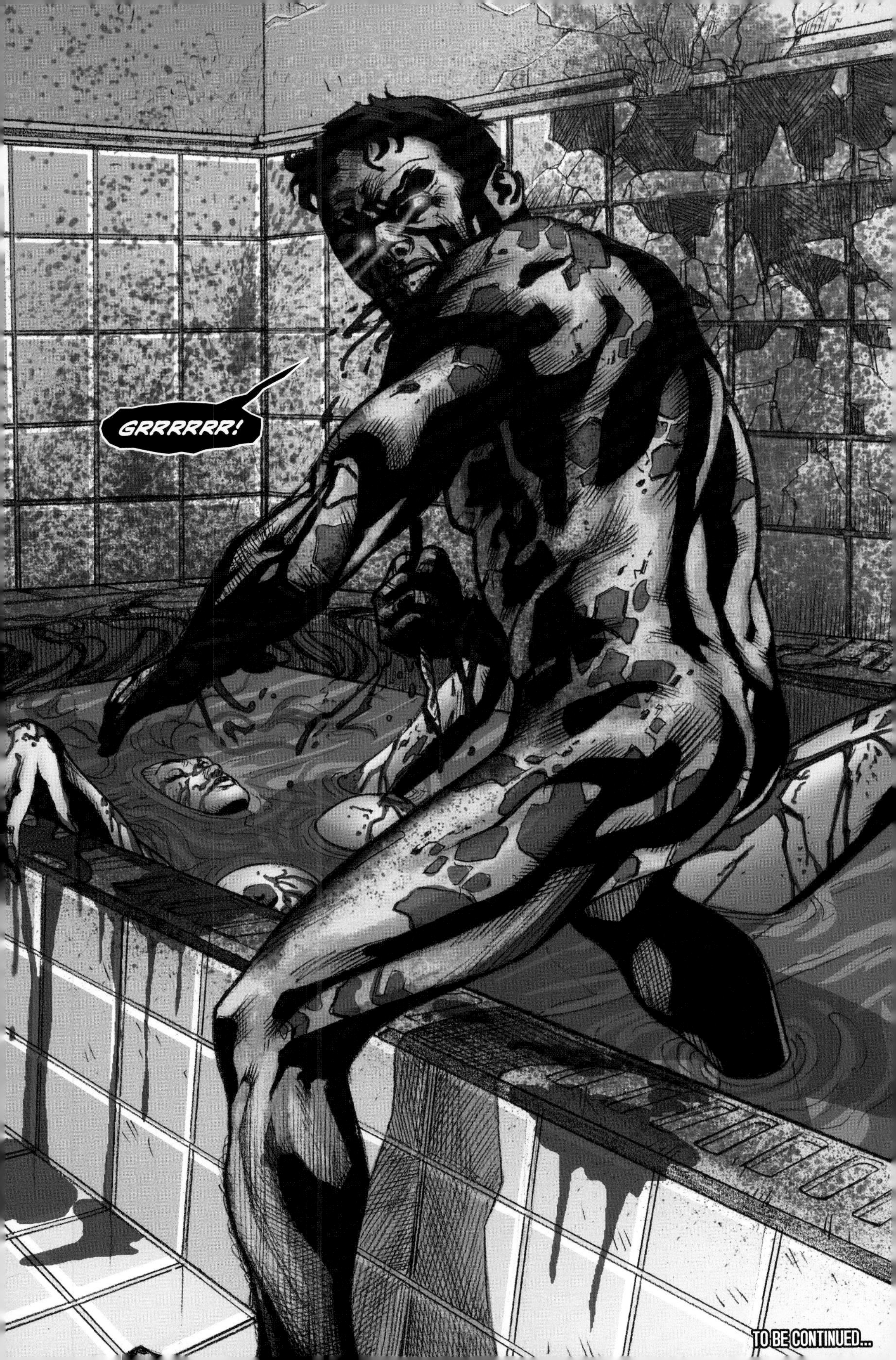
GRRRRRR!
TO BE CONTINUED...

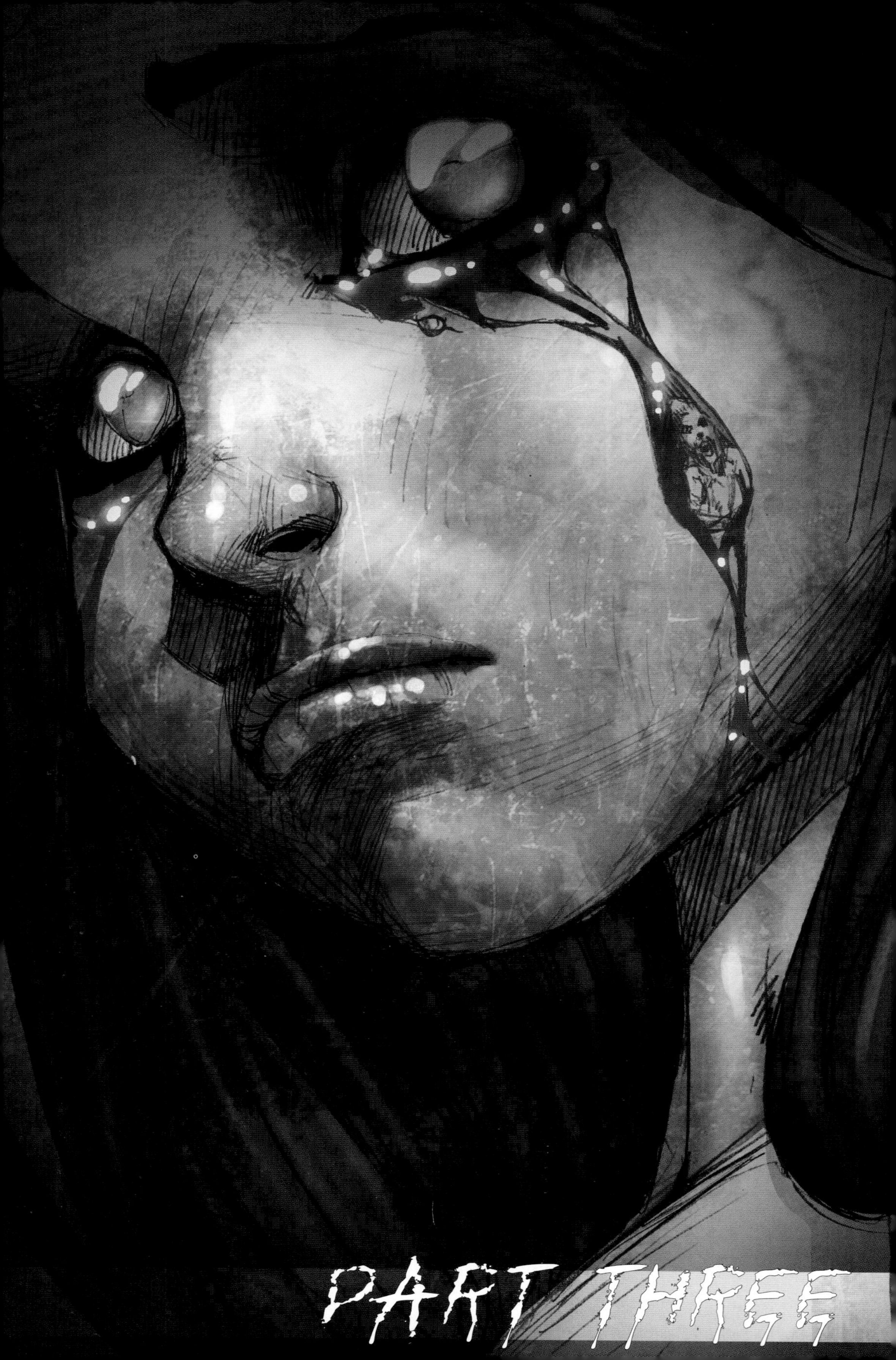
PART THREE

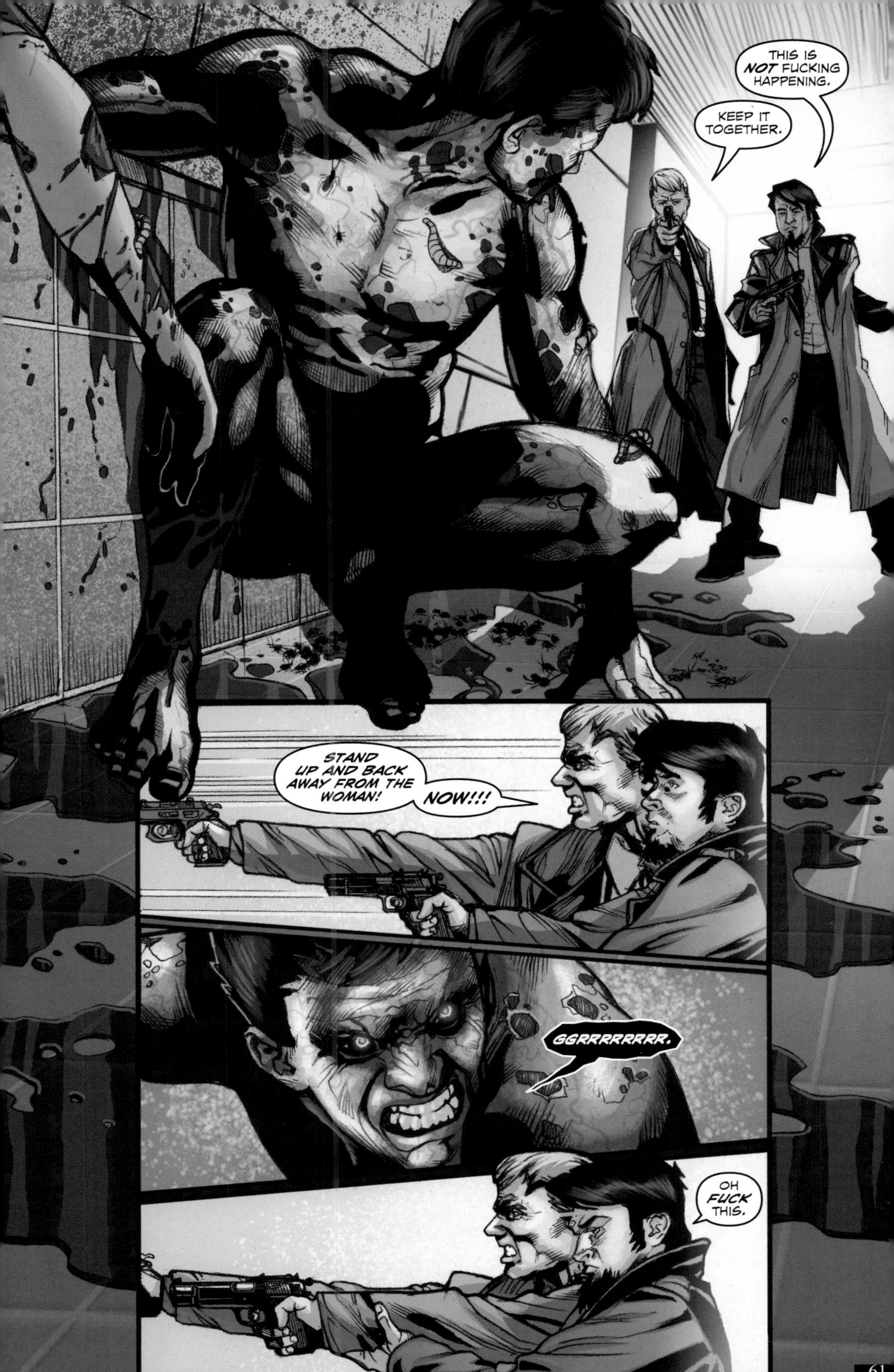
THIS IS NOT FUCKING HAPPENING.
KEEP IT TOGETHER.
STAND UP AND BACK AWAY FROM THE WOMAN!
NOW!!!
GGRRRRRRRR.
OH FUCK THIS.

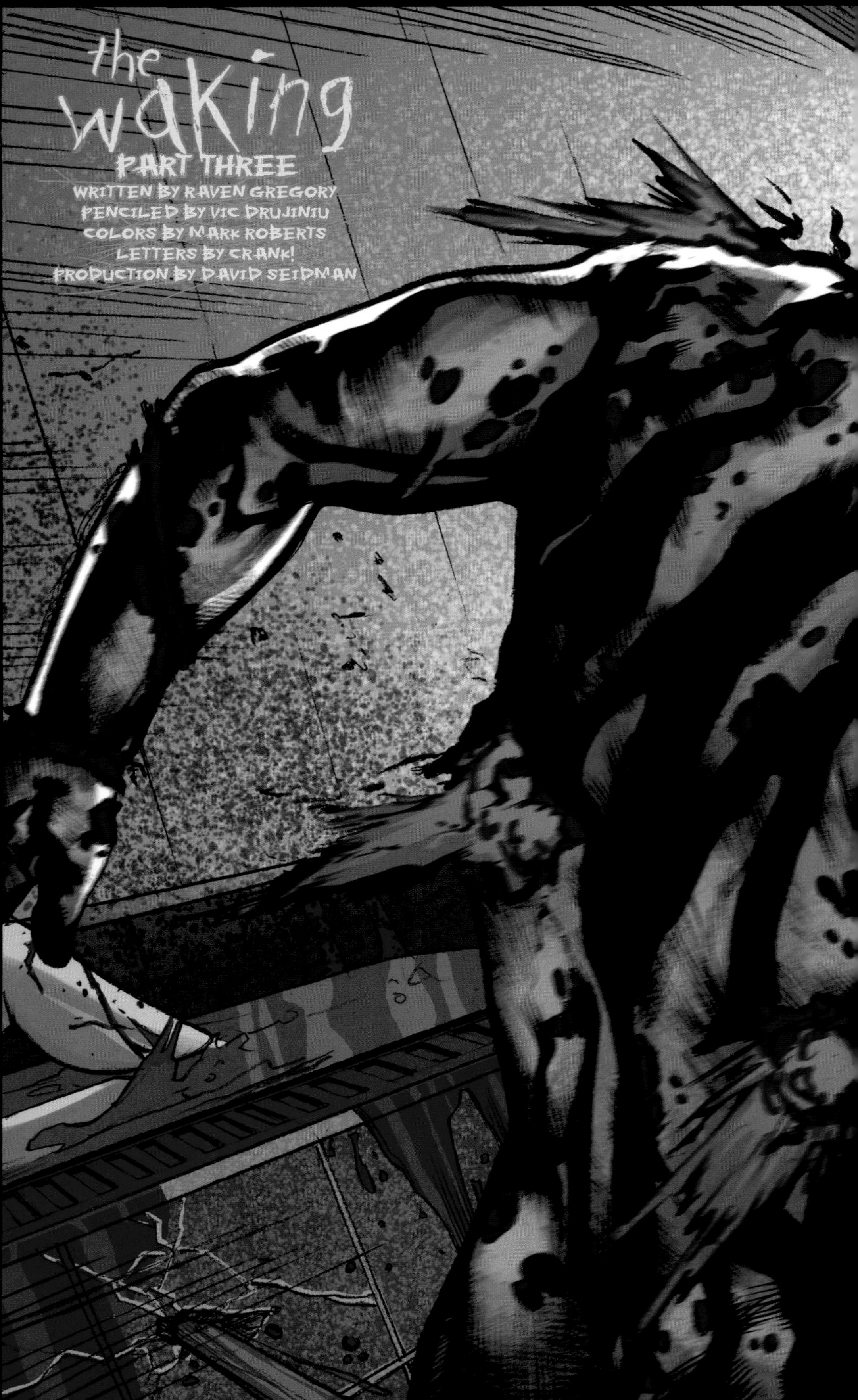
the waking
PART THREE
WRITTEN BY RAVEN GREGORY
PENCILED BY VIC DRUJINIU
COLORS BY MARK ROBERTS
LETTERS BY CRANK!
PRODUCTION BY DAVID SEIDMAN

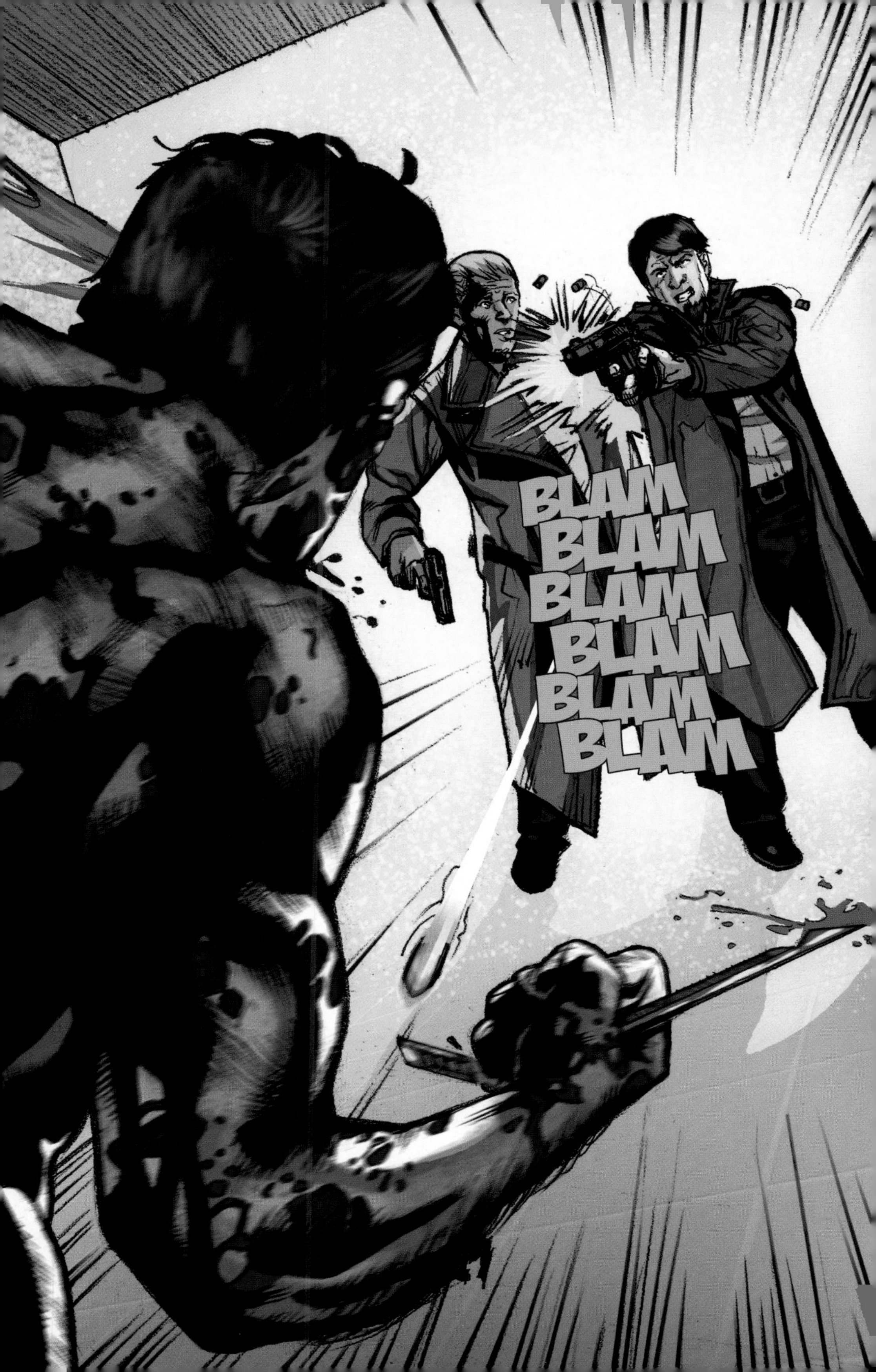
BLAM
BLAM
BLAM
BLAM
BLAM
BLAM

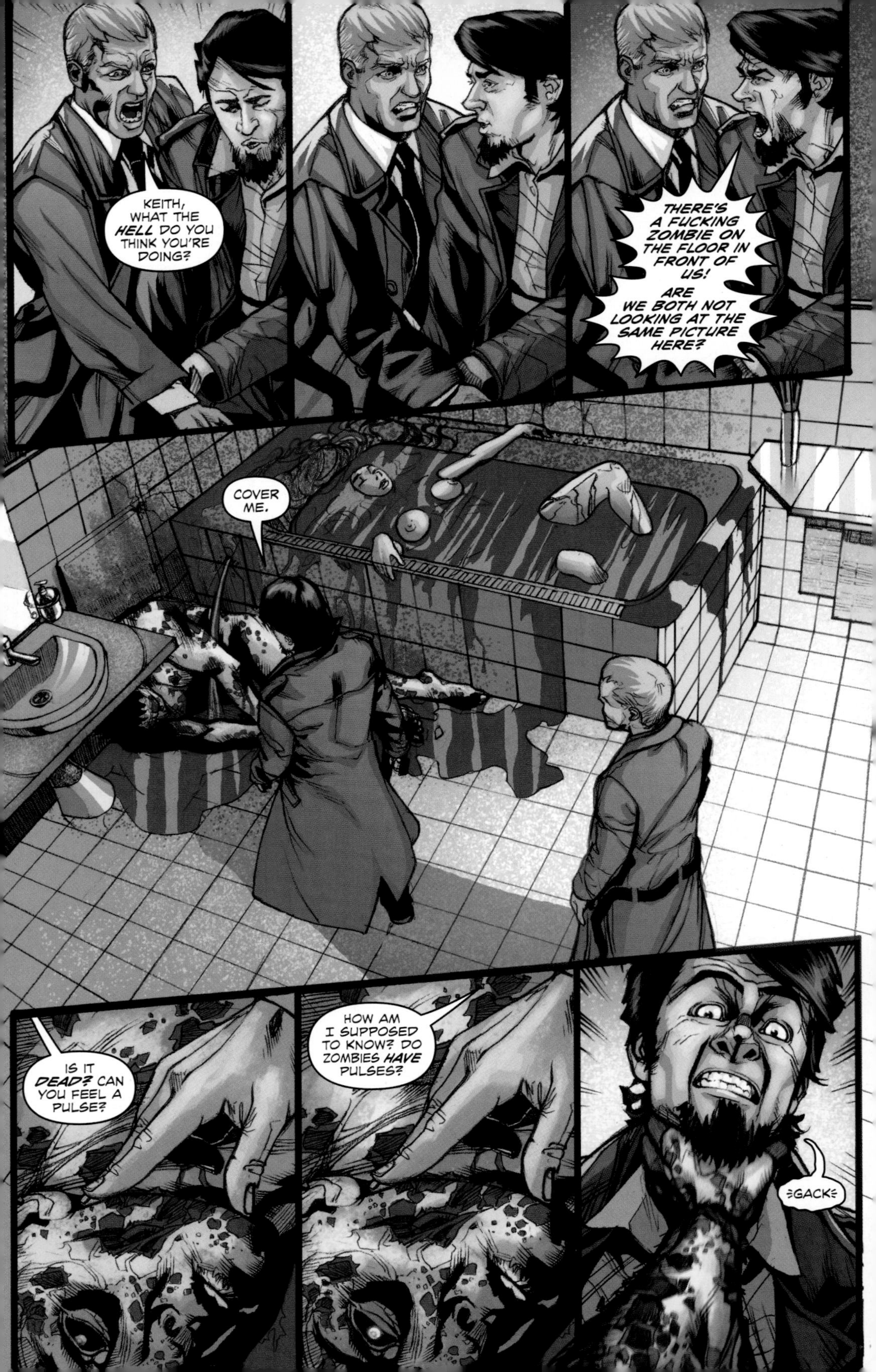
KEITH, WHAT THE *HELL* DO YOU THINK YOU'RE DOING?
THERE'S A FUCKING ZOMBIE ON THE FLOOR IN FRONT OF US!
ARE WE BOTH NOT LOOKING AT THE SAME PICTURE HERE?
COVER ME.
IS IT *DEAD?* CAN YOU FEEL A PULSE?
HOW AM I SUPPOSED TO KNOW? DO ZOMBIES *HAVE* PULSES?
GACK

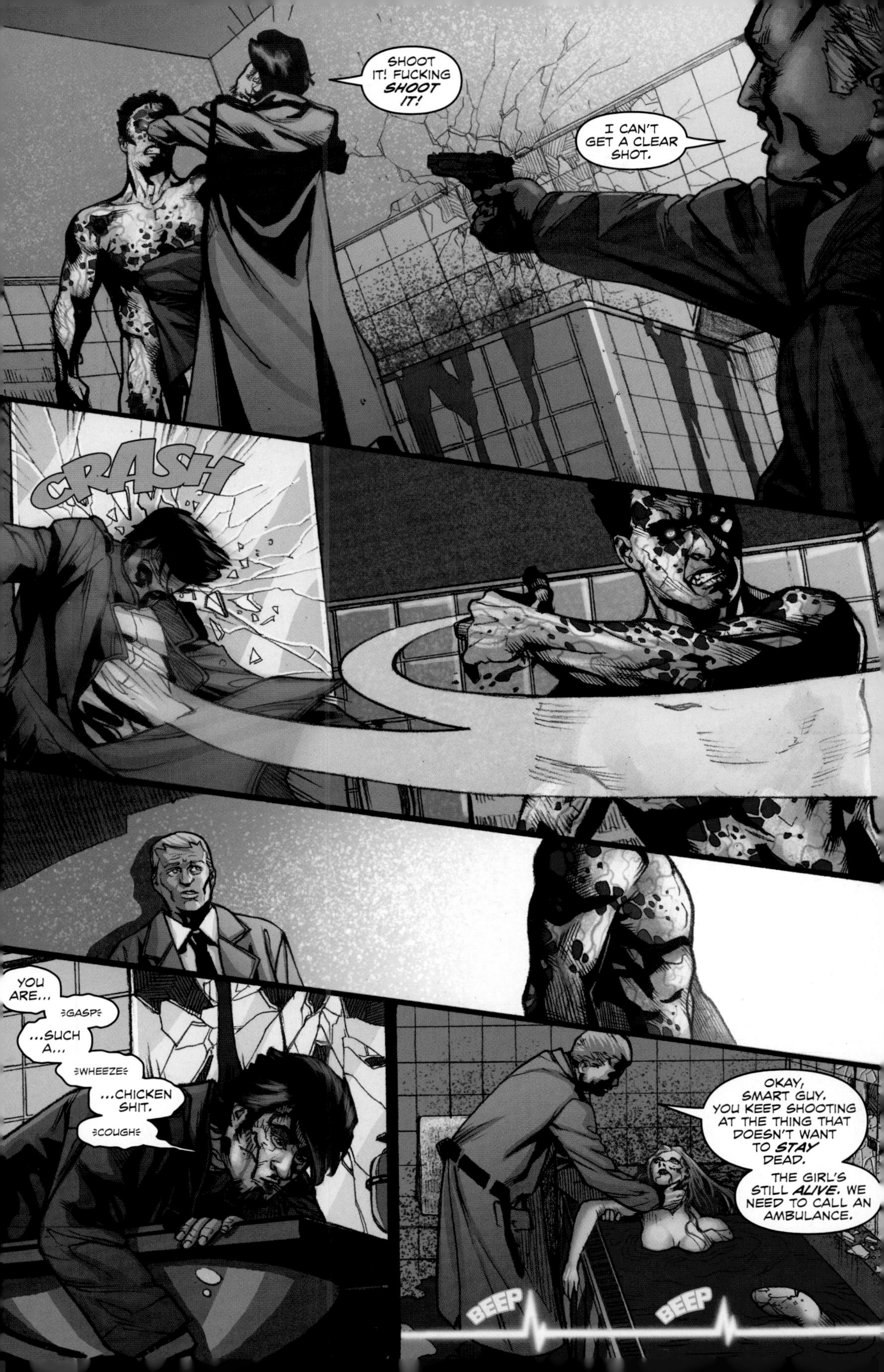

SHOOT IT! FUCKING SHOOT IT!
I CAN'T GET A CLEAR SHOT.
CRASH
YOU ARE...
GASP
...SUCH A...
WHEEZE
...CHICKEN SHIT.
COUGH
OKAY, SMART GUY. YOU KEEP SHOOTING AT THE THING THAT DOESN'T WANT TO STAY DEAD.
THE GIRL'S STILL ALIVE. WE NEED TO CALL AN AMBULANCE.
BEEP
BEEP

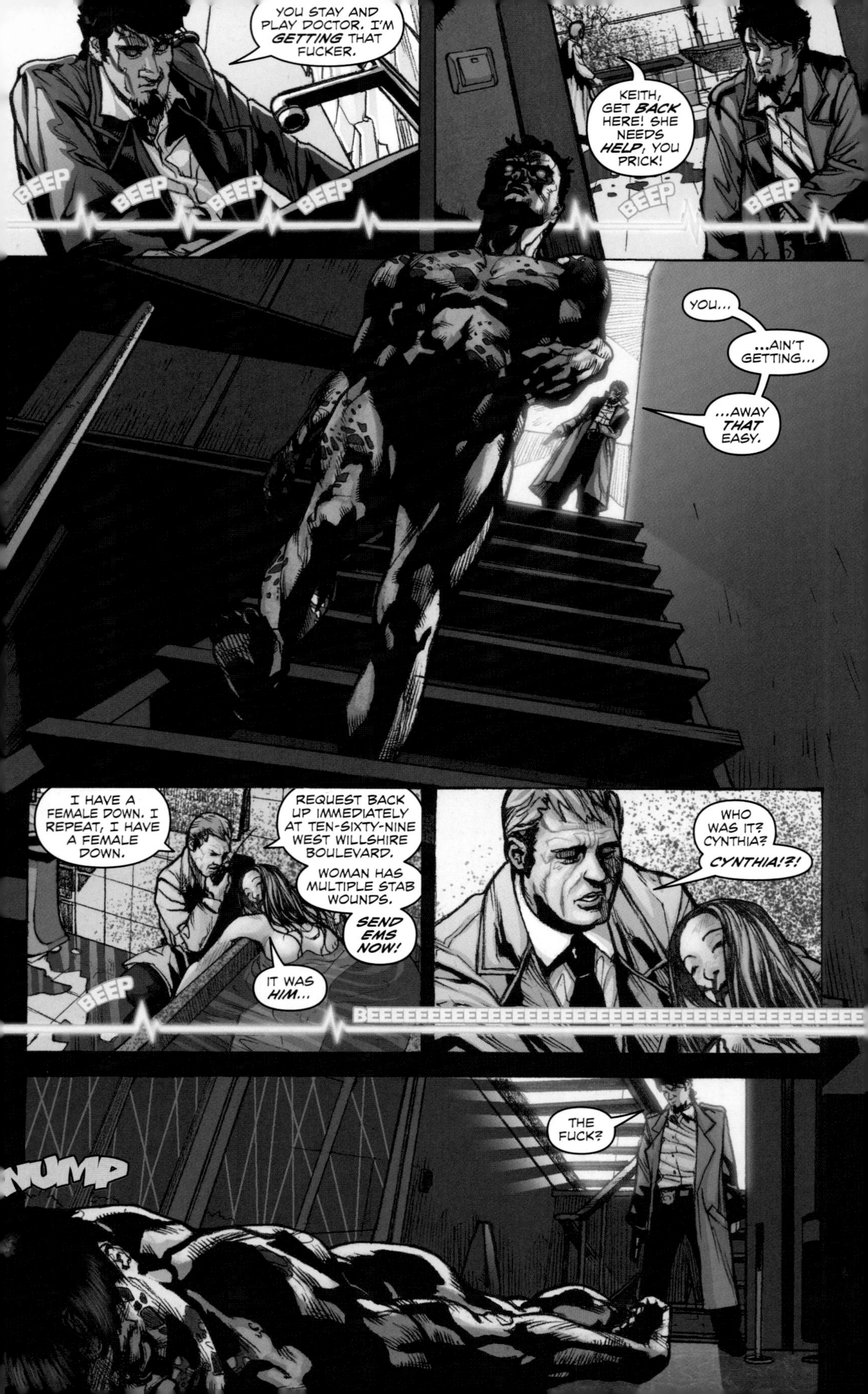
YOU STAY AND PLAY DOCTOR. I'M GETTING THAT FUCKER.
BEEP BEEP BEEP BEEP
KEITH, GET BACK HERE! SHE NEEDS HELP, YOU PRICK!
BEEP BEEP
YOU...
...AIN'T GETTING...
...AWAY THAT EASY.
I HAVE A FEMALE DOWN. I REPEAT, I HAVE A FEMALE DOWN.
REQUEST BACK UP IMMEDIATELY AT TEN-SIXTY-NINE WEST WILLSHIRE BOULEVARD.
WOMAN HAS MULTIPLE STAB WOUNDS.
SEND EMS NOW!
IT WAS HIM...
BEEP
WHO WAS IT? CYNTHIA?
CYNTHIA!?!
BEEEEEEEEEEEEEEEEEEEEEEEEEEEEEEEEEEEEEEEEEEEEEEE
THE FUCK?
NUMP

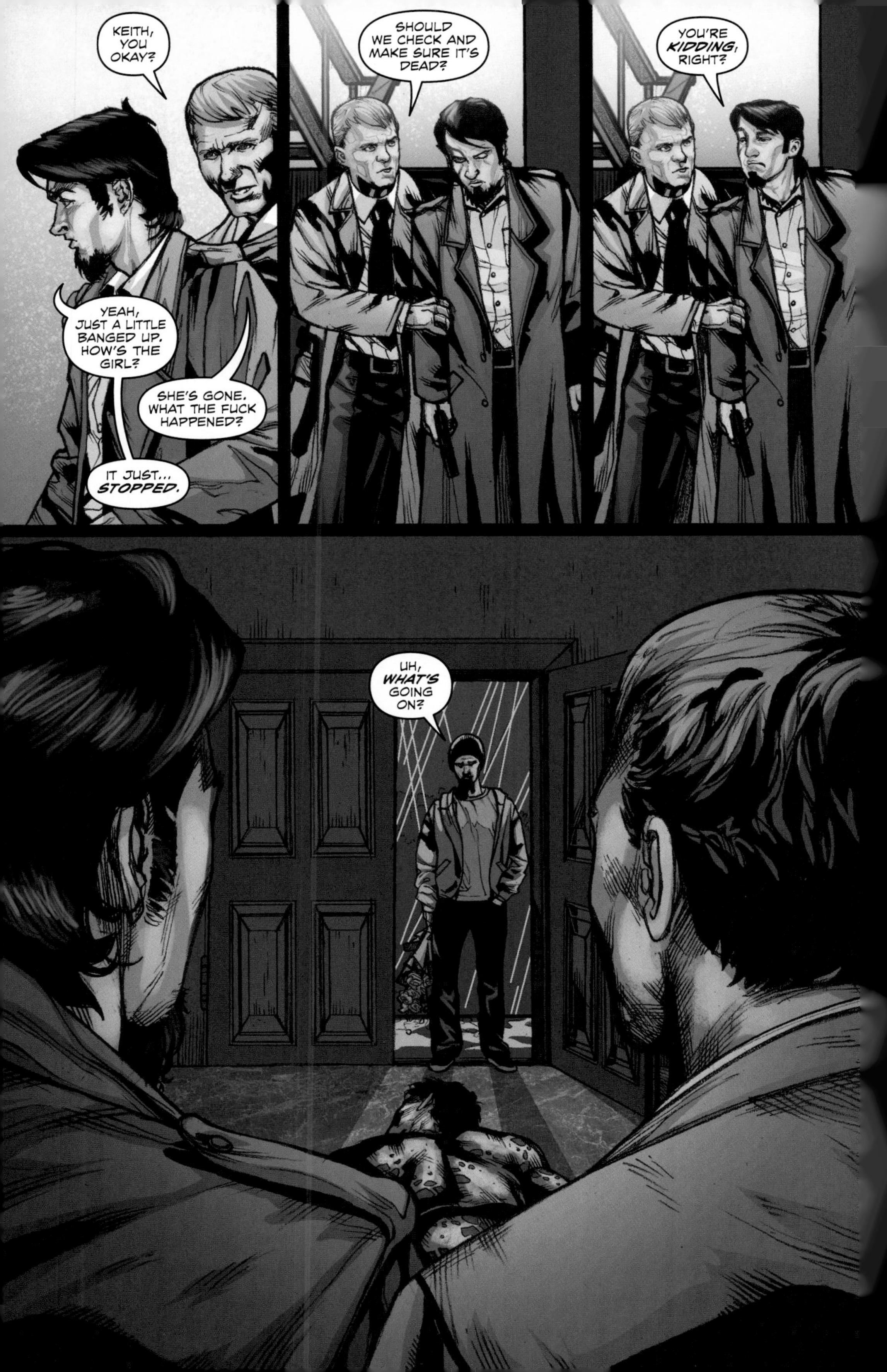
KEITH, YOU OKAY?
YEAH, JUST A LITTLE BANGED UP. HOW'S THE GIRL?
SHE'S GONE. WHAT THE FUCK HAPPENED?
IT JUST... STOPPED.
SHOULD WE CHECK AND MAKE SURE IT'S DEAD?
YOU'RE KIDDING, RIGHT?
UH, WHAT'S GOING ON?

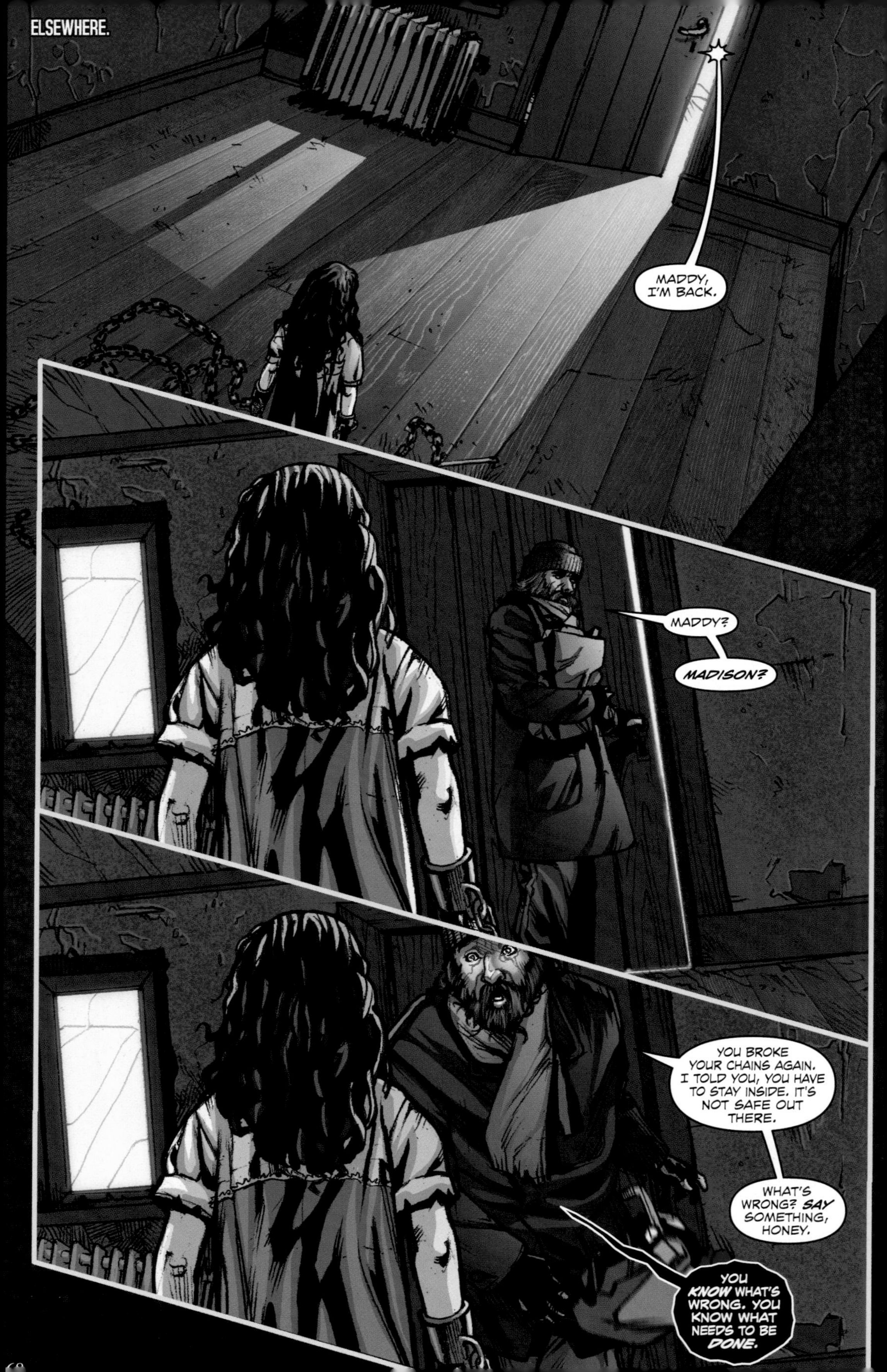
ELSEWHERE.
MADDY, I'M BACK.
MADDY?
MADISON?
YOU BROKE YOUR CHAINS AGAIN. I TOLD YOU, YOU HAVE TO STAY INSIDE. IT'S NOT SAFE OUT THERE.
WHAT'S WRONG? SAY SOMETHING, HONEY.
YOU KNOW WHAT'S WRONG. YOU KNOW WHAT NEEDS TO BE DONE.

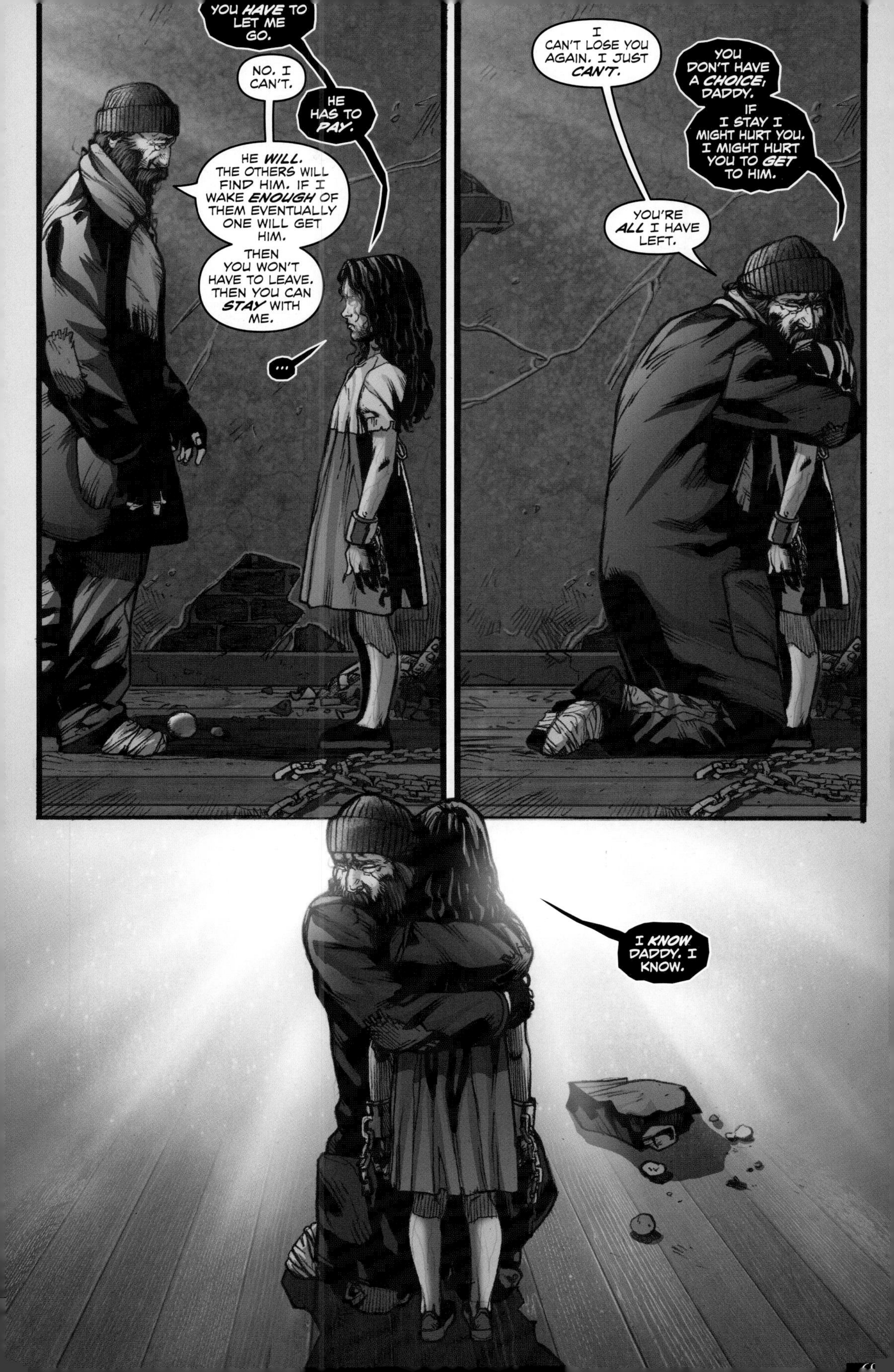
YOU HAVE TO LET ME GO.
NO. I CAN'T.
HE HAS TO PAY.
HE WILL. THE OTHERS WILL FIND HIM. IF I WAKE ENOUGH OF THEM EVENTUALLY ONE WILL GET HIM.
THEN YOU WON'T HAVE TO LEAVE. THEN YOU CAN STAY WITH ME.
...
I CAN'T LOSE YOU AGAIN. I JUST CAN'T.
YOU DON'T HAVE A CHOICE, DADDY.
IF I STAY I MIGHT HURT YOU. I MIGHT HURT YOU TO GET TO HIM.
YOU'RE ALL I HAVE LEFT.
I KNOW. DADDY. I KNOW.

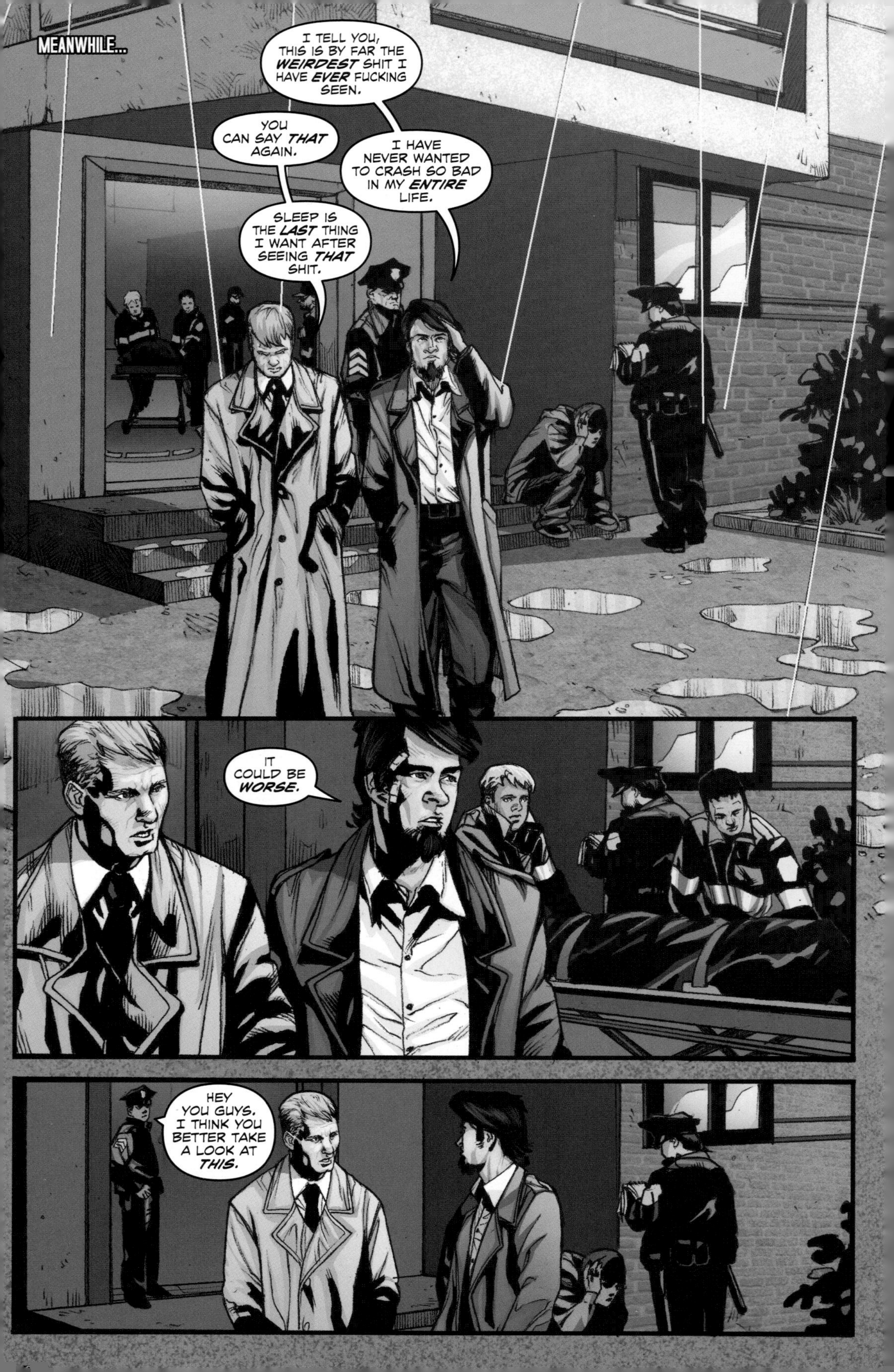
MEANWHILE...
I TELL YOU, THIS IS BY FAR THE WEIRDEST SHIT I HAVE EVER FUCKING SEEN.
YOU CAN SAY THAT AGAIN.
I HAVE NEVER WANTED TO CRASH SO BAD IN MY ENTIRE LIFE.
SLEEP IS THE LAST THING I WANT AFTER SEEING THAT SHIT.
IT COULD BE WORSE.
HEY YOU GUYS. I THINK YOU BETTER TAKE A LOOK AT THIS.

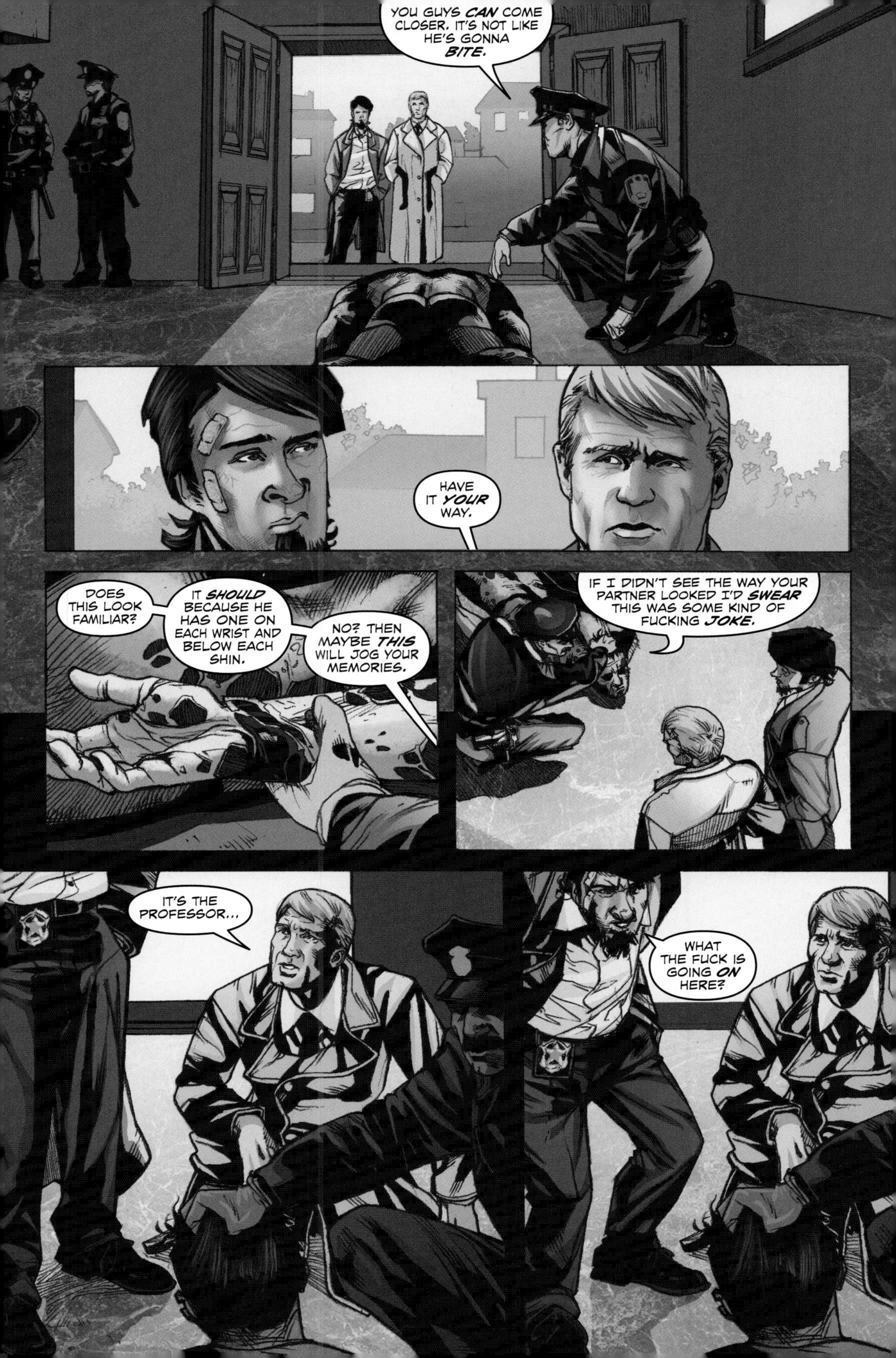
YOU GUYS CAN COME CLOSER. IT'S NOT LIKE HE'S GONNA BITE.
HAVE IT YOUR WAY.
DOES THIS LOOK FAMILIAR?
IT SHOULD BECAUSE HE HAS ONE ON EACH WRIST AND BELOW EACH SHIN.
NO? THEN MAYBE THIS WILL JOG YOUR MEMORIES.
IF I DIDN'T SEE THE WAY YOUR PARTNER LOOKED I'D SWEAR THIS WAS SOME KIND OF FUCKING JOKE.
IT'S THE PROFESSOR...
WHAT THE FUCK IS GOING ON HERE?

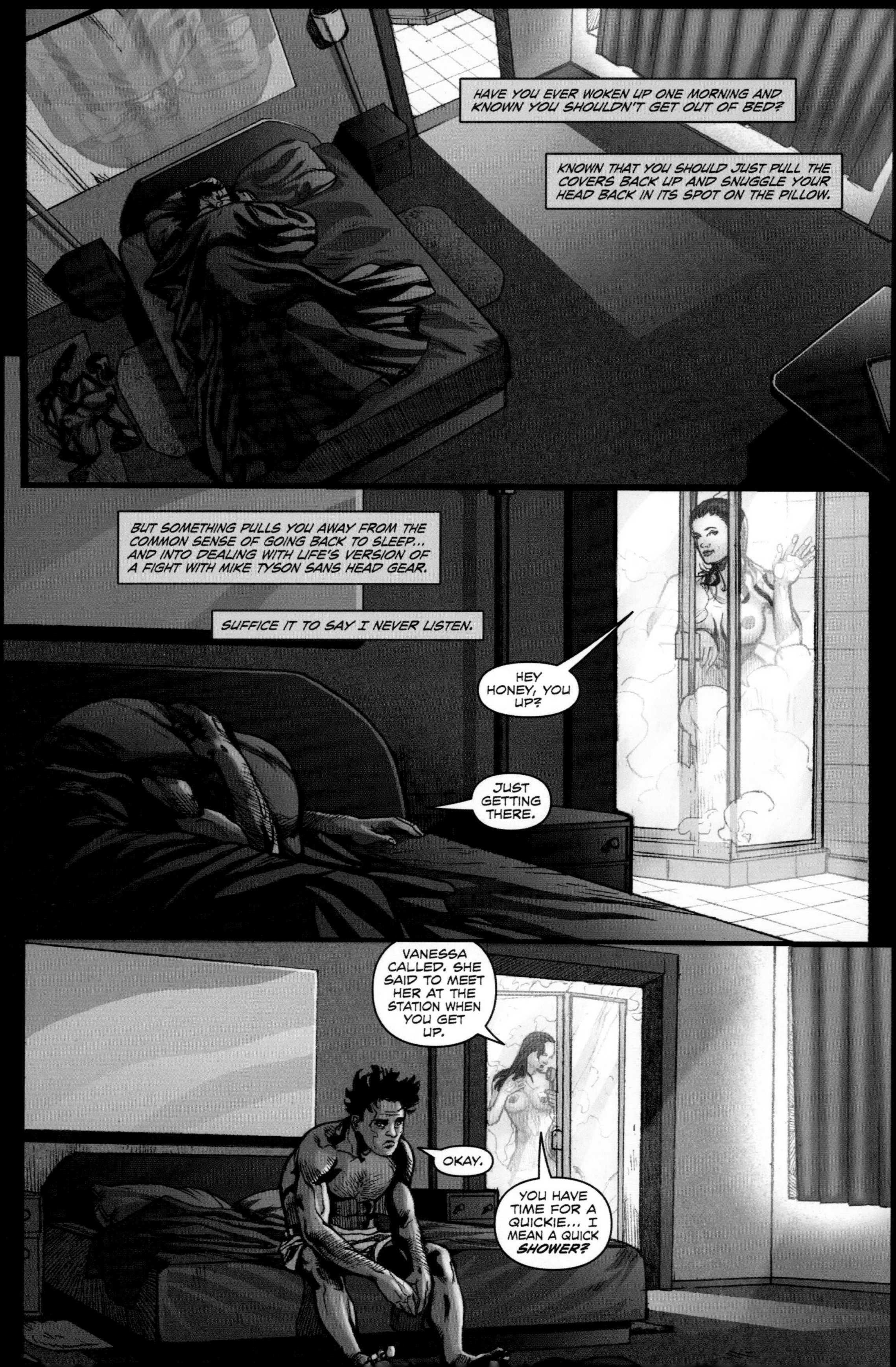
HAVE YOU EVER WOKEN UP ONE MORNING AND KNOWN YOU SHOULDN'T GET OUT OF BED?
KNOWN THAT YOU SHOULD JUST PULL THE COVERS BACK UP AND SNUGGLE YOUR HEAD BACK IN ITS SPOT ON THE PILLOW.
BUT SOMETHING PULLS YOU AWAY FROM THE COMMON SENSE OF GOING BACK TO SLEEP... AND INTO DEALING WITH LIFE'S VERSION OF A FIGHT WITH MIKE TYSON SANS HEAD GEAR.
SUFFICE IT TO SAY I NEVER LISTEN.
HEY HONEY, YOU UP?
JUST GETTING THERE.
VANESSA CALLED. SHE SAID TO MEET HER AT THE STATION WHEN YOU GET UP.
OKAY.
YOU HAVE TIME FOR A QUICKIE... I MEAN A QUICK SHOWER?

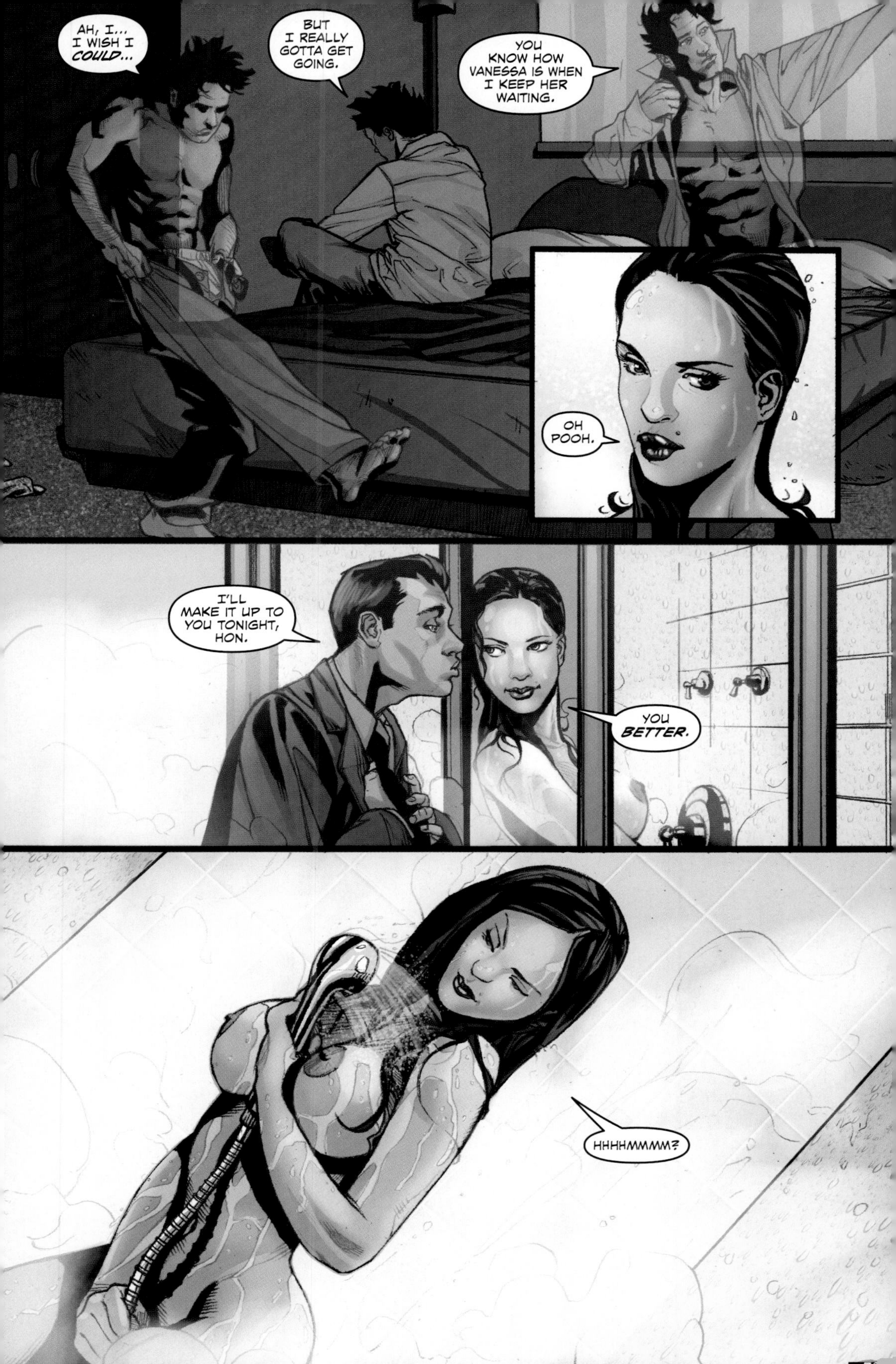
AH, I... I WISH I *COULD*...
BUT I REALLY GOTTA GET GOING.
YOU KNOW HOW VANESSA IS WHEN I KEEP HER WAITING.
OH POOH.
I'LL MAKE IT UP TO YOU TONIGHT, HON.
YOU *BETTER*.
HHHHMMMM?

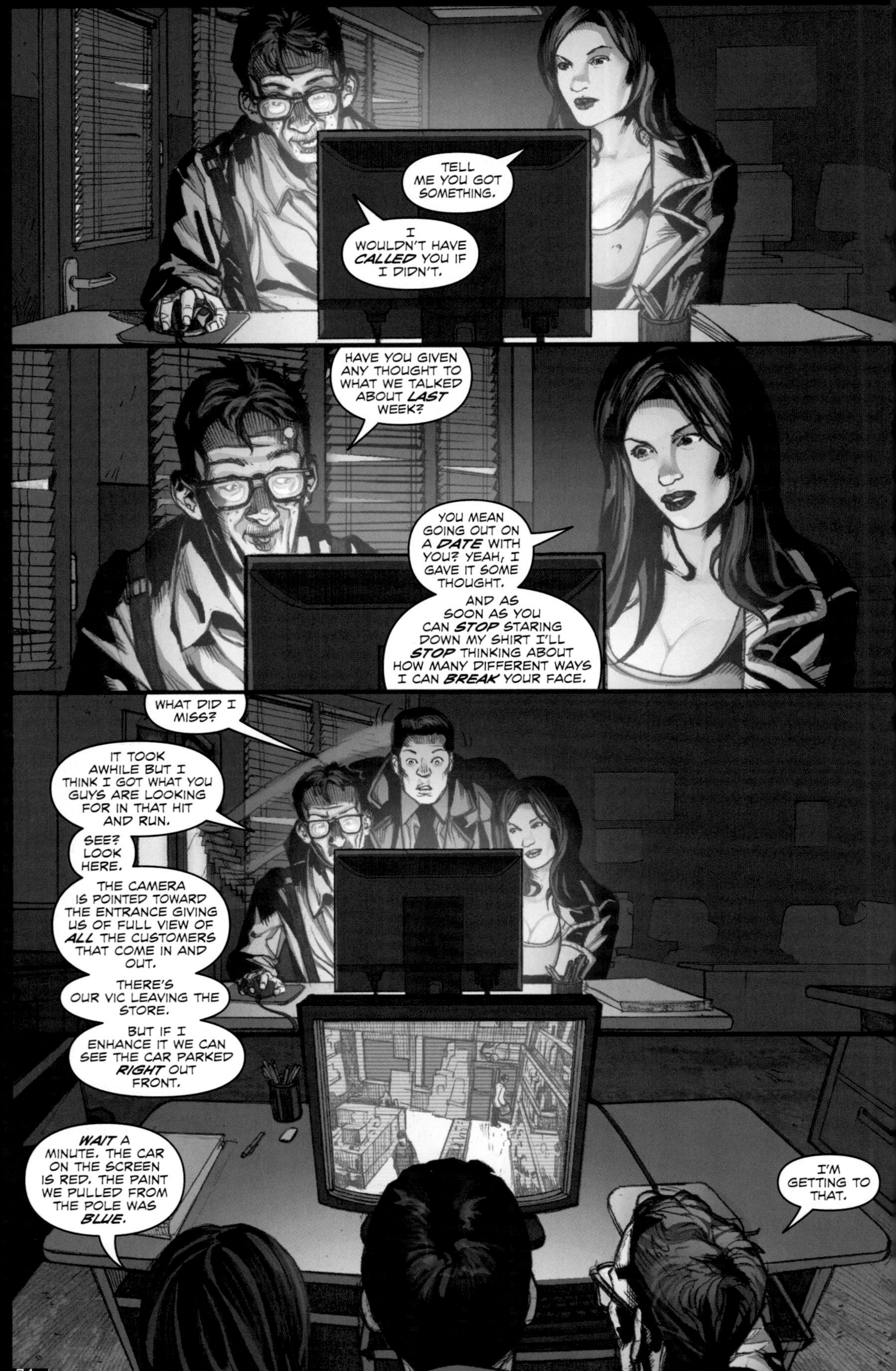
TELL ME YOU GOT SOMETHING.
I WOULDN'T HAVE *CALLED* YOU IF I DIDN'T.
HAVE YOU GIVEN ANY THOUGHT TO WHAT WE TALKED ABOUT *LAST* WEEK?
YOU MEAN GOING OUT ON A *DATE* WITH YOU? YEAH, I GAVE IT SOME THOUGHT.
AND AS SOON AS YOU CAN *STOP* STARING DOWN MY SHIRT I'LL *STOP* THINKING ABOUT HOW MANY DIFFERENT WAYS I CAN *BREAK* YOUR FACE.
WHAT DID I MISS?
IT TOOK AWHILE BUT I THINK I GOT WHAT YOU GUYS ARE LOOKING FOR IN THAT HIT AND RUN.
SEE? LOOK HERE.
THE CAMERA IS POINTED TOWARD THE ENTRANCE GIVING US OF FULL VIEW OF *ALL* THE CUSTOMERS THAT COME IN AND OUT.
THERE'S OUR VIC LEAVING THE STORE.
BUT IF I ENHANCE IT WE CAN SEE THE CAR PARKED *RIGHT* OUT FRONT.
WAIT A MINUTE. THE CAR ON THE SCREEN IS RED. THE PAINT WE PULLED FROM THE POLE WAS *BLUE*.
I'M GETTING TO THAT.

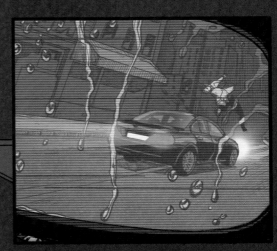

SEE IF WE ENHANCE IT EVEN *MORE* AND FOCUS ON THE SIDE MIRROR OF THE CAR... AND LET IT RUN FORWARD JUST A LITTLE. *VOILA.*

THERE'S YOUR HIT AND RUN *ALL* ON TAPE.

I EVEN PULLED THE *LICENSE.*

I COULD *KISS* YOU IF YOU WEREN'T SUCH A *DIRTBAG.*

AH, WHAT THE HELL.

SMACK!

SO DOES THIS MEAN YOU'LL GO *OUT* WITH ME?

NOT A *CHANCE.*

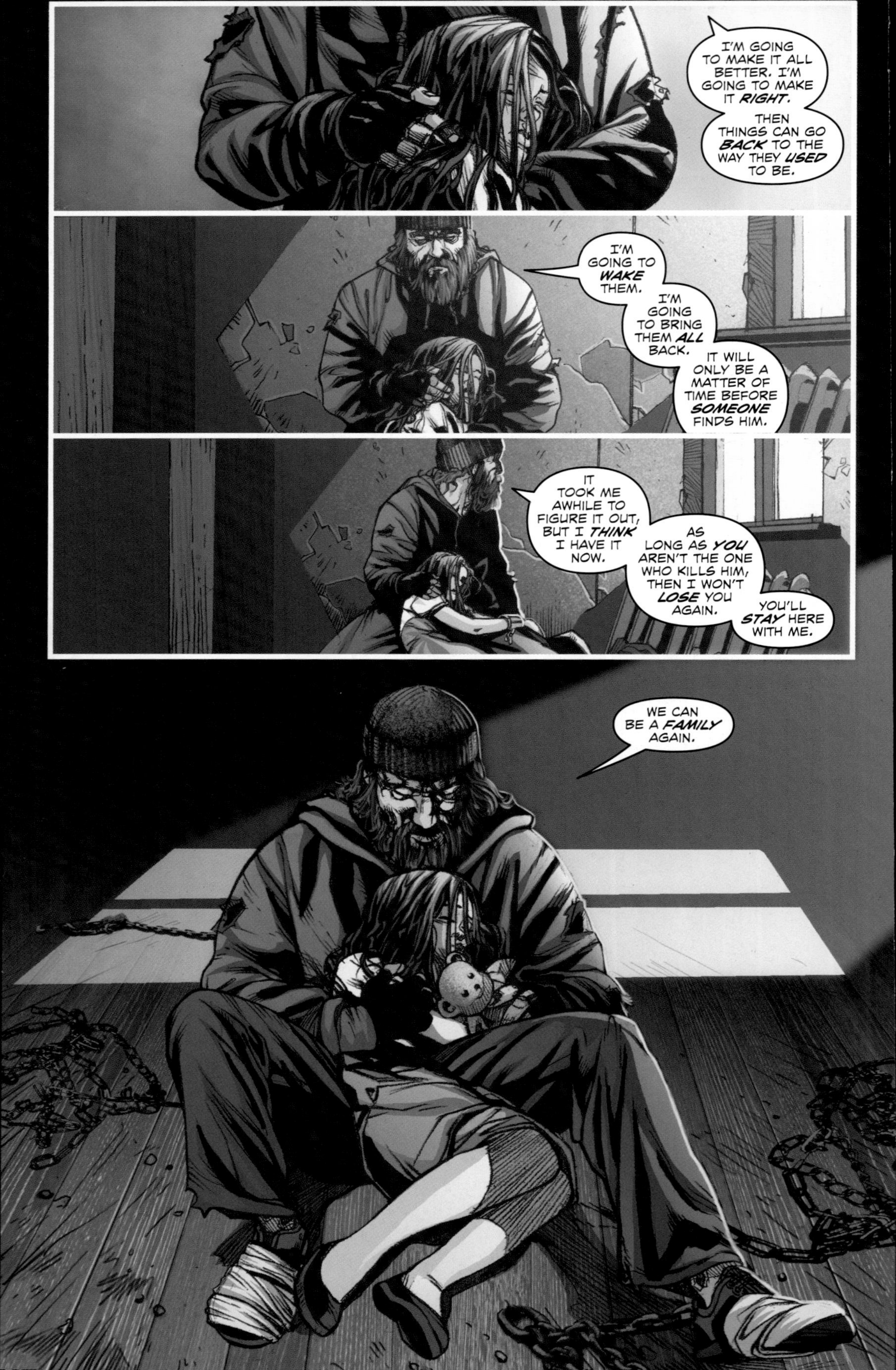
I'M GOING TO MAKE IT ALL BETTER. I'M GOING TO MAKE IT RIGHT.
THEN THINGS CAN GO BACK TO THE WAY THEY USED TO BE.
I'M GOING TO WAKE THEM.
I'M GOING TO BRING THEM ALL BACK.
IT WILL ONLY BE A MATTER OF TIME BEFORE SOMEONE FINDS HIM.
IT TOOK ME AWHILE TO FIGURE IT OUT, BUT I THINK I HAVE IT NOW.
AS LONG AS YOU AREN'T THE ONE WHO KILLS HIM, THEN I WON'T LOSE YOU AGAIN.
YOU'LL STAY HERE WITH ME.
WE CAN BE A FAMILY AGAIN.

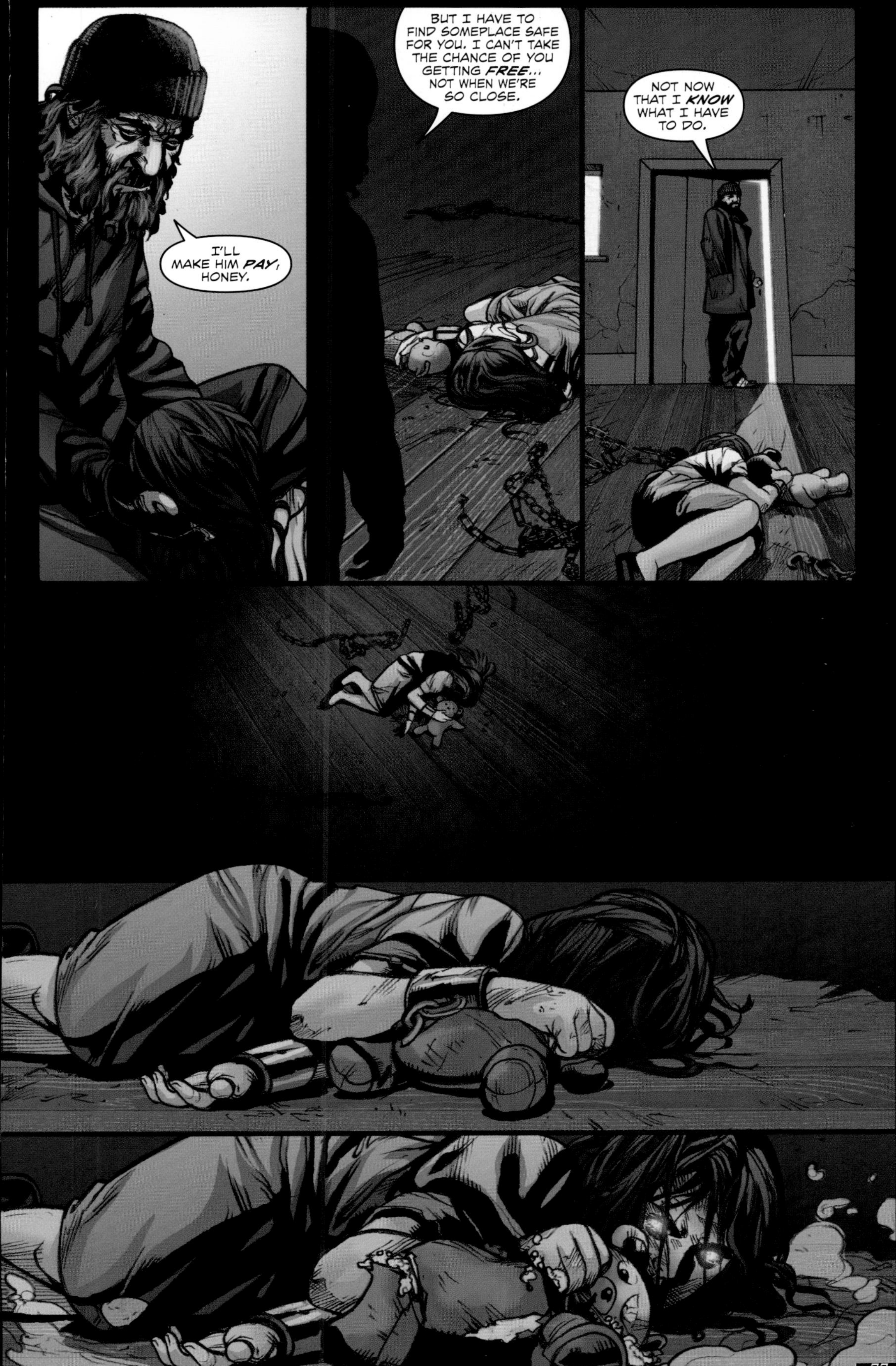
I'LL MAKE HIM PAY, HONEY.
BUT I HAVE TO FIND SOMEPLACE SAFE FOR YOU. I CAN'T TAKE THE CHANCE OF YOU GETTING FREE... NOT WHEN WE'RE SO CLOSE.
NOT NOW THAT I KNOW WHAT I HAVE TO DO.

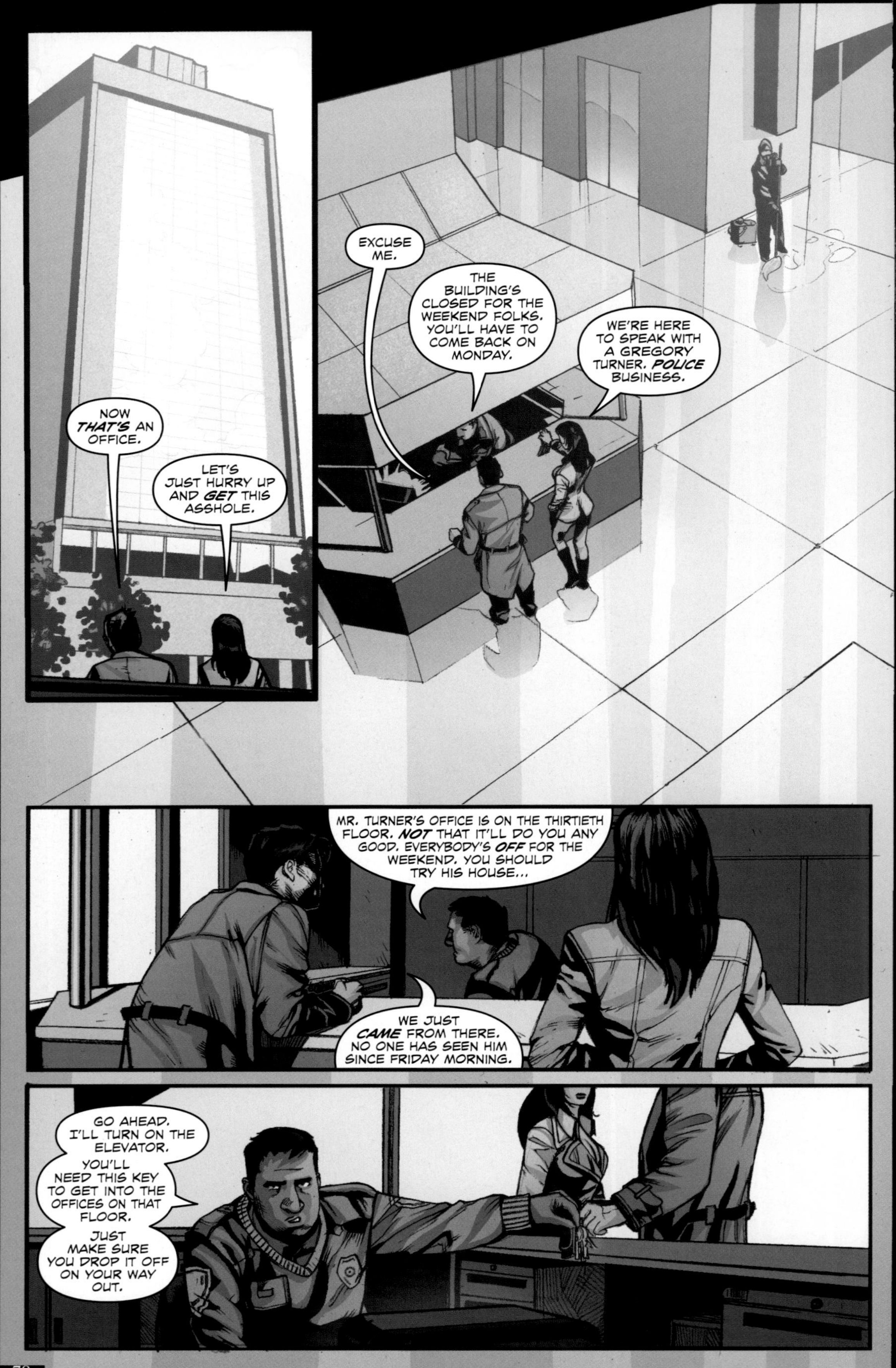

NOW *THAT'S* AN OFFICE.
LET'S JUST HURRY UP AND *GET* THIS ASSHOLE.
EXCUSE ME.
THE BUILDING'S CLOSED FOR THE WEEKEND FOLKS. YOU'LL HAVE TO COME BACK ON MONDAY.
WE'RE HERE TO SPEAK WITH A GREGORY TURNER. *POLICE* BUSINESS.
MR. TURNER'S OFFICE IS ON THE THIRTIETH FLOOR. *NOT* THAT IT'LL DO YOU ANY GOOD. EVERYBODY'S *OFF* FOR THE WEEKEND. YOU SHOULD TRY HIS HOUSE...
WE JUST *CAME* FROM THERE. NO ONE HAS SEEN HIM SINCE FRIDAY MORNING.
GO AHEAD. I'LL TURN ON THE ELEVATOR.
YOU'LL NEED THIS KEY TO GET INTO THE OFFICES ON THAT FLOOR.
JUST MAKE SURE YOU DROP IT OFF ON YOUR WAY OUT.

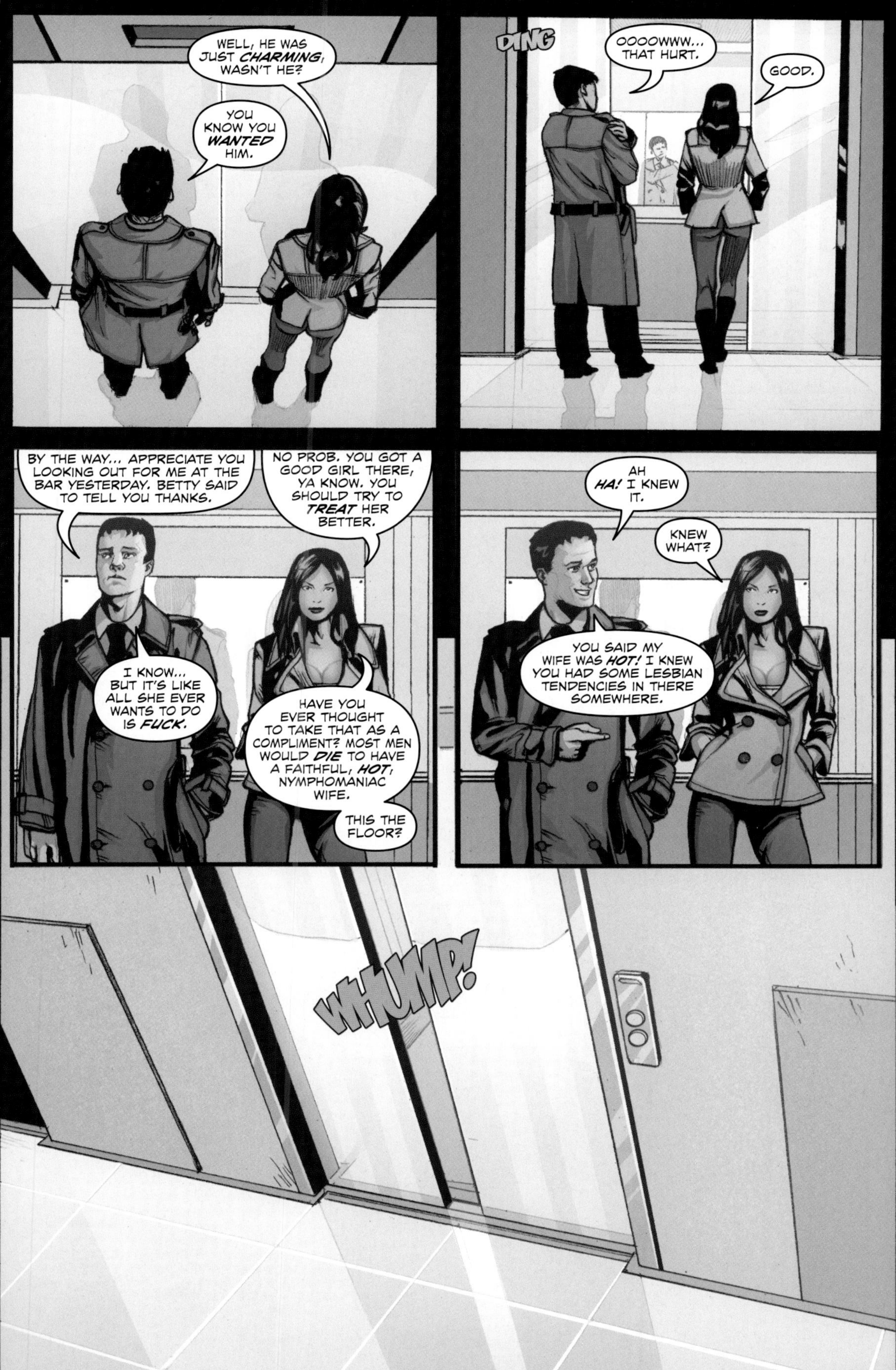
WELL, HE WAS JUST CHARMING, WASN'T HE?
YOU KNOW YOU WANTED HIM.
DING
OOOOWWW... THAT HURT.
GOOD.
BY THE WAY... APPRECIATE YOU LOOKING OUT FOR ME AT THE BAR YESTERDAY. BETTY SAID TO TELL YOU THANKS.
NO PROB. YOU GOT A GOOD GIRL THERE, YA KNOW. YOU SHOULD TRY TO TREAT HER BETTER.
I KNOW... BUT IT'S LIKE ALL SHE EVER WANTS TO DO IS FUCK.
HAVE YOU EVER THOUGHT TO TAKE THAT AS A COMPLIMENT? MOST MEN WOULD DIE TO HAVE A FAITHFUL, HOT, NYMPHOMANIAC WIFE.
THIS THE FLOOR?
AH HA! I KNEW IT.
KNEW WHAT?
YOU SAID MY WIFE WAS HOT! I KNEW YOU HAD SOME LESBIAN TENDENCIES IN THERE SOMEWHERE.
WHUMP!

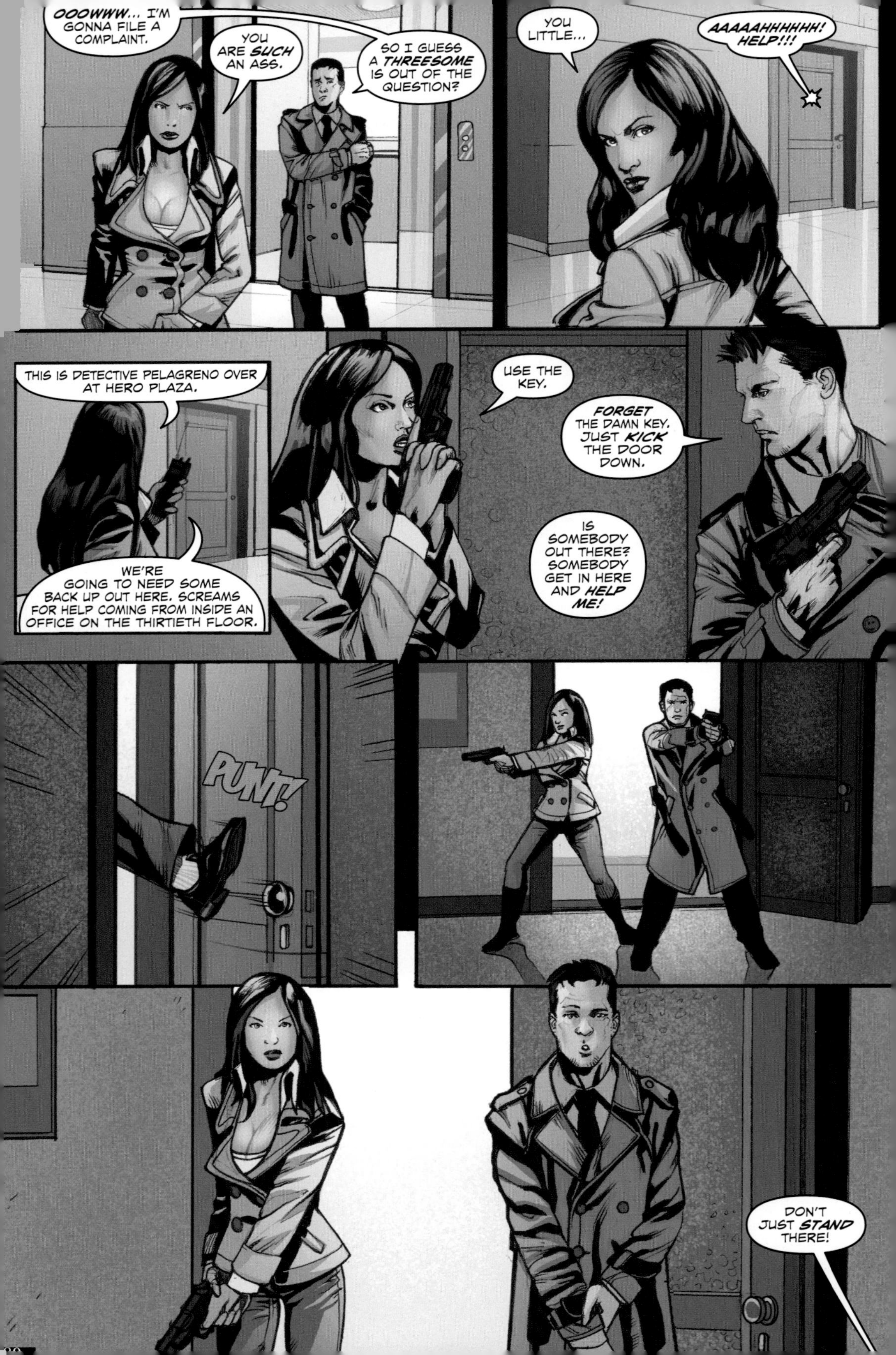
OOOWWW... I'M GONNA FILE A COMPLAINT.
YOU ARE SUCH AN ASS.
SO I GUESS A THREESOME IS OUT OF THE QUESTION?
YOU LITTLE...
AAAAAHHHHHH! HELP!!!
THIS IS DETECTIVE PELAGRENO OVER AT HERO PLAZA.
WE'RE GOING TO NEED SOME BACK UP OUT HERE. SCREAMS FOR HELP COMING FROM INSIDE AN OFFICE ON THE THIRTIETH FLOOR.
USE THE KEY.
FORGET THE DAMN KEY. JUST KICK THE DOOR DOWN.
IS SOMEBODY OUT THERE? SOMEBODY GET IN HERE AND HELP ME!
PUNT!
DON'T JUST STAND THERE!

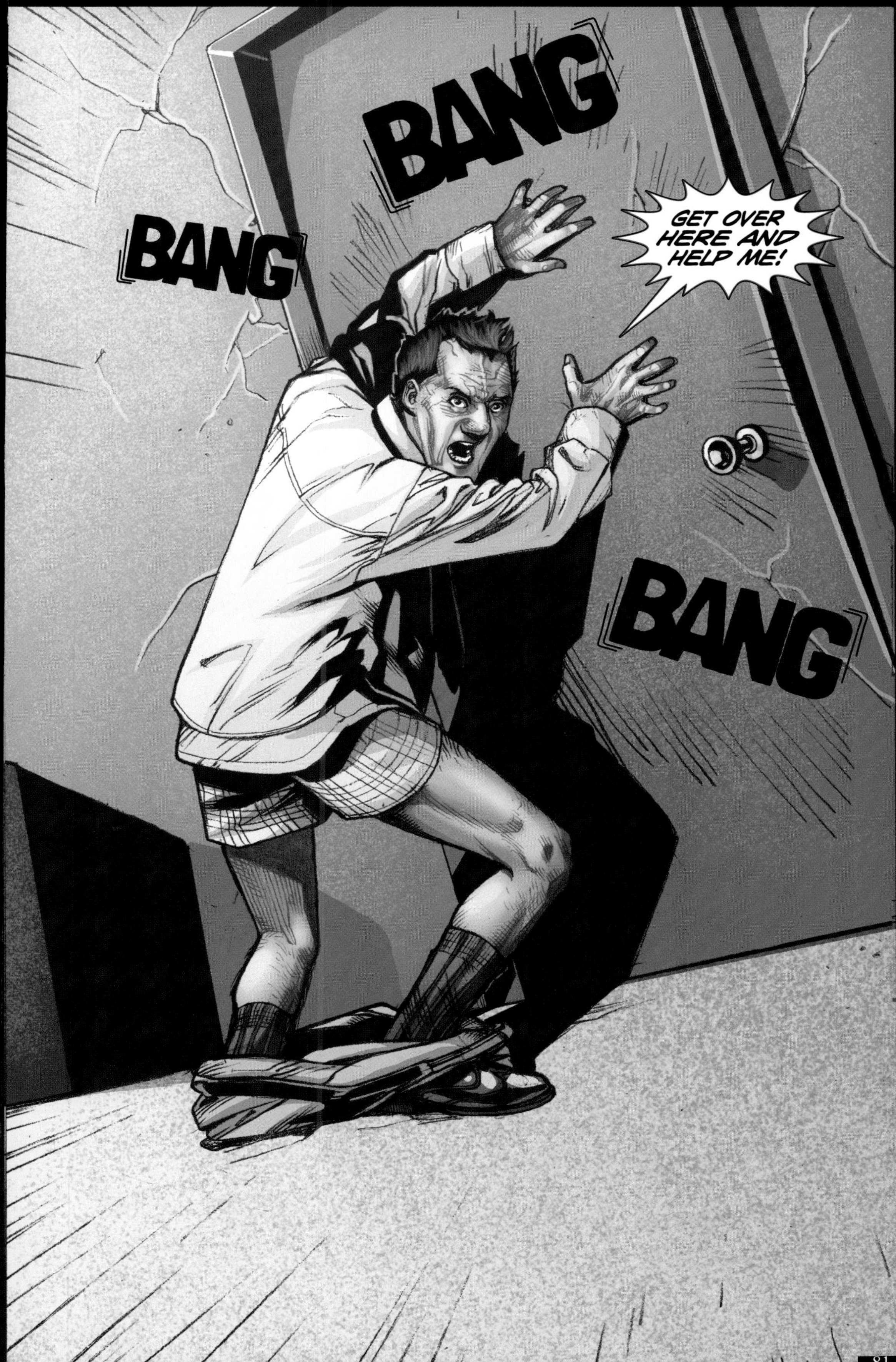
BANG
BANG
GET OVER HERE AND HELP ME!
BANG

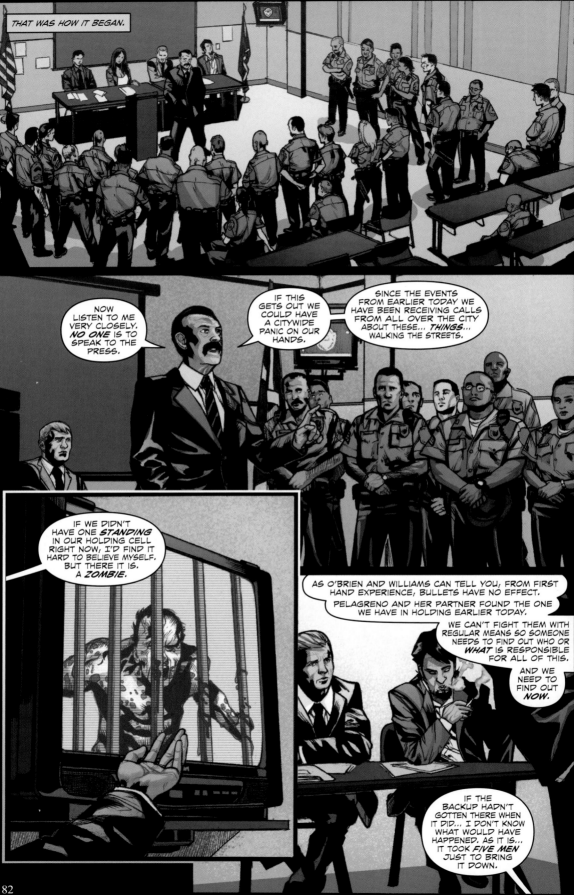

THAT WAS HOW IT BEGAN.

NOW LISTEN TO ME VERY CLOSELY. *NO ONE* IS TO SPEAK TO THE PRESS.

IF THIS GETS OUT WE COULD HAVE A CITYWIDE PANIC ON OUR HANDS.

SINCE THE EVENTS FROM EARLIER TODAY WE HAVE BEEN RECEIVING CALLS FROM ALL OVER THE CITY ABOUT THESE... *THINGS*... WALKING THE STREETS.

IF WE DIDN'T HAVE ONE *STANDING* IN OUR HOLDING CELL RIGHT NOW, I'D FIND IT HARD TO BELIEVE MYSELF. BUT THERE IT IS. A *ZOMBIE*.

AS O'BRIEN AND WILLIAMS CAN TELL YOU, FROM FIRST HAND EXPERIENCE, BULLETS HAVE NO EFFECT. PELAGRENO AND HER PARTNER FOUND THE ONE WE HAVE IN HOLDING EARLIER TODAY.

WE CAN'T FIGHT THEM WITH REGULAR MEANS SO SOMEONE NEEDS TO FIND OUT WHO OR *WHAT* IS RESPONSIBLE FOR ALL OF THIS.

AND WE NEED TO FIND OUT *NOW*.

IF THE BACKUP HADN'T GOTTEN THERE WHEN IT DID... I DON'T KNOW WHAT WOULD HAVE HAPPENED. AS IT IS... IT TOOK *FIVE MEN* JUST TO BRING IT DOWN.

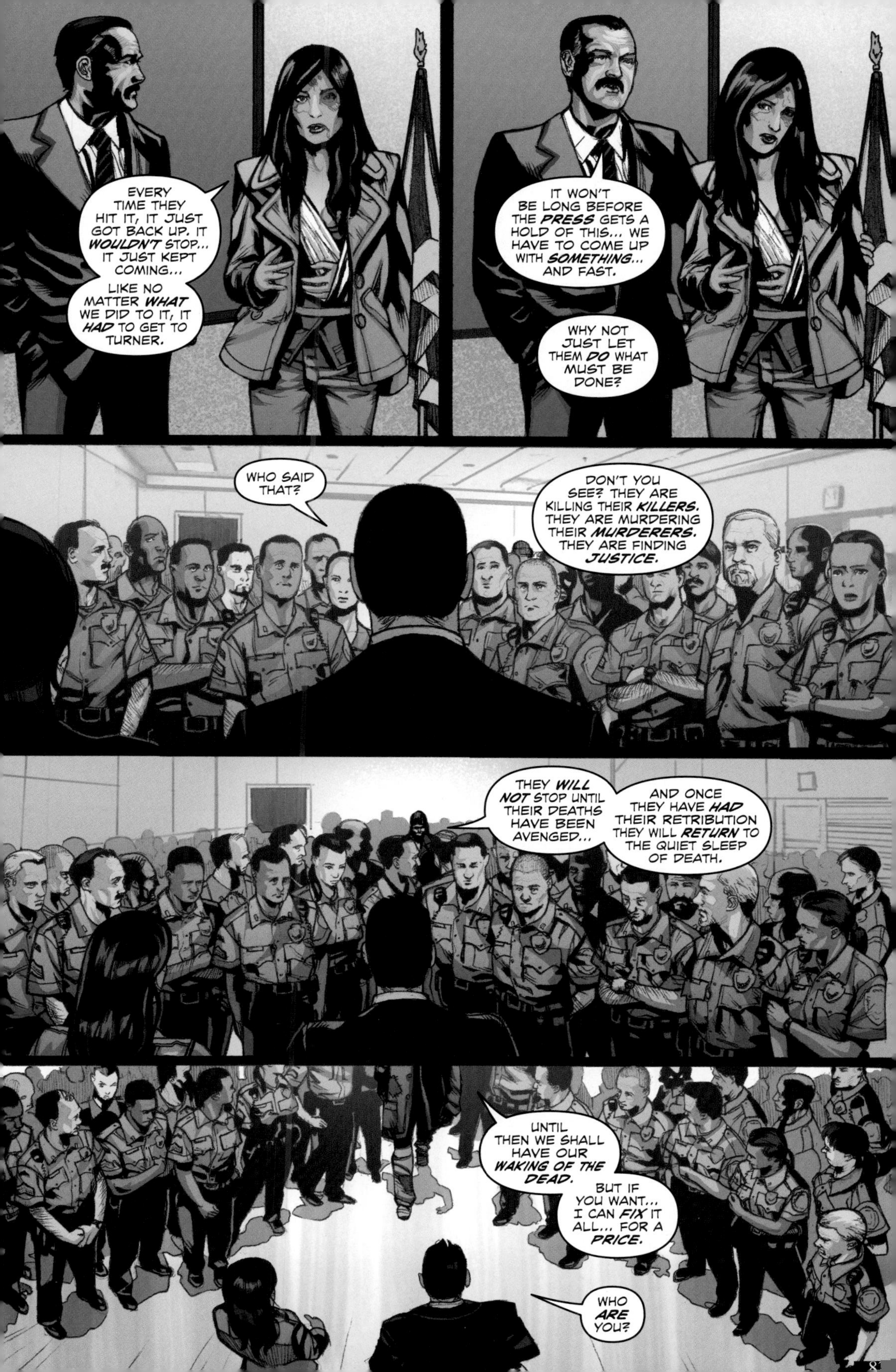
EVERY TIME THEY HIT IT, IT JUST GOT BACK UP. IT WOULDN'T STOP... IT JUST KEPT COMING...
LIKE NO MATTER WHAT WE DID TO IT, IT HAD TO GET TO TURNER.
IT WON'T BE LONG BEFORE THE PRESS GETS A HOLD OF THIS... WE HAVE TO COME UP WITH SOMETHING... AND FAST.
WHY NOT JUST LET THEM DO WHAT MUST BE DONE?
WHO SAID THAT?
DON'T YOU SEE? THEY ARE KILLING THEIR KILLERS. THEY ARE MURDERING THEIR MURDERERS. THEY ARE FINDING JUSTICE.
THEY WILL NOT STOP UNTIL THEIR DEATHS HAVE BEEN AVENGED...
AND ONCE THEY HAVE HAD THEIR RETRIBUTION THEY WILL RETURN TO THE QUIET SLEEP OF DEATH.
UNTIL THEN WE SHALL HAVE OUR WAKING OF THE DEAD.
BUT IF YOU WANT... I CAN FIX IT ALL... FOR A PRICE.
WHO ARE YOU?

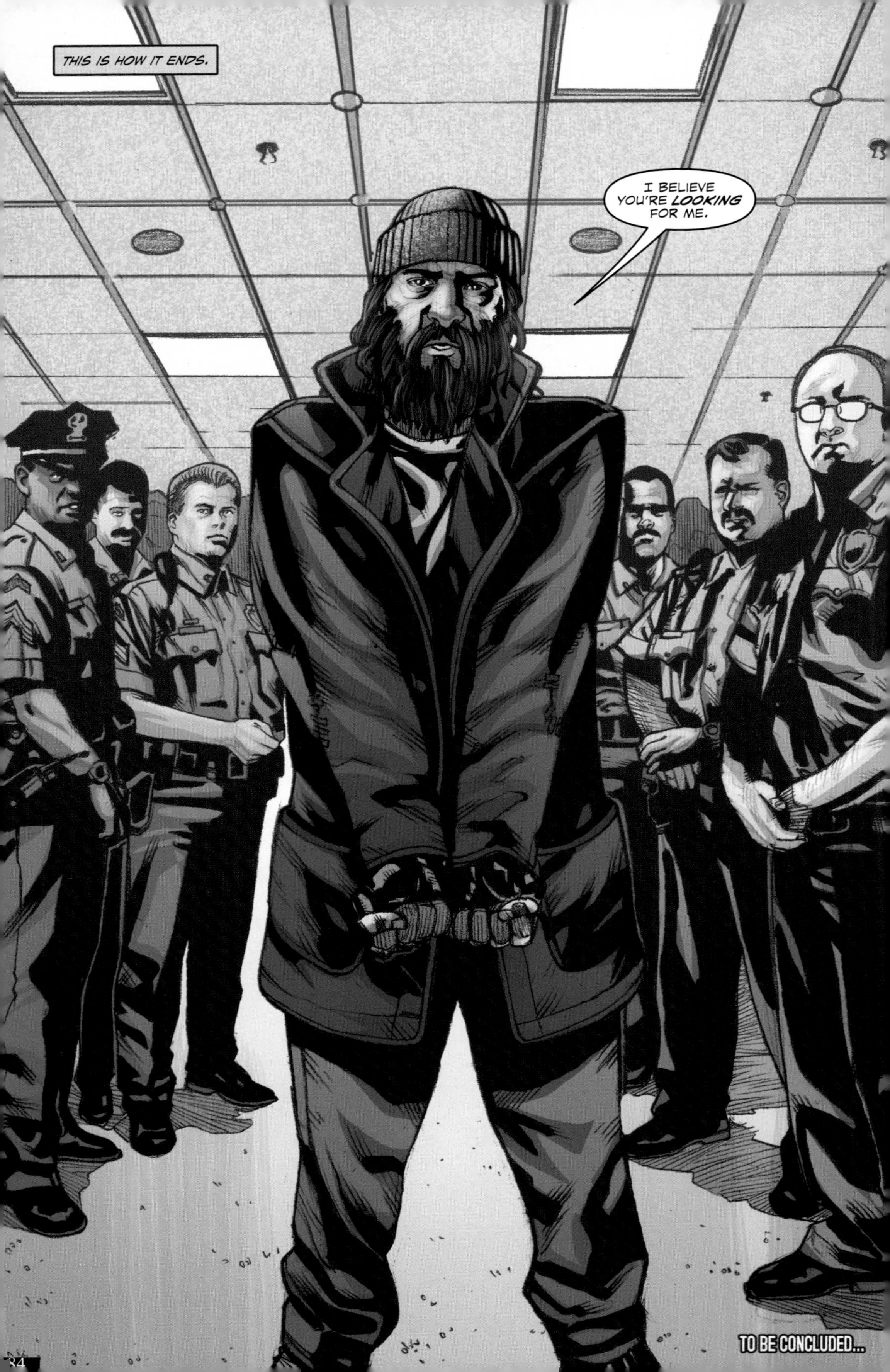
THIS IS HOW IT ENDS.
I BELIEVE YOU'RE **LOOKING** FOR ME.
TO BE CONCLUDED...

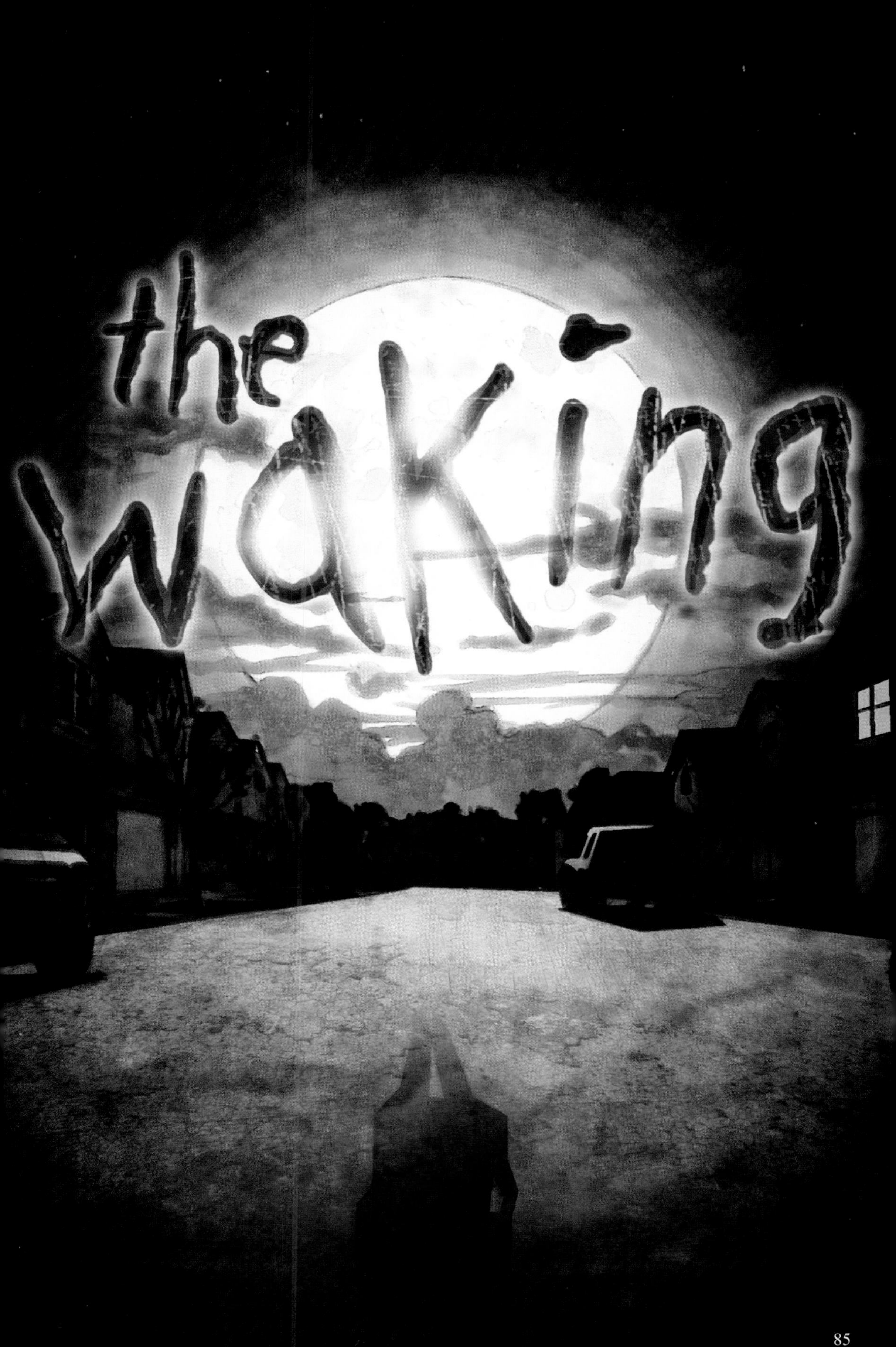
the waKing

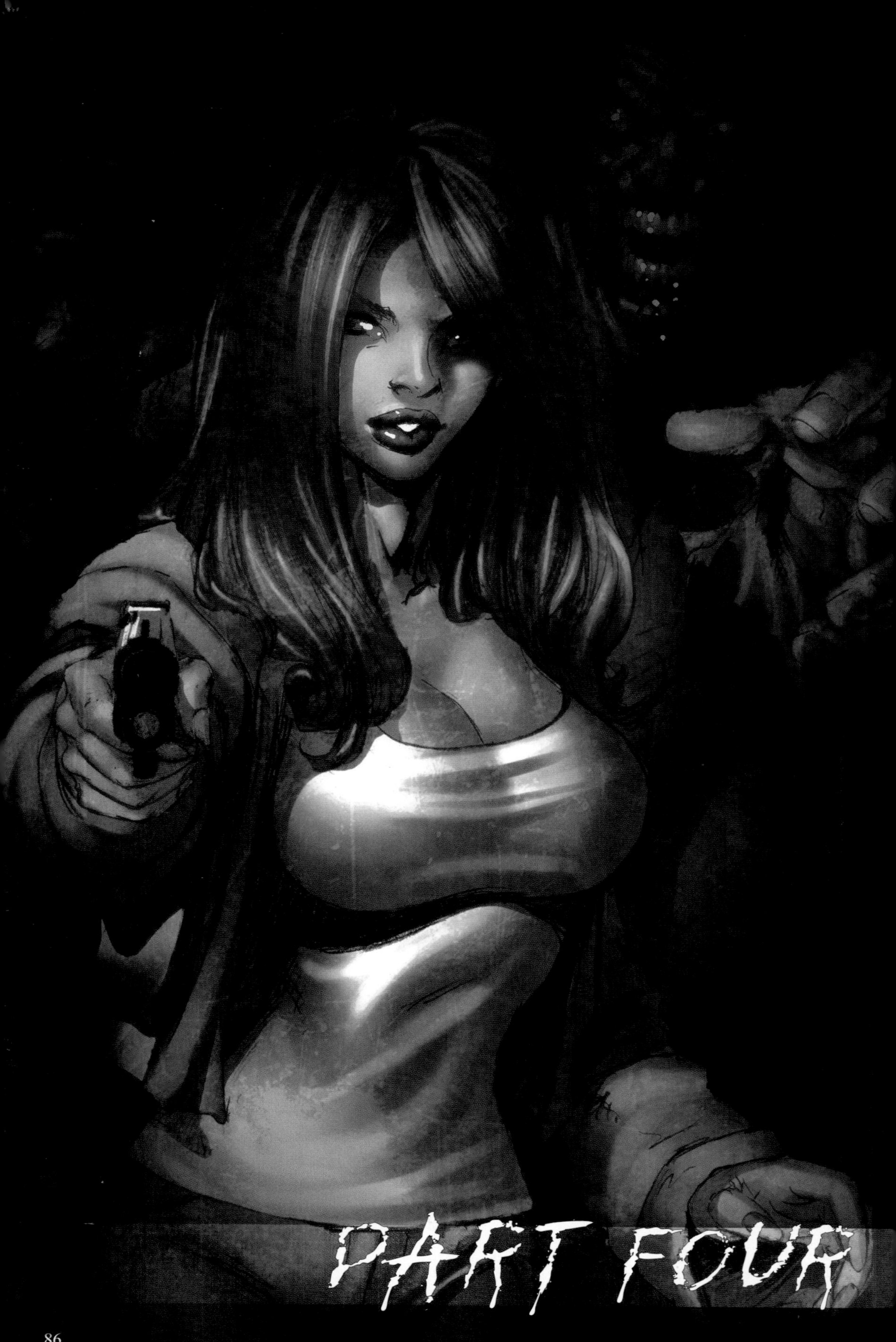
PART FOUR

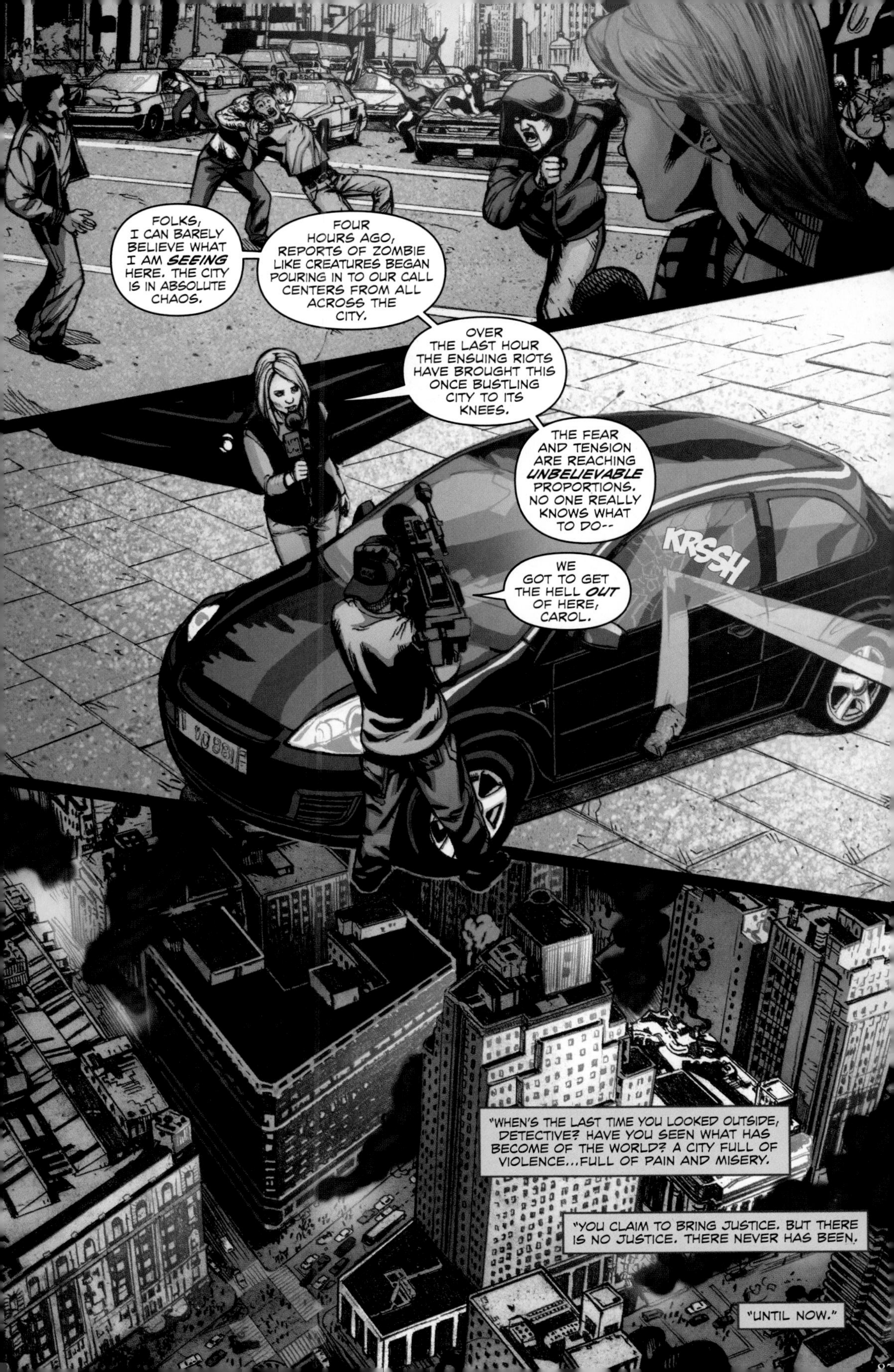

FOLKS, I CAN BARELY BELIEVE WHAT I AM SEEING HERE. THE CITY IS IN ABSOLUTE CHAOS.
FOUR HOURS AGO, REPORTS OF ZOMBIE LIKE CREATURES BEGAN POURING IN TO OUR CALL CENTERS FROM ALL ACROSS THE CITY.
OVER THE LAST HOUR THE ENSUING RIOTS HAVE BROUGHT THIS ONCE BUSTLING CITY TO ITS KNEES.
THE FEAR AND TENSION ARE REACHING UNBELIEVABLE PROPORTIONS. NO ONE REALLY KNOWS WHAT TO DO--
KRSSH
WE GOT TO GET THE HELL OUT OF HERE, CAROL.
"WHEN'S THE LAST TIME YOU LOOKED OUTSIDE, DETECTIVE? HAVE YOU SEEN WHAT HAS BECOME OF THE WORLD? A CITY FULL OF VIOLENCE...FULL OF PAIN AND MISERY.
"YOU CLAIM TO BRING JUSTICE. BUT THERE IS NO JUSTICE. THERE NEVER HAS BEEN.
"UNTIL NOW."

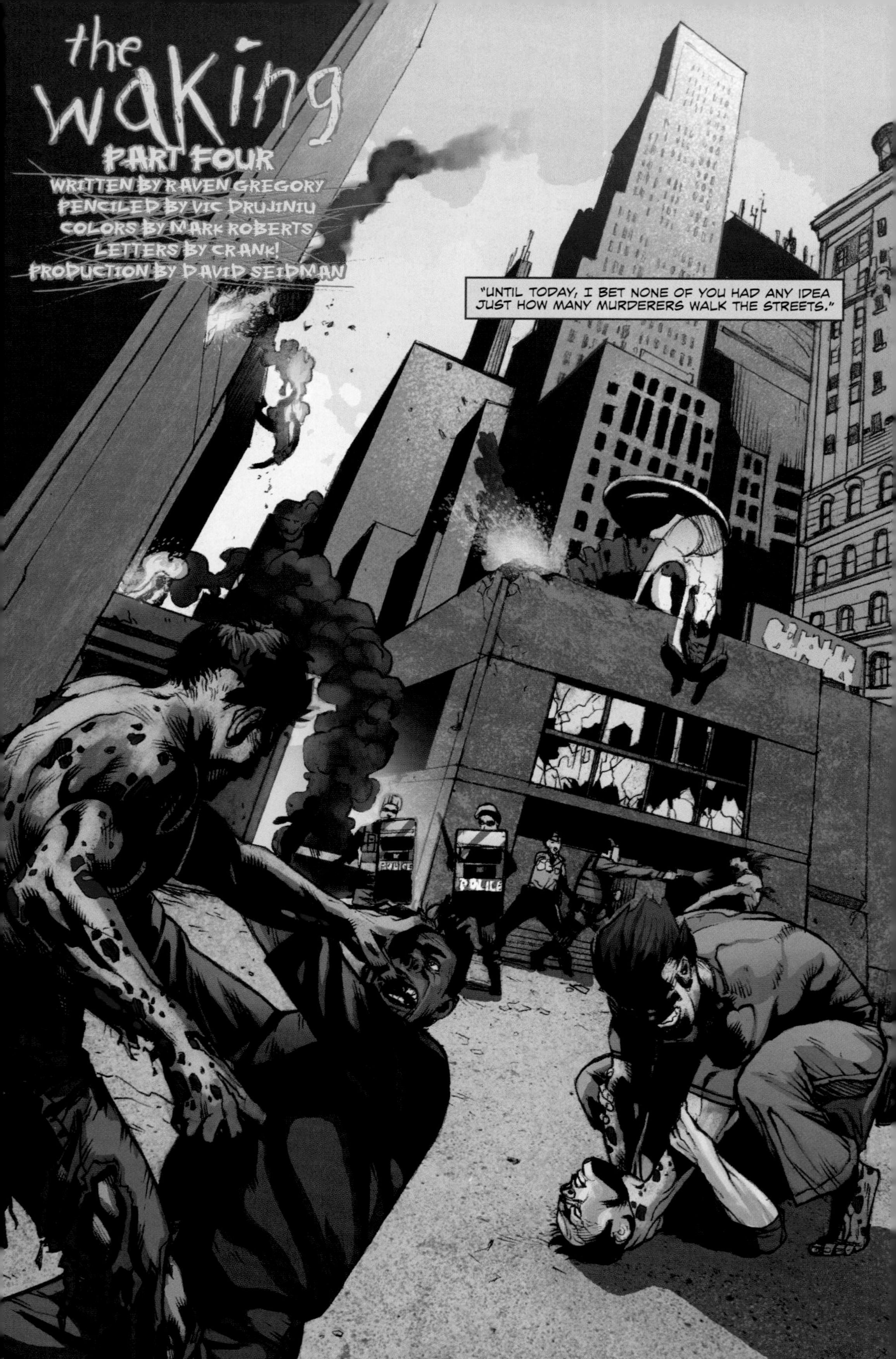
the waking
PART FOUR
WRITTEN BY RAVEN GREGORY
PENCILED BY VIC DRUJINIU
COLORS BY MARK ROBERTS
LETTERS BY CRANK!
PRODUCTION BY DAVID SEIDMAN
"UNTIL TODAY, I BET NONE OF YOU HAD ANY IDEA JUST HOW MANY MURDERERS WALK THE STREETS."
POLICE
POLICE

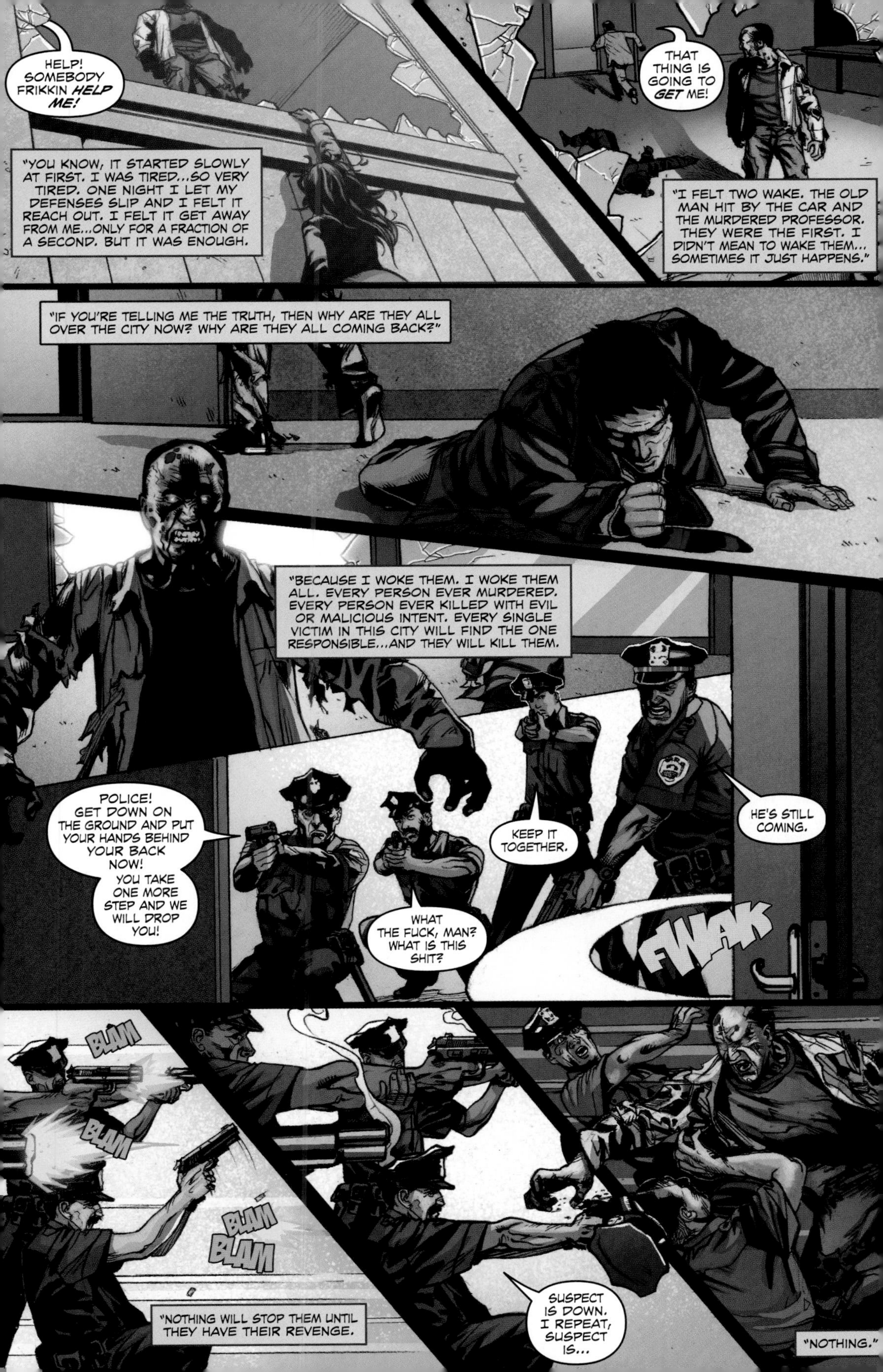

HELP! SOMEBODY FRIKKIN *HELP ME!*
"YOU KNOW, IT STARTED SLOWLY AT FIRST. I WAS TIRED...SO VERY TIRED. ONE NIGHT I LET MY DEFENSES SLIP AND I FELT IT REACH OUT. I FELT IT GET AWAY FROM ME...ONLY FOR A FRACTION OF A SECOND. BUT IT WAS ENOUGH.
THAT THING IS GOING TO *GET* ME!
"I FELT TWO WAKE. THE OLD MAN HIT BY THE CAR AND THE MURDERED PROFESSOR. THEY WERE THE FIRST. I DIDN'T MEAN TO WAKE THEM... SOMETIMES IT JUST HAPPENS."
"IF YOU'RE TELLING ME THE TRUTH, THEN WHY ARE THEY ALL OVER THE CITY NOW? WHY ARE THEY ALL COMING BACK?"
"BECAUSE I WOKE THEM. I WOKE THEM ALL. EVERY PERSON EVER MURDERED. EVERY PERSON EVER KILLED WITH EVIL OR MALICIOUS INTENT. EVERY SINGLE VICTIM IN THIS CITY WILL FIND THE ONE RESPONSIBLE...AND THEY WILL KILL THEM.
POLICE! GET DOWN ON THE GROUND AND PUT YOUR HANDS BEHIND YOUR BACK NOW!
YOU TAKE ONE MORE STEP AND WE WILL DROP YOU!
WHAT THE FUCK, MAN? WHAT IS THIS SHIT?
KEEP IT TOGETHER.
HE'S STILL COMING.
FWAK
BLAM
BLAM
BLAM
BLAM
"NOTHING WILL STOP THEM UNTIL THEY HAVE THEIR REVENGE.
SUSPECT IS DOWN. I REPEAT, SUSPECT IS...
"NOTHING."

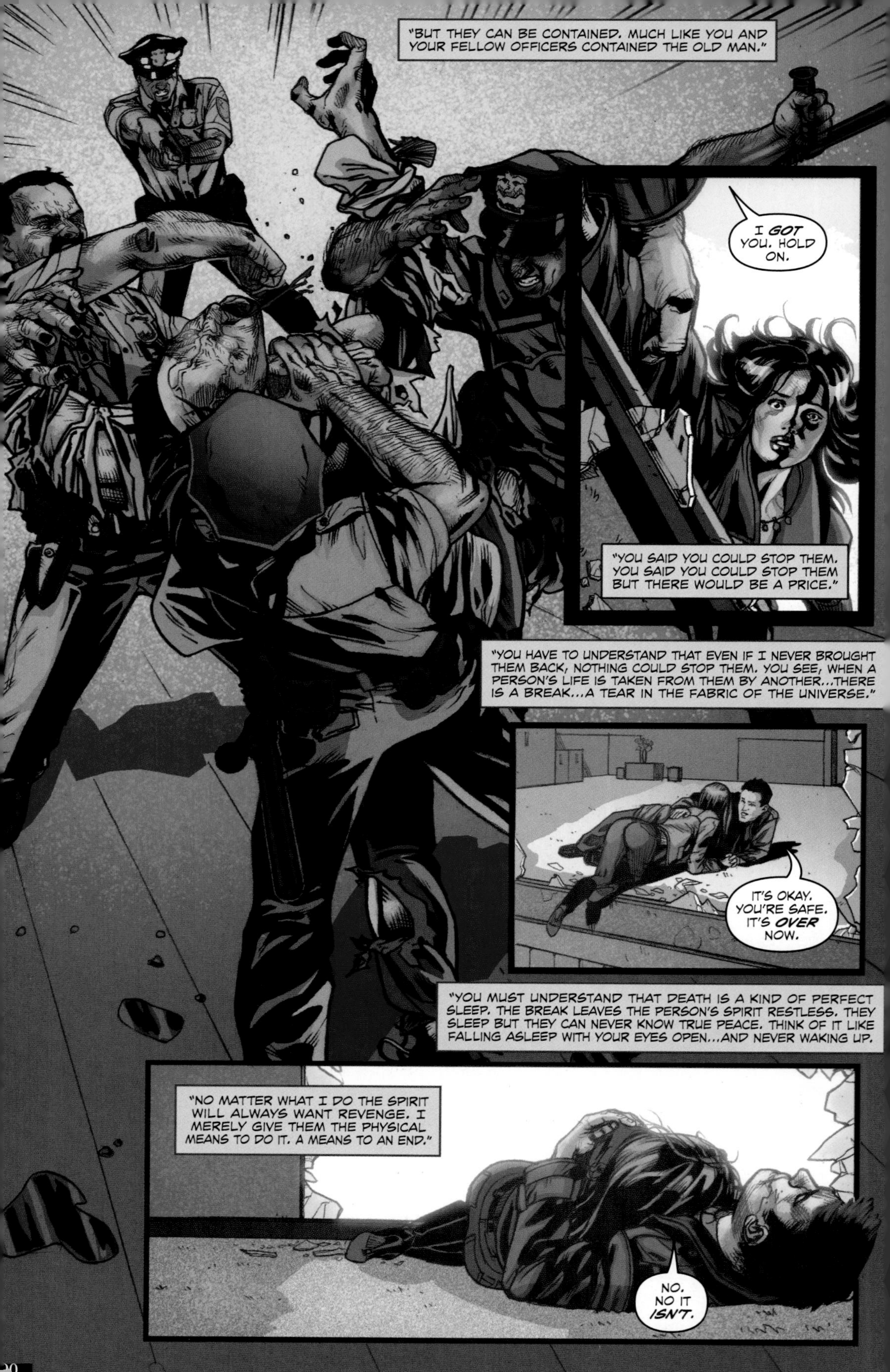
"BUT THEY CAN BE CONTAINED. MUCH LIKE YOU AND YOUR FELLOW OFFICERS CONTAINED THE OLD MAN."
I GOT YOU. HOLD ON.
"YOU SAID YOU COULD STOP THEM. YOU SAID YOU COULD STOP THEM BUT THERE WOULD BE A PRICE."
"YOU HAVE TO UNDERSTAND THAT EVEN IF I NEVER BROUGHT THEM BACK, NOTHING COULD STOP THEM. YOU SEE, WHEN A PERSON'S LIFE IS TAKEN FROM THEM BY ANOTHER...THERE IS A BREAK...A TEAR IN THE FABRIC OF THE UNIVERSE."
IT'S OKAY. YOU'RE SAFE. IT'S OVER NOW.
"YOU MUST UNDERSTAND THAT DEATH IS A KIND OF PERFECT SLEEP. THE BREAK LEAVES THE PERSON'S SPIRIT RESTLESS. THEY SLEEP BUT THEY CAN NEVER KNOW TRUE PEACE. THINK OF IT LIKE FALLING ASLEEP WITH YOUR EYES OPEN...AND NEVER WAKING UP."
"NO MATTER WHAT I DO THE SPIRIT WILL ALWAYS WANT REVENGE. I MERELY GIVE THEM THE PHYSICAL MEANS TO DO IT. A MEANS TO AN END."
NO. NO IT ISN'T.

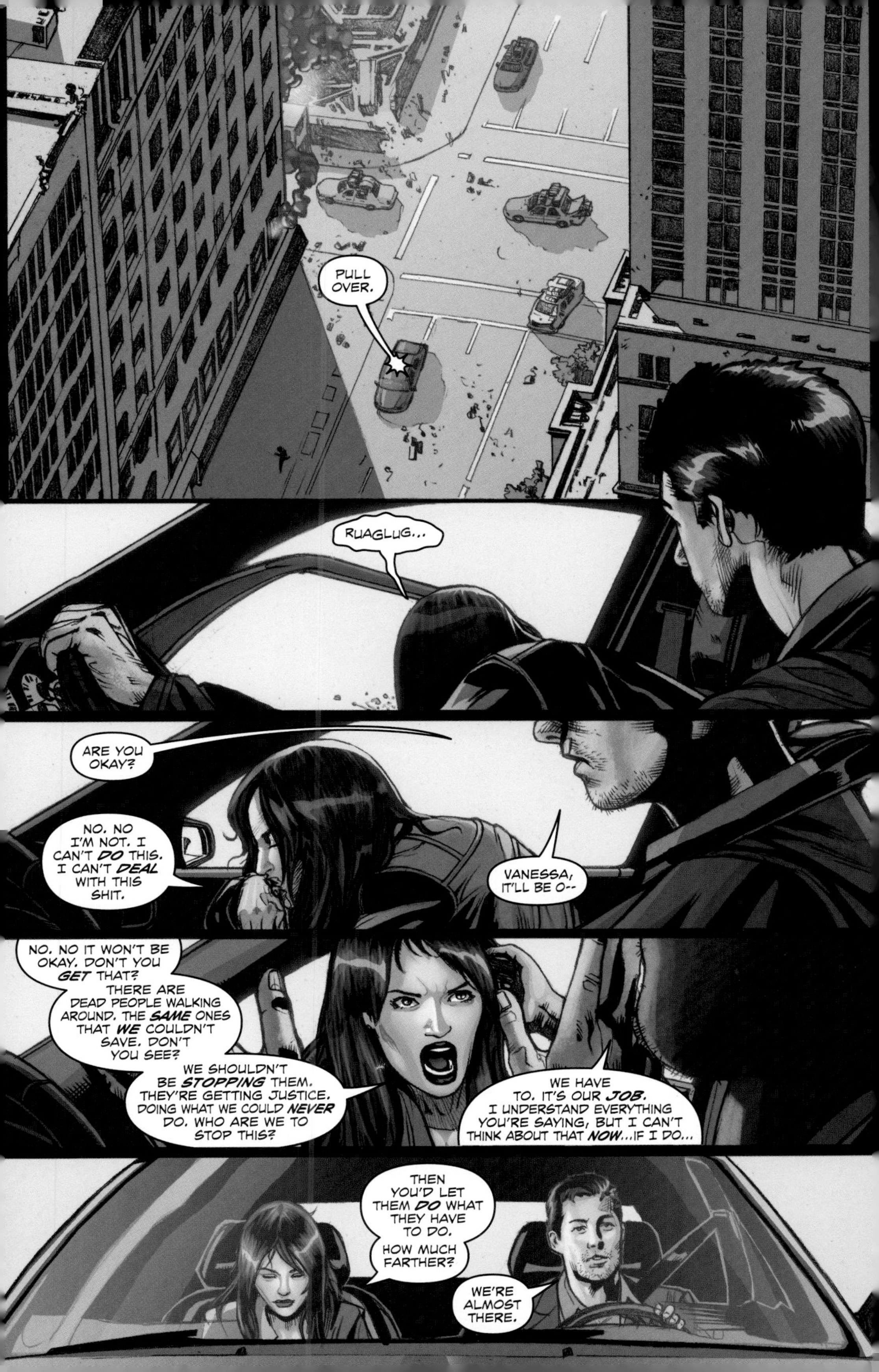
PULL OVER.
RUAGLUG...
ARE YOU OKAY?
NO. NO I'M NOT. I CAN'T DO THIS. I CAN'T DEAL WITH THIS SHIT.
VANESSA, IT'LL BE O--
NO. NO IT WON'T BE OKAY. DON'T YOU GET THAT?
THERE ARE DEAD PEOPLE WALKING AROUND. THE SAME ONES THAT WE COULDN'T SAVE. DON'T YOU SEE?
WE SHOULDN'T BE STOPPING THEM. THEY'RE GETTING JUSTICE. DOING WHAT WE COULD NEVER DO. WHO ARE WE TO STOP THIS?
WE HAVE TO. IT'S OUR JOB. I UNDERSTAND EVERYTHING YOU'RE SAYING, BUT I CAN'T THINK ABOUT THAT NOW...IF I DO...
THEN YOU'D LET THEM DO WHAT THEY HAVE TO DO.
HOW MUCH FARTHER?
WE'RE ALMOST THERE.

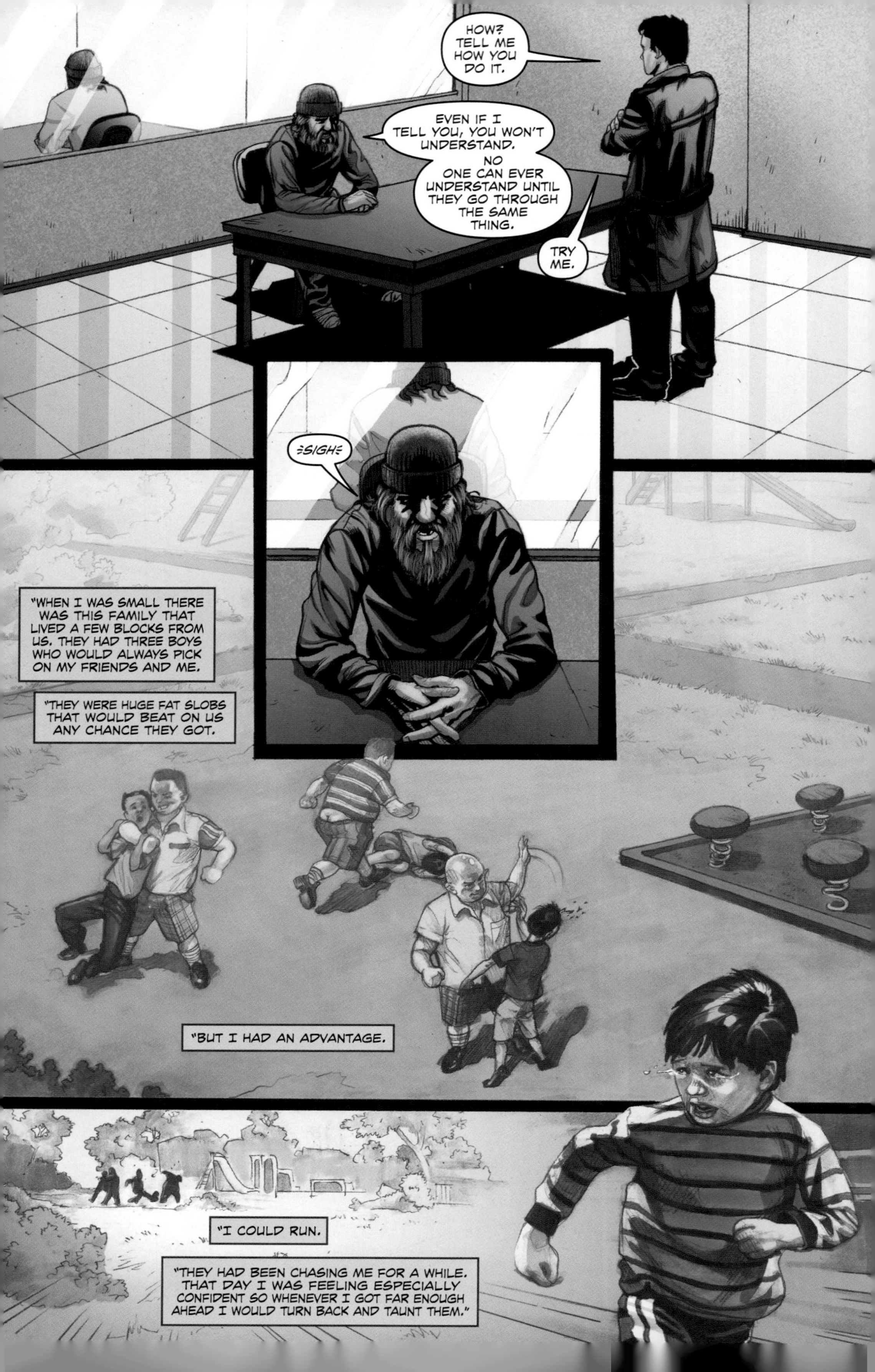
HOW? TELL ME HOW YOU DO IT.
EVEN IF I TELL YOU, YOU WON'T UNDERSTAND.
NO ONE CAN EVER UNDERSTAND UNTIL THEY GO THROUGH THE SAME THING.
TRY ME.
SIGH
"WHEN I WAS SMALL THERE WAS THIS FAMILY THAT LIVED A FEW BLOCKS FROM US. THEY HAD THREE BOYS WHO WOULD ALWAYS PICK ON MY FRIENDS AND ME.
"THEY WERE HUGE FAT SLOBS THAT WOULD BEAT ON US ANY CHANCE THEY GOT.
"BUT I HAD AN ADVANTAGE.
"I COULD RUN.
"THEY HAD BEEN CHASING ME FOR A WHILE. THAT DAY I WAS FEELING ESPECIALLY CONFIDENT SO WHENEVER I GOT FAR ENOUGH AHEAD I WOULD TURN BACK AND TAUNT THEM."

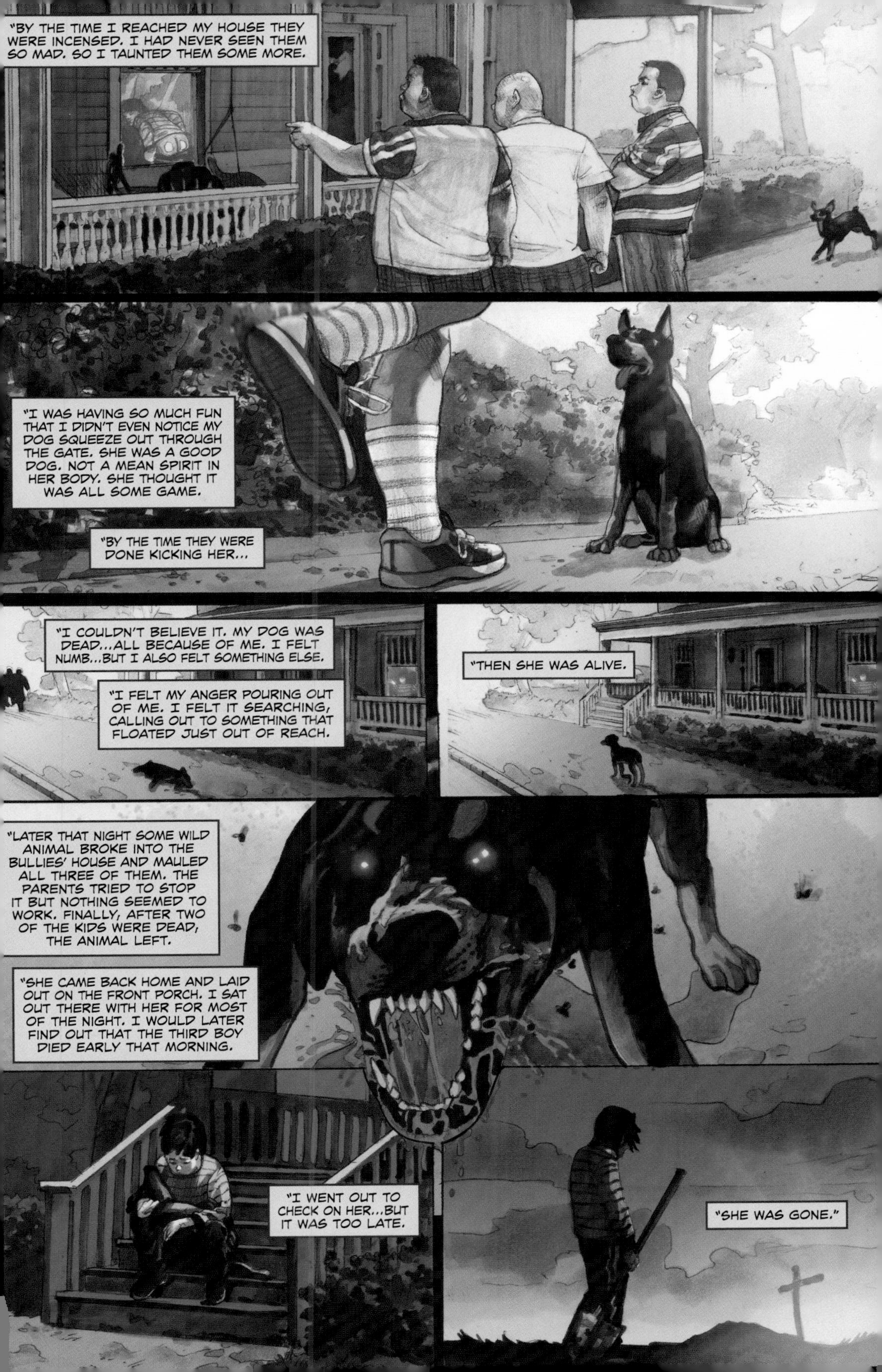
"BY THE TIME I REACHED MY HOUSE THEY WERE INCENSED. I HAD NEVER SEEN THEM SO MAD. SO I TAUNTED THEM SOME MORE.
"I WAS HAVING SO MUCH FUN THAT I DIDN'T EVEN NOTICE MY DOG SQUEEZE OUT THROUGH THE GATE. SHE WAS A GOOD DOG. NOT A MEAN SPIRIT IN HER BODY. SHE THOUGHT IT WAS ALL SOME GAME.
"BY THE TIME THEY WERE DONE KICKING HER...
"I COULDN'T BELIEVE IT. MY DOG WAS DEAD...ALL BECAUSE OF ME. I FELT NUMB...BUT I ALSO FELT SOMETHING ELSE.
"I FELT MY ANGER POURING OUT OF ME. I FELT IT SEARCHING, CALLING OUT TO SOMETHING THAT FLOATED JUST OUT OF REACH.
"THEN SHE WAS ALIVE.
"LATER THAT NIGHT SOME WILD ANIMAL BROKE INTO THE BULLIES' HOUSE AND MAULED ALL THREE OF THEM. THE PARENTS TRIED TO STOP IT BUT NOTHING SEEMED TO WORK. FINALLY, AFTER TWO OF THE KIDS WERE DEAD, THE ANIMAL LEFT.
"SHE CAME BACK HOME AND LAID OUT ON THE FRONT PORCH. I SAT OUT THERE WITH HER FOR MOST OF THE NIGHT. I WOULD LATER FIND OUT THAT THE THIRD BOY DIED EARLY THAT MORNING.
"I WENT OUT TO CHECK ON HER...BUT IT WAS TOO LATE.
"SHE WAS GONE."

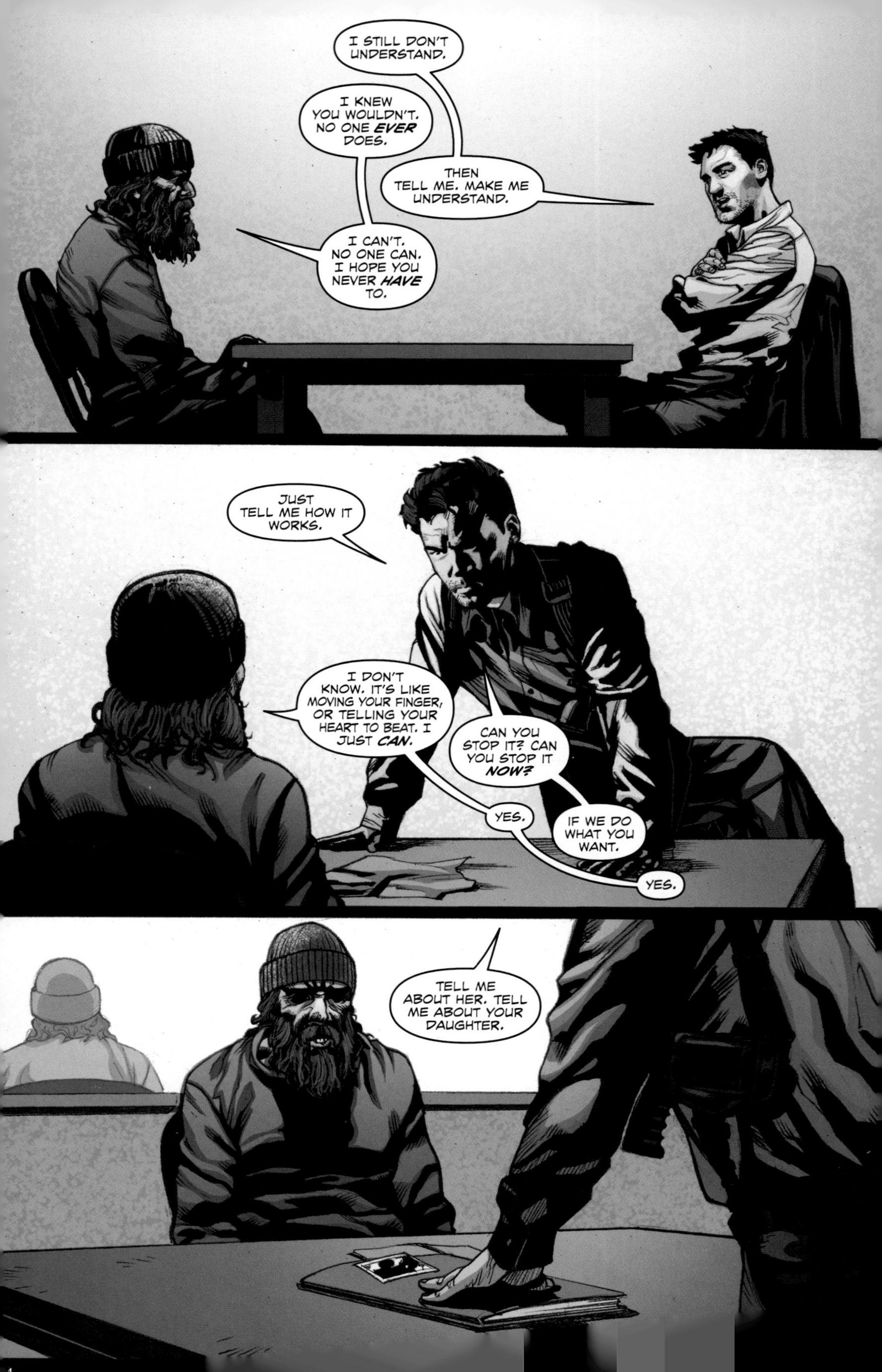
I STILL DON'T UNDERSTAND.
I KNEW YOU WOULDN'T. NO ONE *EVER* DOES.
THEN TELL ME. MAKE ME UNDERSTAND.
I CAN'T. NO ONE CAN. I HOPE YOU NEVER *HAVE* TO.
JUST TELL ME HOW IT WORKS.
I DON'T KNOW. IT'S LIKE MOVING YOUR FINGER, OR TELLING YOUR HEART TO BEAT. I JUST *CAN*.
CAN YOU STOP IT? CAN YOU STOP IT *NOW?*
YES.
IF WE DO WHAT YOU WANT.
YES.
TELL ME ABOUT HER. TELL ME ABOUT YOUR DAUGHTER.

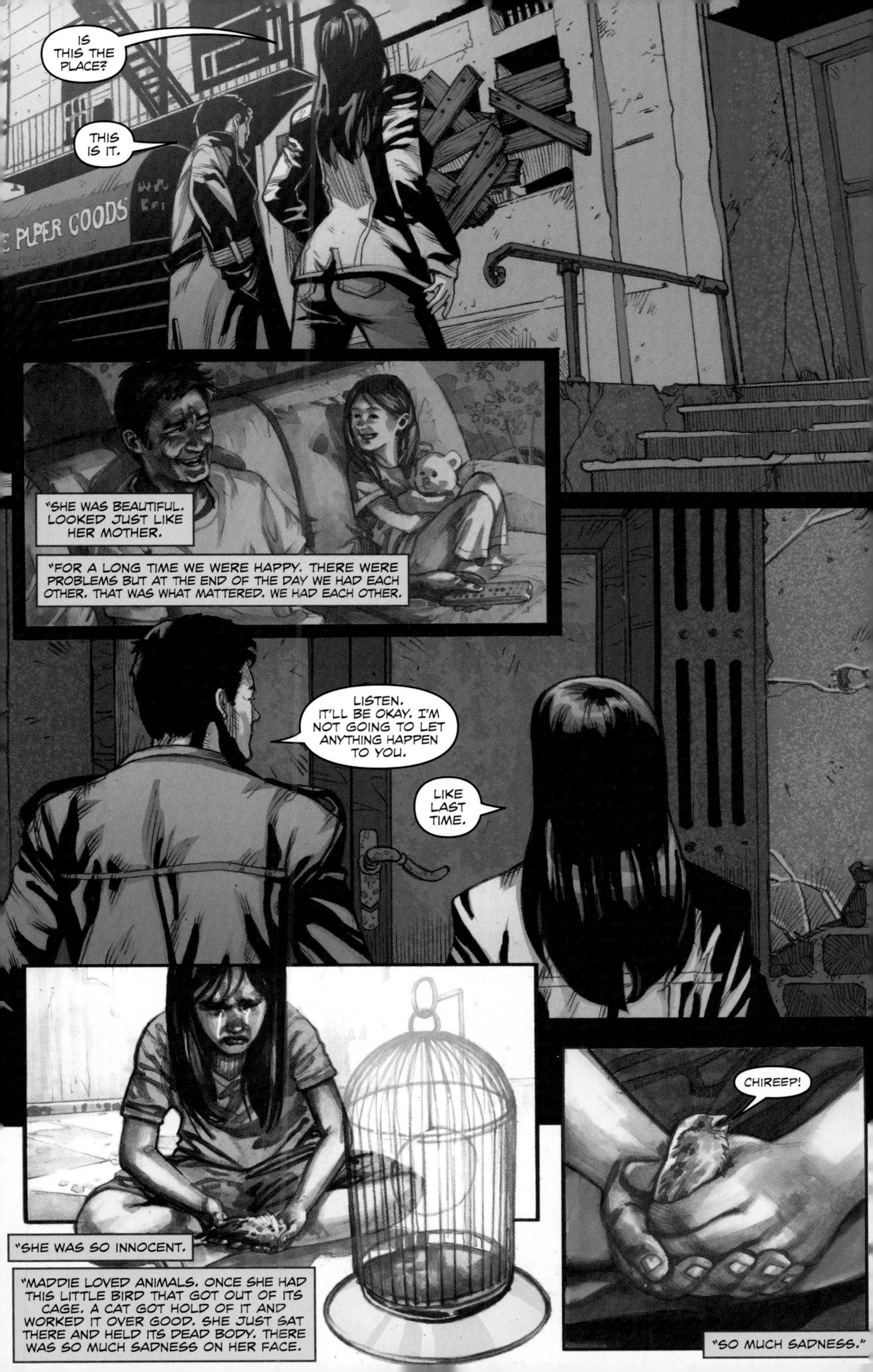
IS THIS THE PLACE?
THIS IS IT.
PIPER GOODS
"SHE WAS BEAUTIFUL. LOOKED JUST LIKE HER MOTHER.
"FOR A LONG TIME WE WERE HAPPY. THERE WERE PROBLEMS BUT AT THE END OF THE DAY WE HAD EACH OTHER. THAT WAS WHAT MATTERED. WE HAD EACH OTHER.
LISTEN. IT'LL BE OKAY. I'M NOT GOING TO LET ANYTHING HAPPEN TO YOU.
LIKE LAST TIME.
"SHE WAS SO INNOCENT.
"MADDIE LOVED ANIMALS. ONCE SHE HAD THIS LITTLE BIRD THAT GOT OUT OF ITS CAGE. A CAT GOT HOLD OF IT AND WORKED IT OVER GOOD. SHE JUST SAT THERE AND HELD ITS DEAD BODY. THERE WAS SO MUCH SADNESS ON HER FACE.
CHIREEP!
"SO MUCH SADNESS."

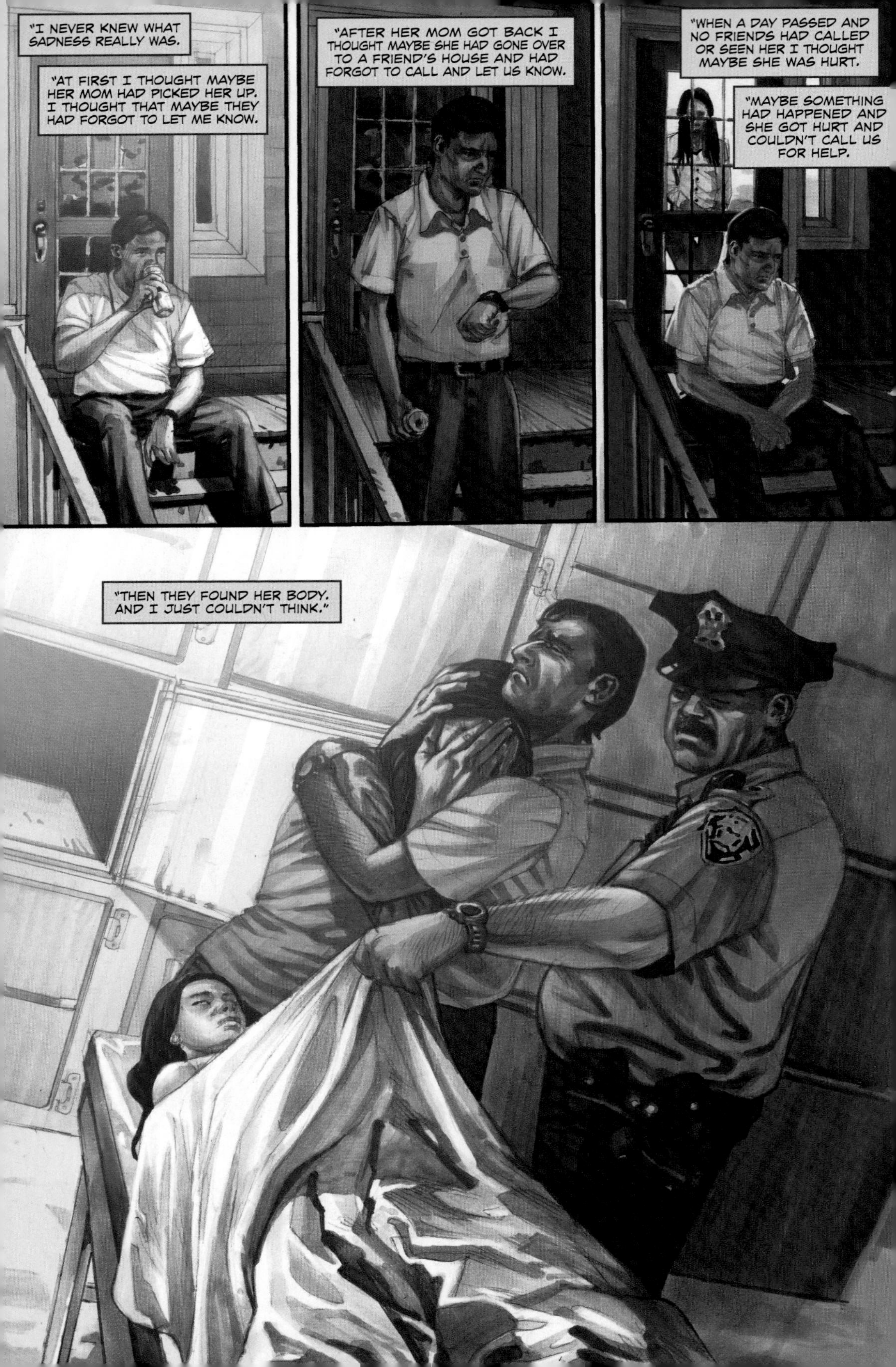
"I NEVER KNEW WHAT SADNESS REALLY WAS.
"AT FIRST I THOUGHT MAYBE HER MOM HAD PICKED HER UP. I THOUGHT THAT MAYBE THEY HAD FORGOT TO LET ME KNOW.
"AFTER HER MOM GOT BACK I THOUGHT MAYBE SHE HAD GONE OVER TO A FRIEND'S HOUSE AND HAD FORGOT TO CALL AND LET US KNOW.
"WHEN A DAY PASSED AND NO FRIENDS HAD CALLED OR SEEN HER I THOUGHT MAYBE SHE WAS HURT.
"MAYBE SOMETHING HAD HAPPENED AND SHE GOT HURT AND COULDN'T CALL US FOR HELP.
"THEN THEY FOUND HER BODY. AND I JUST COULDN'T THINK."

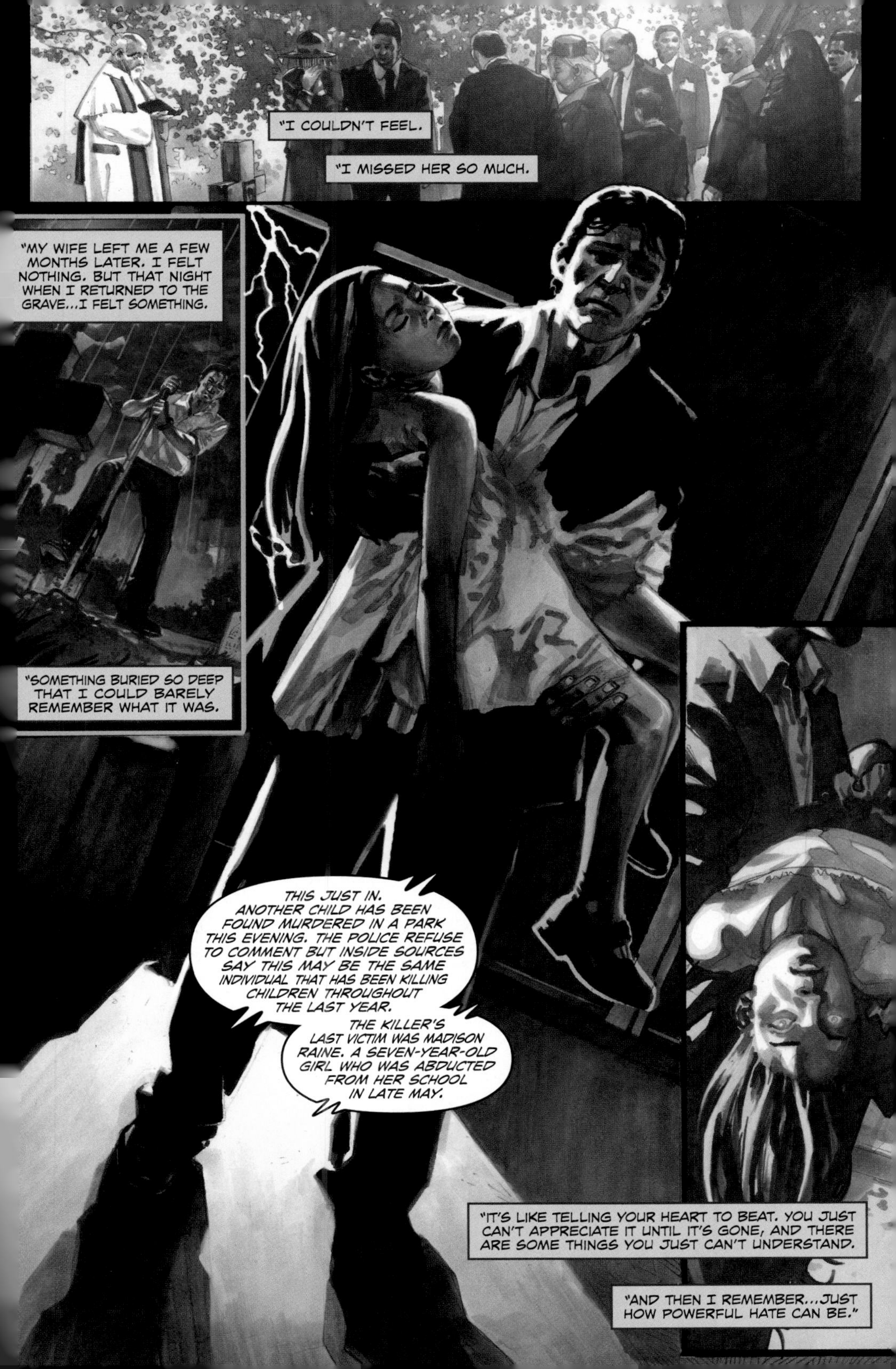
"I COULDN'T FEEL.
"I MISSED HER SO MUCH.
"MY WIFE LEFT ME A FEW MONTHS LATER. I FELT NOTHING. BUT THAT NIGHT WHEN I RETURNED TO THE GRAVE...I FELT SOMETHING.
"SOMETHING BURIED SO DEEP THAT I COULD BARELY REMEMBER WHAT IT WAS.
THIS JUST IN. ANOTHER CHILD HAS BEEN FOUND MURDERED IN A PARK THIS EVENING. THE POLICE REFUSE TO COMMENT BUT INSIDE SOURCES SAY THIS MAY BE THE SAME INDIVIDUAL THAT HAS BEEN KILLING CHILDREN THROUGHOUT THE LAST YEAR.
THE KILLER'S LAST VICTIM WAS MADISON RAINE. A SEVEN-YEAR-OLD GIRL WHO WAS ABDUCTED FROM HER SCHOOL IN LATE MAY.
"IT'S LIKE TELLING YOUR HEART TO BEAT. YOU JUST CAN'T APPRECIATE IT UNTIL IT'S GONE, AND THERE ARE SOME THINGS YOU JUST CAN'T UNDERSTAND.
"AND THEN I REMEMBER...JUST HOW POWERFUL HATE CAN BE."

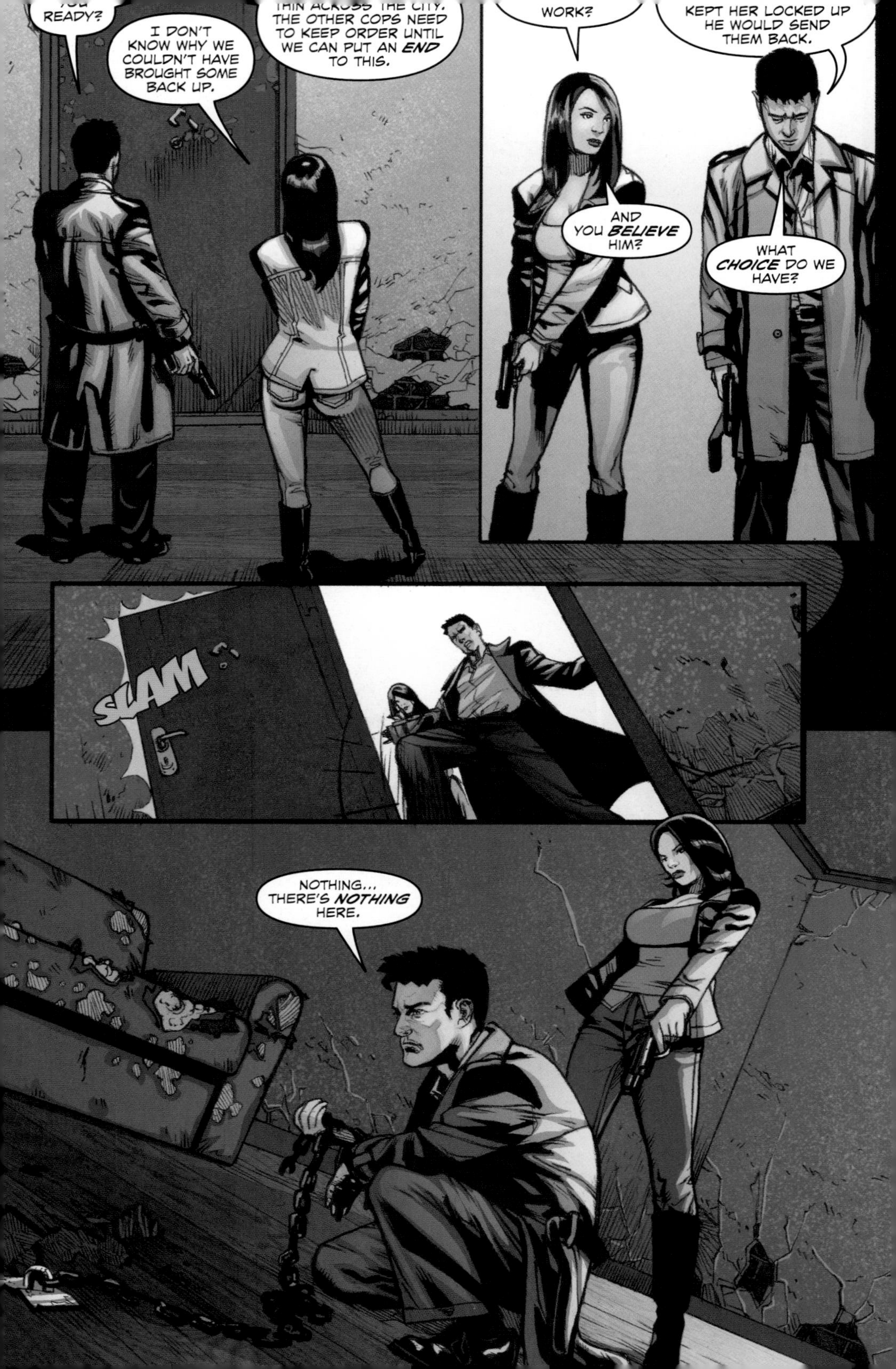

READY?
I DON'T KNOW WHY WE COULDN'T HAVE BROUGHT SOME BACK UP.
THIN ACROSS THE CITY. THE OTHER COPS NEED TO KEEP ORDER UNTIL WE CAN PUT AN *END* TO THIS.
WORK?
KEPT HER LOCKED UP HE WOULD SEND THEM BACK.
AND YOU *BELIEVE* HIM?
WHAT *CHOICE* DO WE HAVE?
SLAM
NOTHING... THERE'S *NOTHING* HERE.

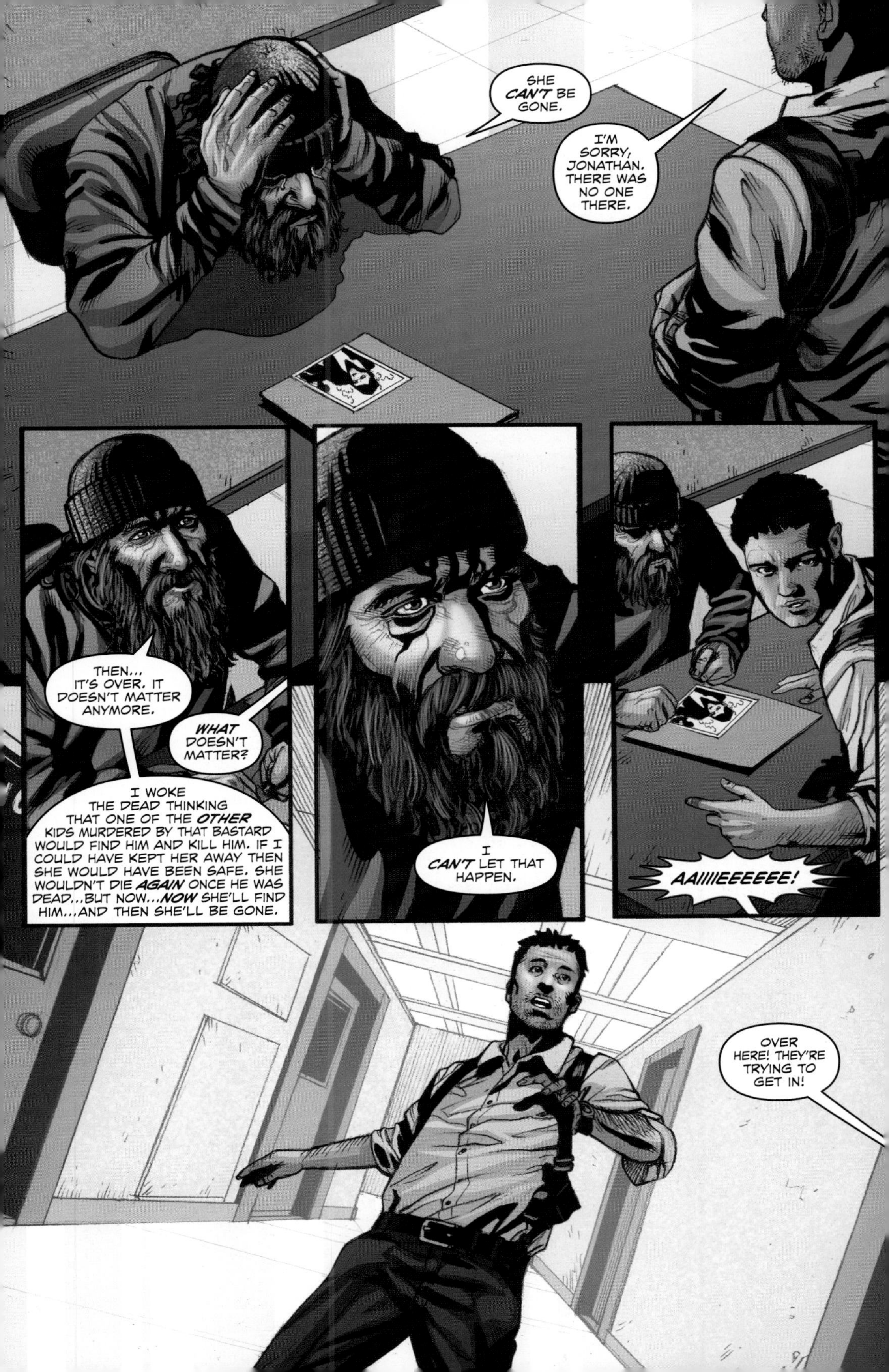
SHE CAN'T BE GONE.
I'M SORRY, JONATHAN. THERE WAS NO ONE THERE.
THEN... IT'S OVER. IT DOESN'T MATTER ANYMORE.
WHAT DOESN'T MATTER?
I WOKE THE DEAD THINKING THAT ONE OF THE OTHER KIDS MURDERED BY THAT BASTARD WOULD FIND HIM AND KILL HIM. IF I COULD HAVE KEPT HER AWAY THEN SHE WOULD HAVE BEEN SAFE. SHE WOULDN'T DIE AGAIN ONCE HE WAS DEAD...BUT NOW...NOW SHE'LL FIND HIM...AND THEN SHE'LL BE GONE.
I CAN'T LET THAT HAPPEN.
AAIIIIEEEEEE!
OVER HERE! THEY'RE TRYING TO GET IN!

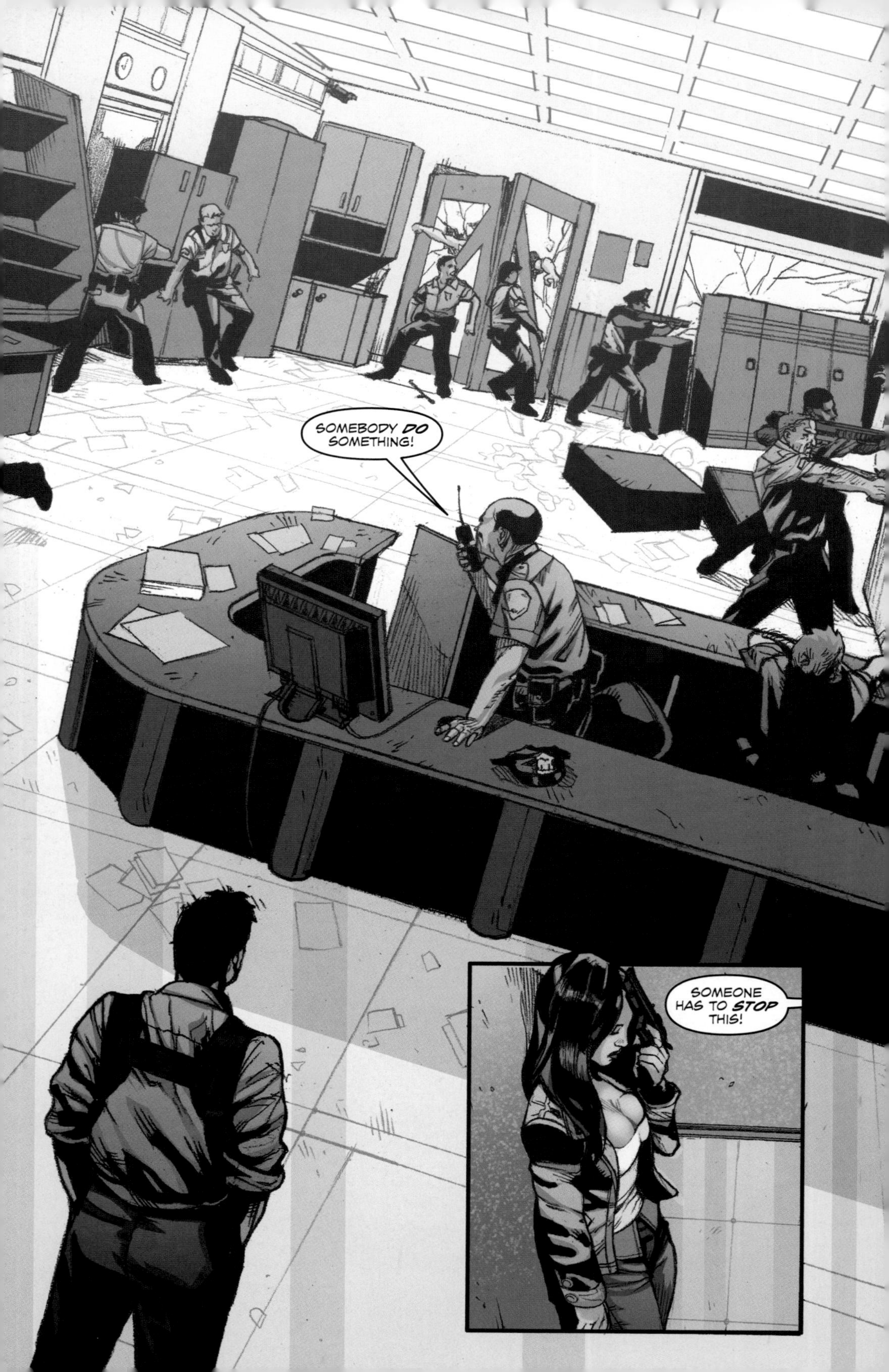
SOMEBODY DO SOMETHING!
SOMEONE HAS TO STOP THIS!

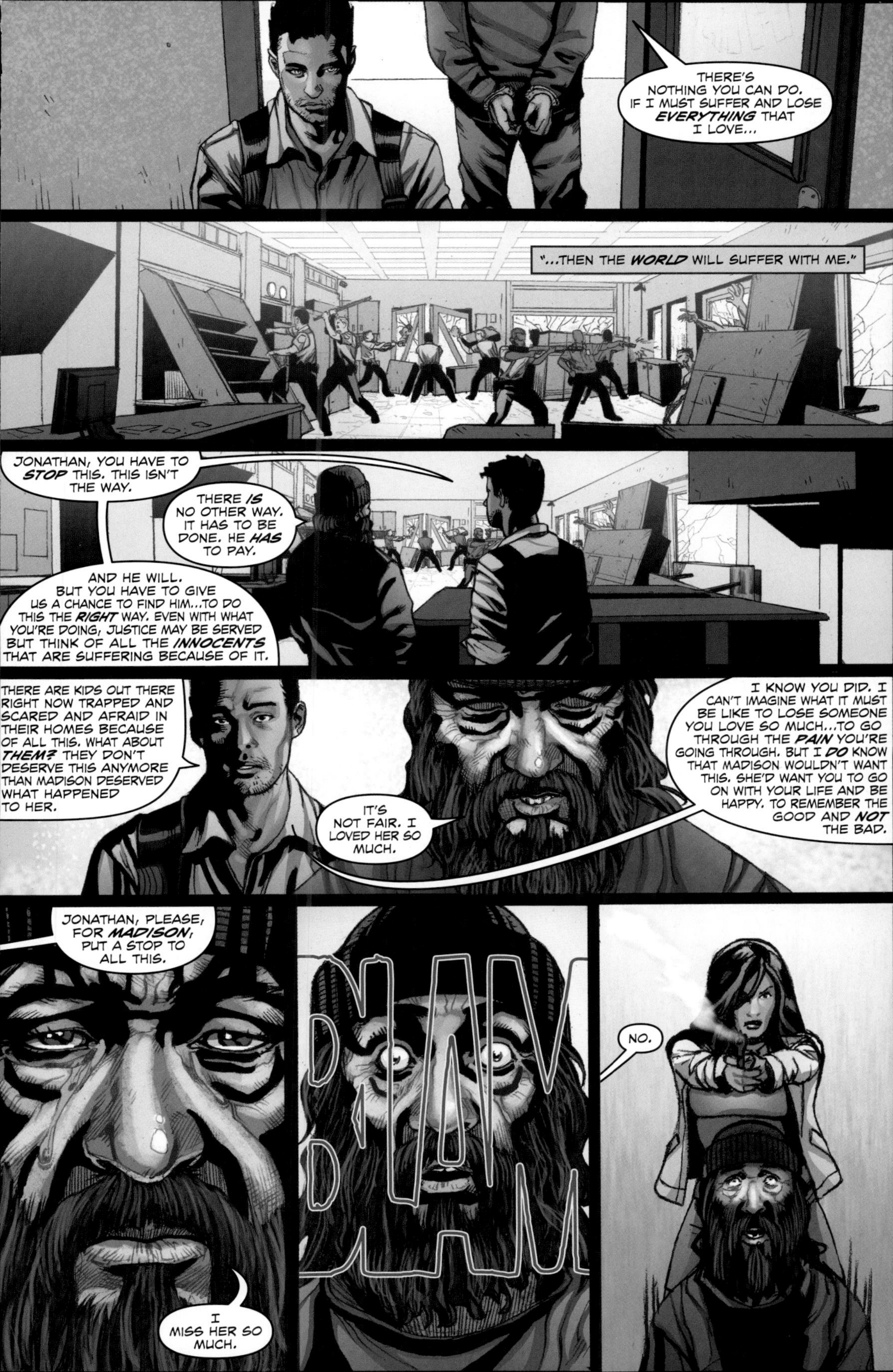

THERE'S NOTHING YOU CAN DO. IF I MUST SUFFER AND LOSE EVERYTHING THAT I LOVE...
"...THEN THE WORLD WILL SUFFER WITH ME."
JONATHAN, YOU HAVE TO STOP THIS. THIS ISN'T THE WAY.
THERE IS NO OTHER WAY. IT HAS TO BE DONE. HE HAS TO PAY.
AND HE WILL. BUT YOU HAVE TO GIVE US A CHANCE TO FIND HIM...TO DO THIS THE RIGHT WAY. EVEN WITH WHAT YOU'RE DOING, JUSTICE MAY BE SERVED BUT THINK OF ALL THE INNOCENTS THAT ARE SUFFERING BECAUSE OF IT.
THERE ARE KIDS OUT THERE RIGHT NOW TRAPPED AND SCARED AND AFRAID IN THEIR HOMES BECAUSE OF ALL THIS. WHAT ABOUT THEM? THEY DON'T DESERVE THIS ANYMORE THAN MADISON DESERVED WHAT HAPPENED TO HER.
IT'S NOT FAIR. I LOVED HER SO MUCH.
I KNOW YOU DID. I CAN'T IMAGINE WHAT IT MUST BE LIKE TO LOSE SOMEONE YOU LOVE SO MUCH...TO GO THROUGH THE PAIN YOU'RE GOING THROUGH. BUT I DO KNOW THAT MADISON WOULDN'T WANT THIS. SHE'D WANT YOU TO GO ON WITH YOUR LIFE AND BE HAPPY. TO REMEMBER THE GOOD AND NOT THE BAD.
JONATHAN, PLEASE, FOR MADISON, PUT A STOP TO ALL THIS.
I MISS HER SO MUCH.
BLAM BLAM
NO.

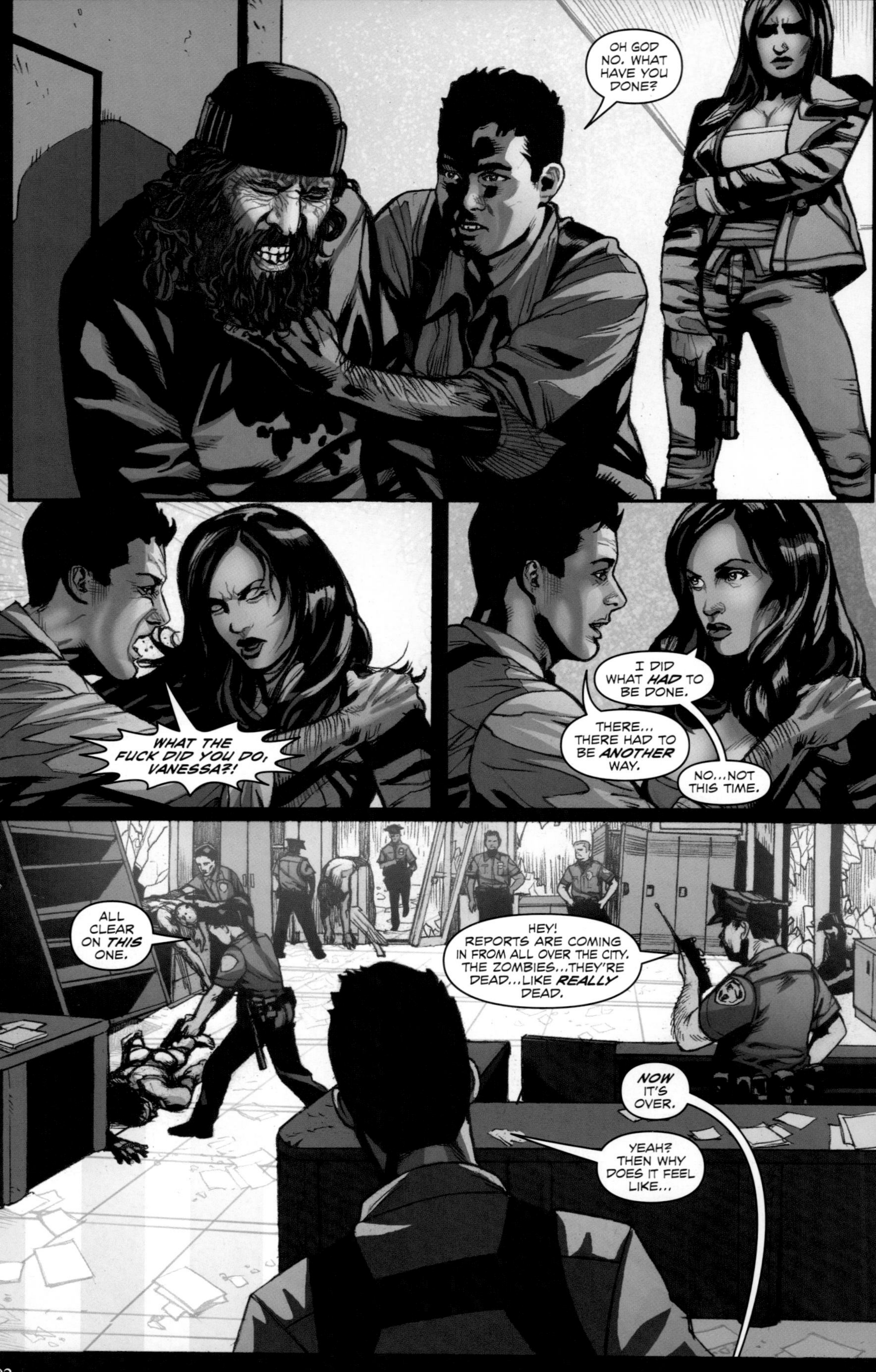
OH GOD NO. WHAT HAVE YOU DONE?
WHAT THE FUCK DID YOU DO, VANESSA?!
I DID WHAT HAD TO BE DONE.
THERE... THERE HAD TO BE ANOTHER WAY.
NO...NOT THIS TIME.
ALL CLEAR ON THIS ONE.
HEY! REPORTS ARE COMING IN FROM ALL OVER THE CITY. THE ZOMBIES...THEY'RE DEAD...LIKE REALLY DEAD.
NOW IT'S OVER.
YEAH? THEN WHY DOES IT FEEL LIKE...

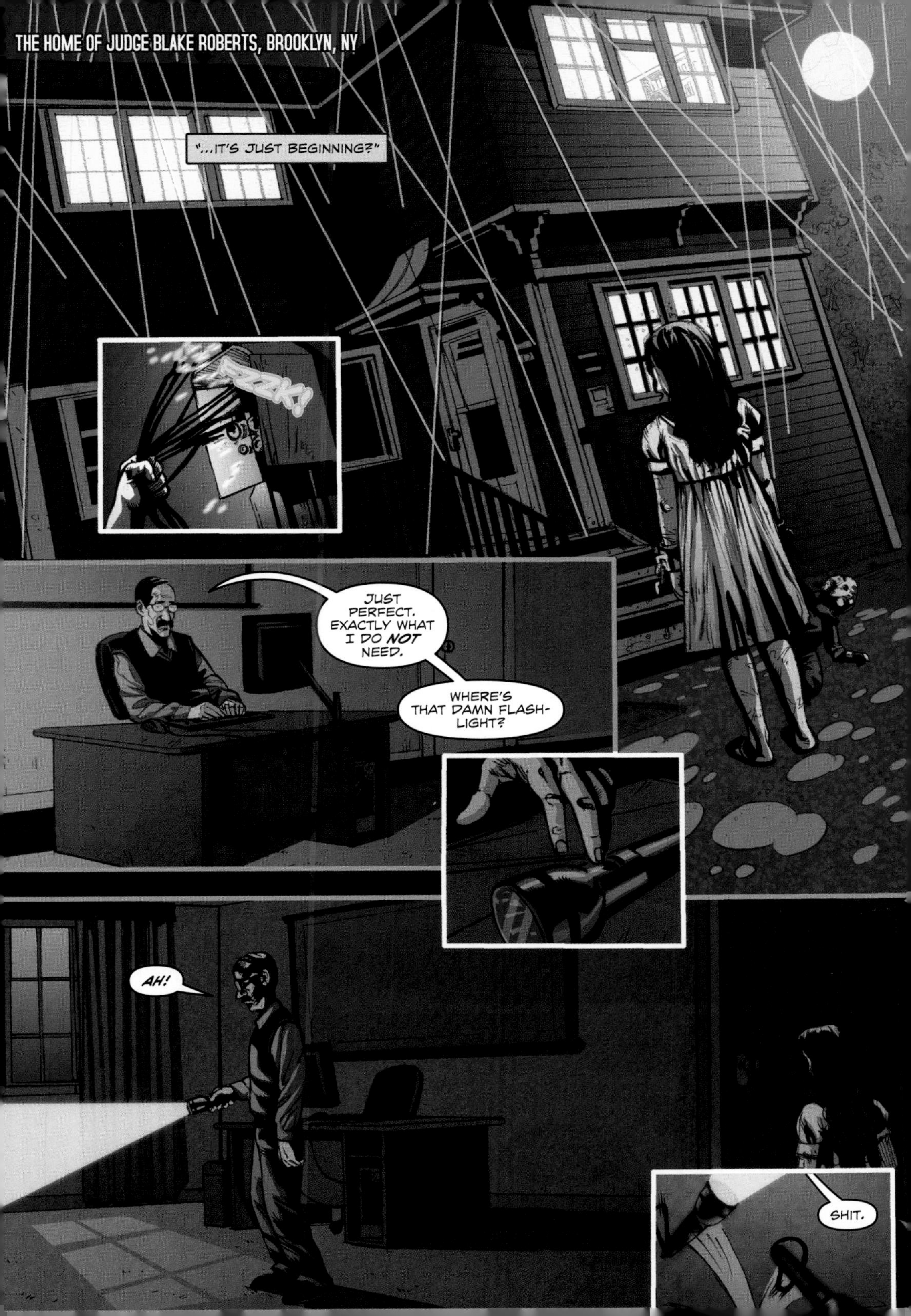

THE HOME OF JUDGE BLAKE ROBERTS, BROOKLYN, NY
"...IT'S JUST BEGINNING?"
FZZZK!
JUST PERFECT. EXACTLY WHAT I DO NOT NEED.
WHERE'S THAT DAMN FLASH-LIGHT?
AH!
SHIT.

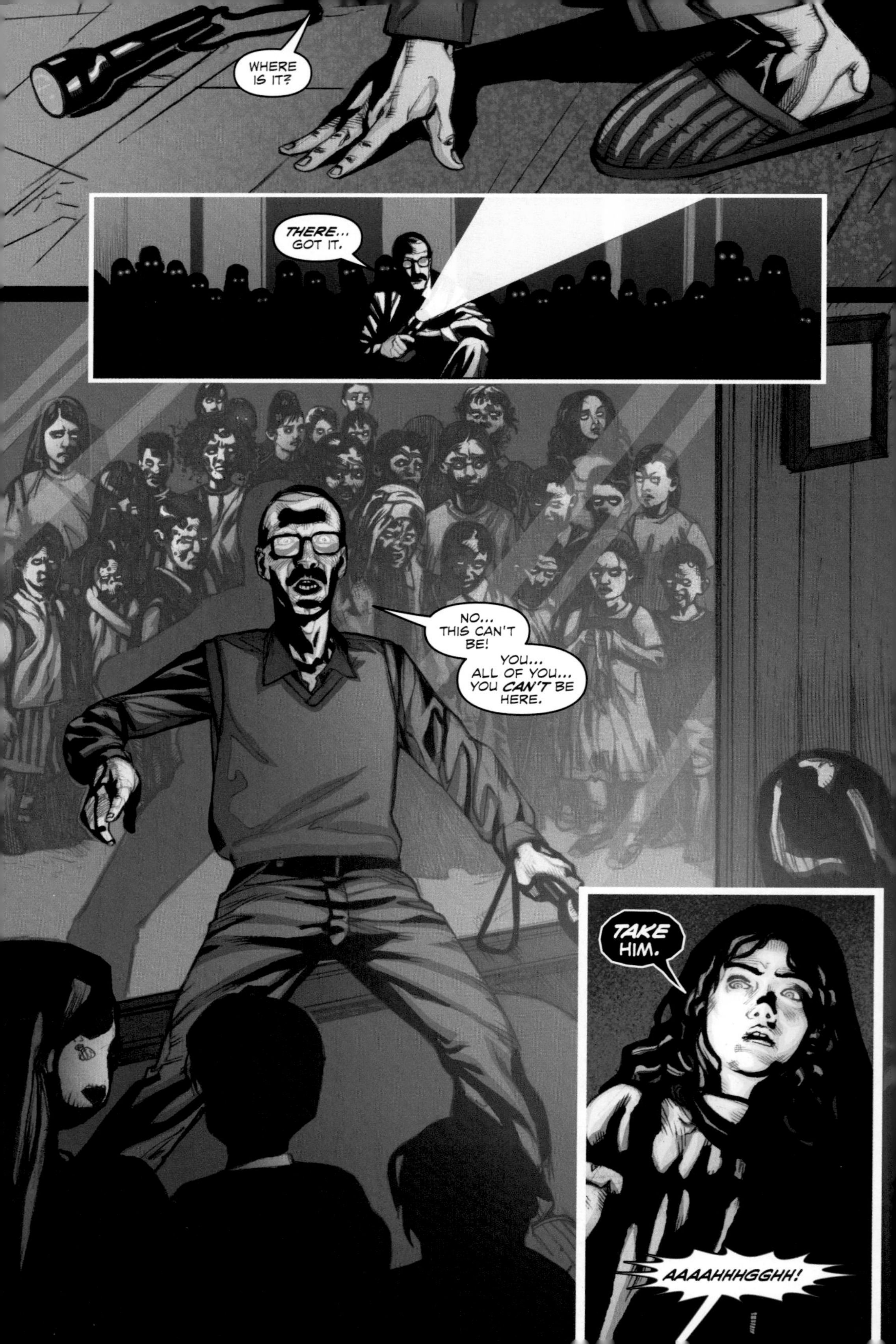
WHERE IS IT?
THERE... GOT IT.
NO... THIS CAN'T BE!
YOU... ALL OF YOU... YOU CAN'T BE HERE.
TAKE HIM.
AAAAHHHGGHH!

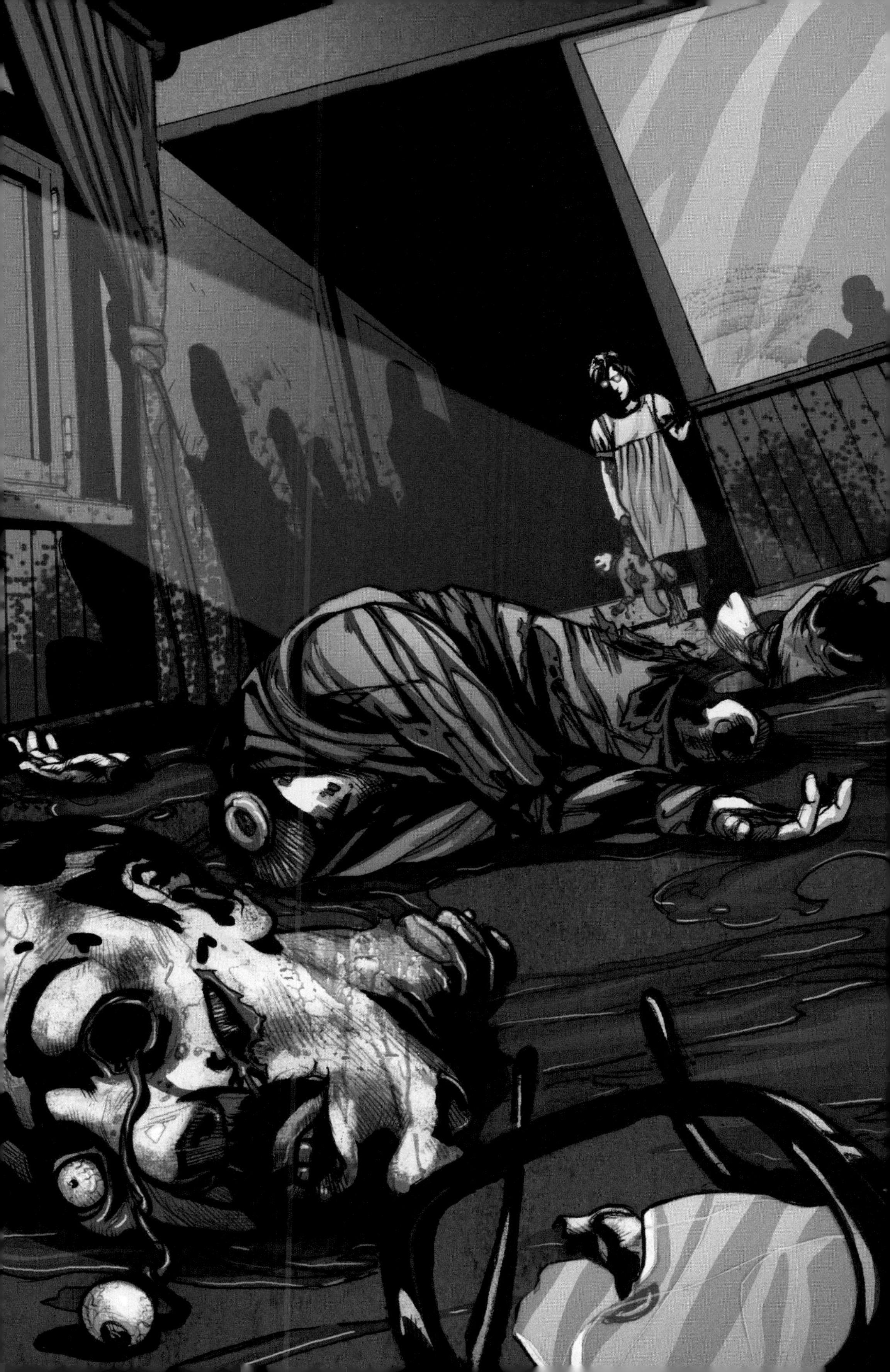

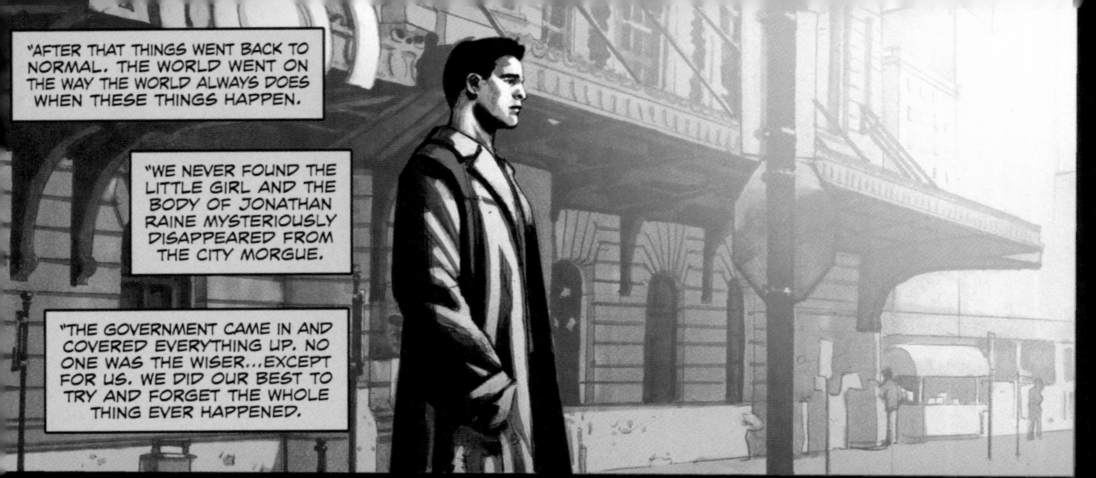
"AFTER THAT THINGS WENT BACK TO NORMAL. THE WORLD WENT ON THE WAY THE WORLD ALWAYS DOES WHEN THESE THINGS HAPPEN.
"WE NEVER FOUND THE LITTLE GIRL AND THE BODY OF JONATHAN RAINE MYSTERIOUSLY DISAPPEARED FROM THE CITY MORGUE.
"THE GOVERNMENT CAME IN AND COVERED EVERYTHING UP. NO ONE WAS THE WISER...EXCEPT FOR US. WE DID OUR BEST TO TRY AND FORGET THE WHOLE THING EVER HAPPENED.

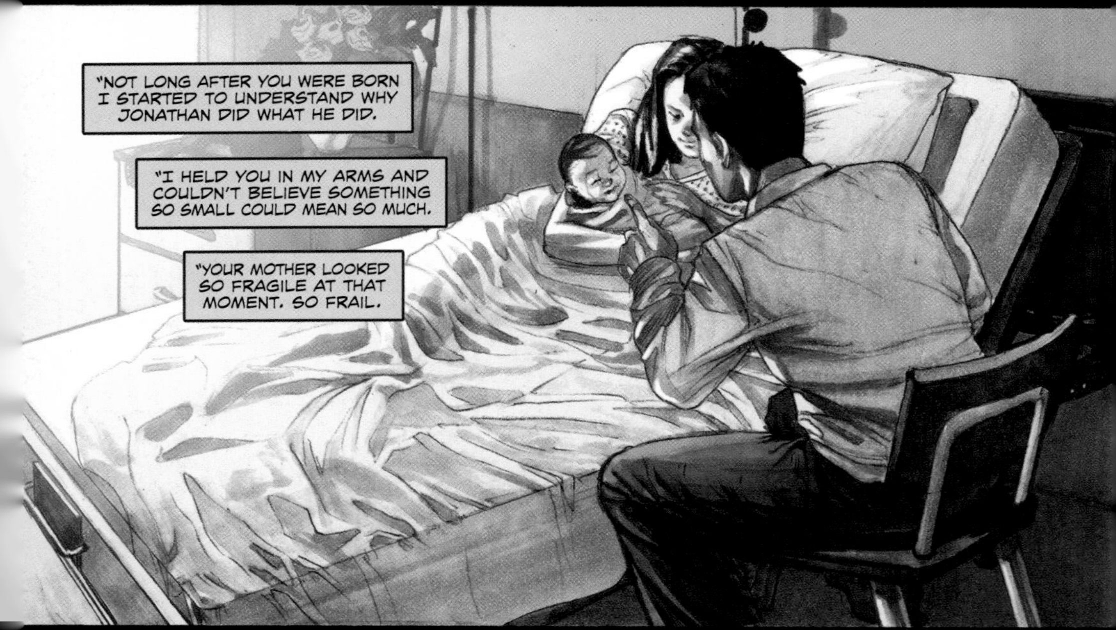
"NOT LONG AFTER YOU WERE BORN I STARTED TO UNDERSTAND WHY JONATHAN DID WHAT HE DID.
"I HELD YOU IN MY ARMS AND COULDN'T BELIEVE SOMETHING SO SMALL COULD MEAN SO MUCH.
"YOUR MOTHER LOOKED SO FRAGILE AT THAT MOMENT. SO FRAIL.

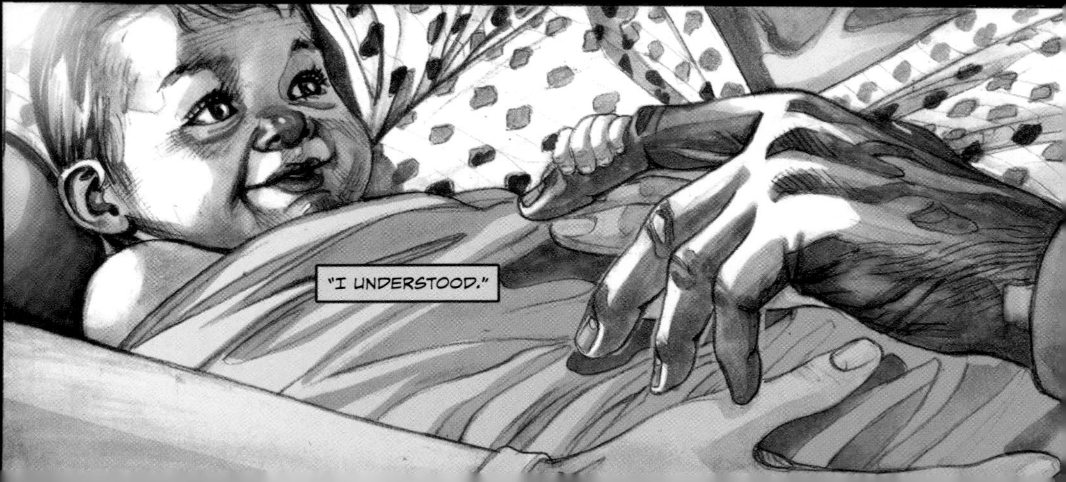
"I UNDERSTOOD."

"A FEW YEARS LATER I LEFT THE FORCE."

"FOR A WHILE THINGS WERE QUIET AND NO ONE HEARD ANYTHING...THEN IT STARTED HAPPENING AGAIN."

"YOU WERE FOUR BY THAT TIME AND I DECIDED SOME PLACE FAR AWAY FROM ALL THAT WOULD BE BETTER FOR YOU."

"SO WE CAME HERE."

"NOT JUST IN NEW YORK, BUT ALL OVER THE COUNTRY."

"ONE AT A TIME, CITY AFTER CITY, STATE AFTER STATE, THE DEAD BEGAN TO WALK THE STREETS SEARCHING FOR THOSE WHO HAD TAKEN THEIR LIGHT AND PLACED THEM IN A RESTLESS SLEEP."

"IT TOOK ONLY A FEW MONTHS BEFORE EVERYTHING CHANGED.

"FROM THAT POINT ON, AFTER PEOPLE DISCOVERED THE TRUTH, THE WORLD BECAME A SAFER PLACE. NO LONGER IS THERE FEAR. NO LONGER DO PEOPLE WAKE AT NIGHT KNOWING THAT SOMETHING TERRIBLE HAS HAPPENED TO A LOVED ONE. MURDER, IN ALL ITS FORMS, IS ESSENTIALLY GONE. THE WORLD IS SAFE.

"BECAUSE SHE IS THERE. SHE HAS THE SAME GIFT IN DEATH...THAT HER FATHER HAD IN LIFE."

"I DON'T REALLY UNDERSTAND IT, BUT EVEN JONATHAN'S DEATH COULDN'T STOP HER. SHE JUST KEPT GOING WHEN ALL THE OTHERS STOPPED.

"HER WALK NEVER ENDS. NONE CAN HIDE FROM HER SIGHT.

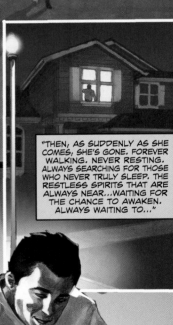

"THEN, AS SUDDENLY AS SHE COMES, SHE'S GONE. FOREVER WALKING. NEVER RESTING. ALWAYS SEARCHING FOR THOSE WHO NEVER TRULY SLEEP. THE RESTLESS SPIRITS THAT ARE ALWAYS NEAR...WAITING FOR THE CHANCE TO AWAKEN. ALWAYS WAITING TO..."

...WAKE THE DEAD.

THAT'S RIGHT. NIGHT, SON.

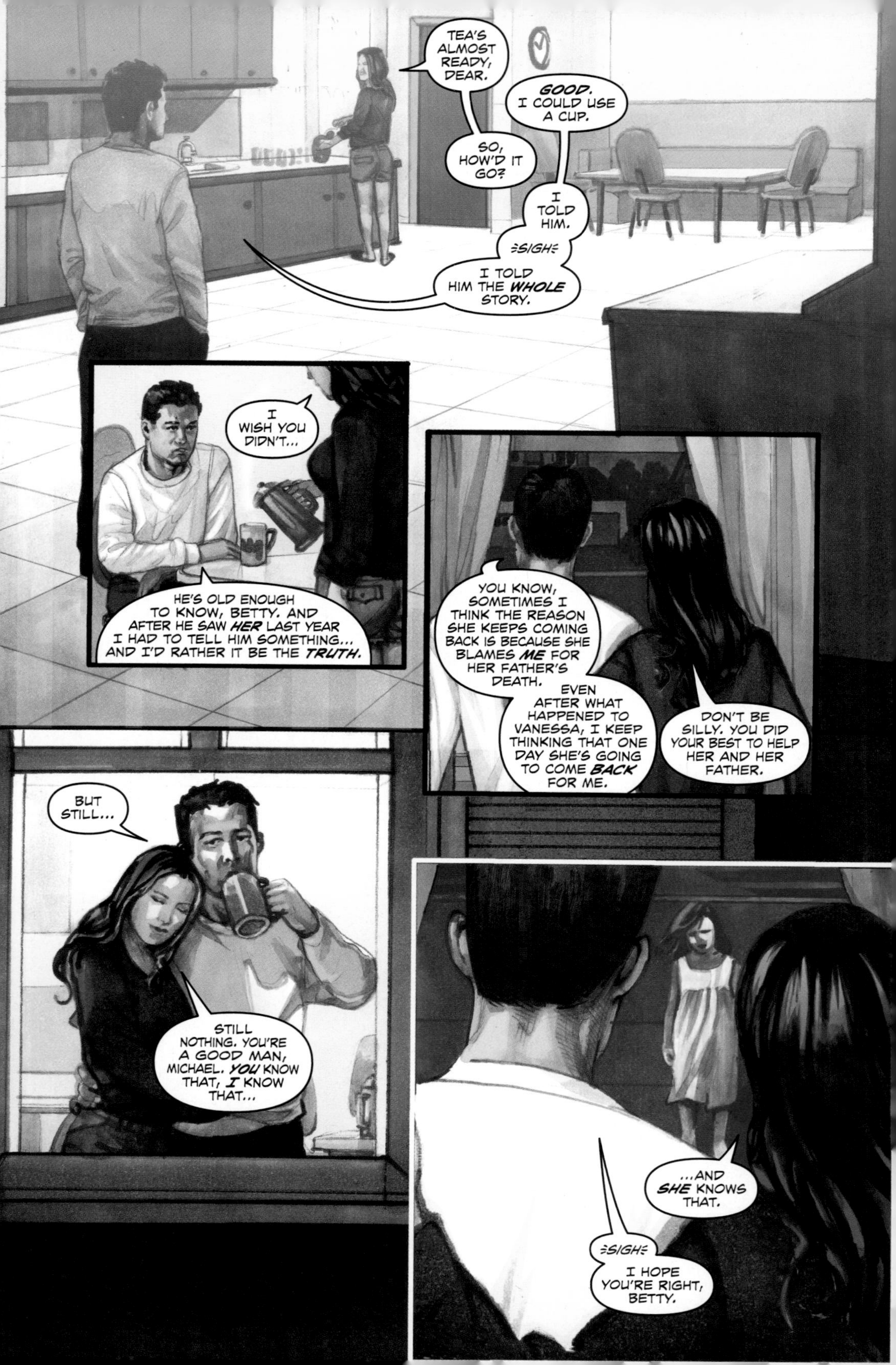
TEA'S ALMOST READY, DEAR.
GOOD. I COULD USE A CUP.
SO, HOW'D IT GO?
I TOLD HIM.
SIGH
I TOLD HIM THE WHOLE STORY.
I WISH YOU DIDN'T...
HE'S OLD ENOUGH TO KNOW, BETTY. AND AFTER HE SAW HER LAST YEAR I HAD TO TELL HIM SOMETHING... AND I'D RATHER IT BE THE TRUTH.
YOU KNOW, SOMETIMES I THINK THE REASON SHE KEEPS COMING BACK IS BECAUSE SHE BLAMES ME FOR HER FATHER'S DEATH.
EVEN AFTER WHAT HAPPENED TO VANESSA, I KEEP THINKING THAT ONE DAY SHE'S GOING TO COME BACK FOR ME.
DON'T BE SILLY. YOU DID YOUR BEST TO HELP HER AND HER FATHER.
BUT STILL...
STILL NOTHING. YOU'RE A GOOD MAN, MICHAEL. YOU KNOW THAT, I KNOW THAT...
...AND SHE KNOWS THAT.
SIGH
I HOPE YOU'RE RIGHT, BETTY.

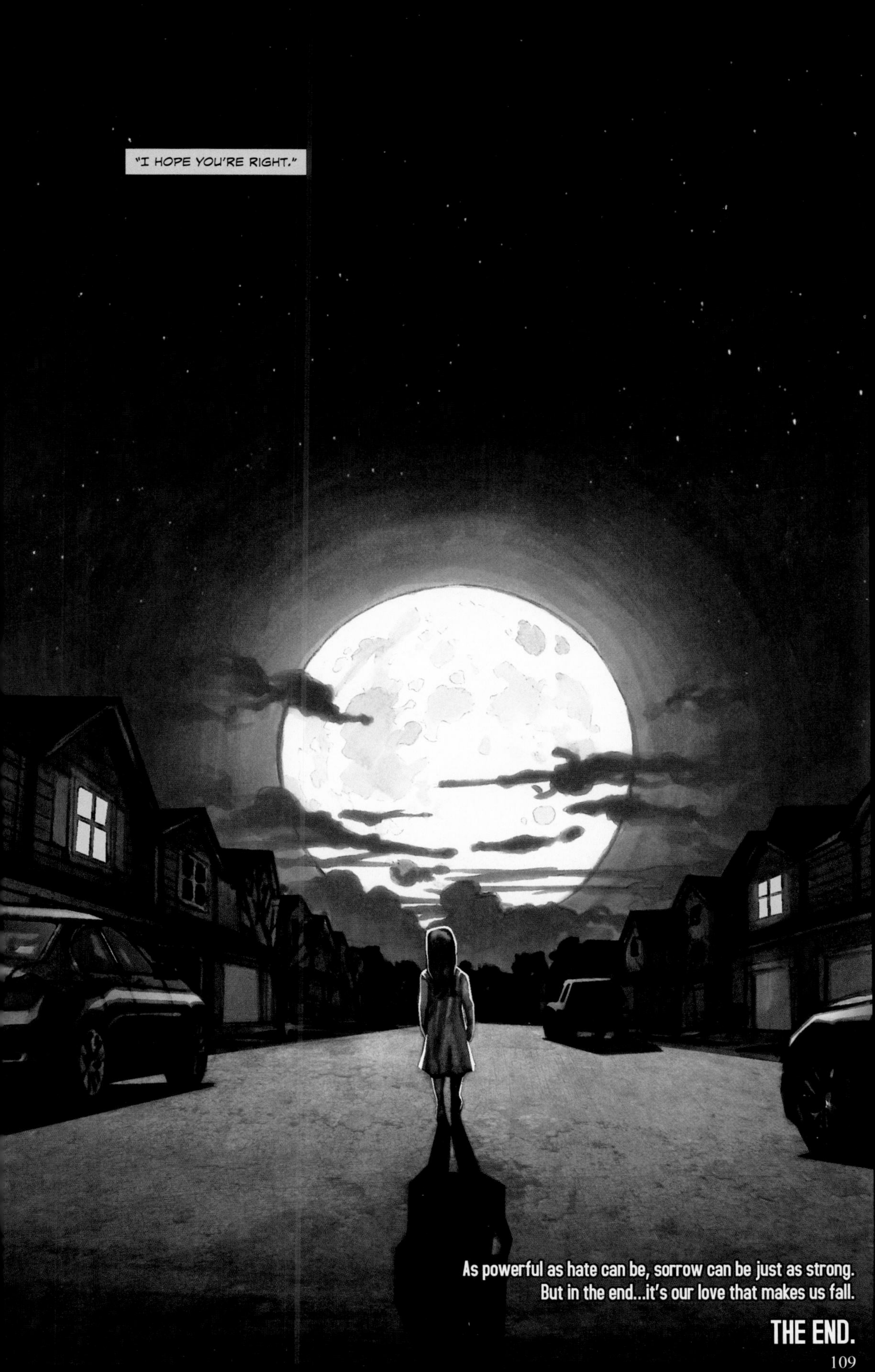
"I HOPE YOU'RE RIGHT."
As powerful as hate can be, sorrow can be just as strong.
But in the end...it's our love that makes us fall.
THE END.

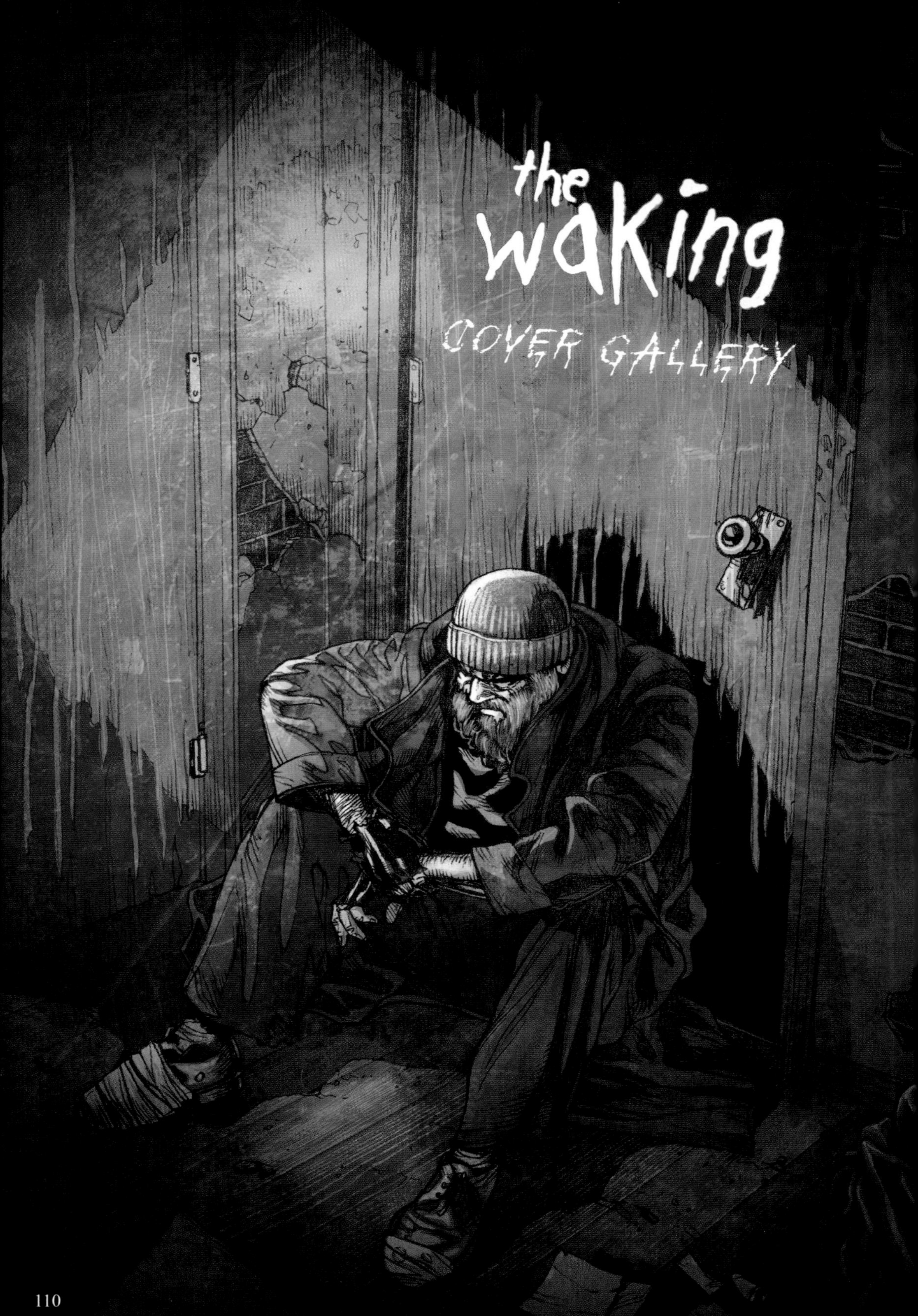
the waking
COVER GALLERY

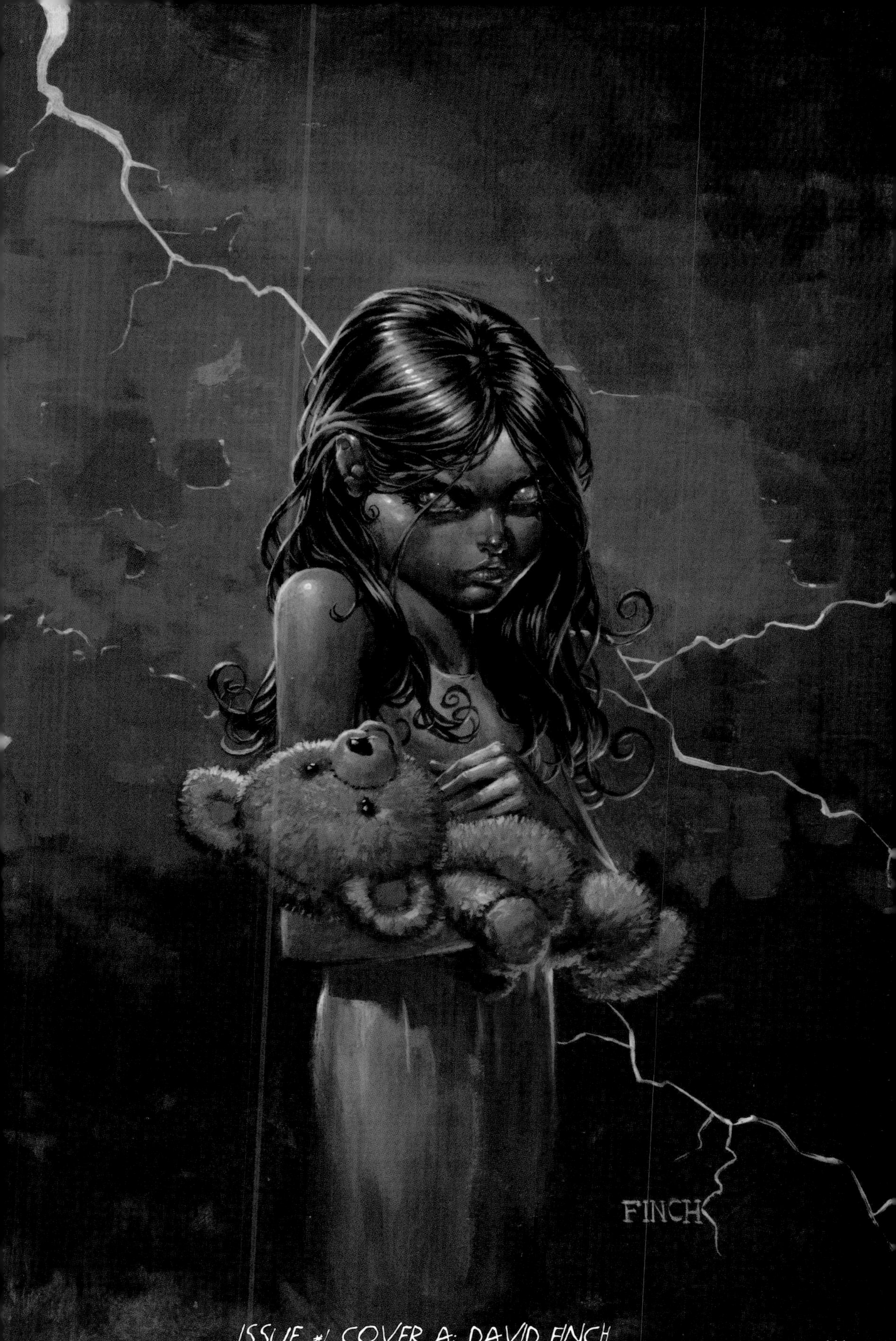
FINCH

ISSUE #1 COVER A: DAVID FINCH

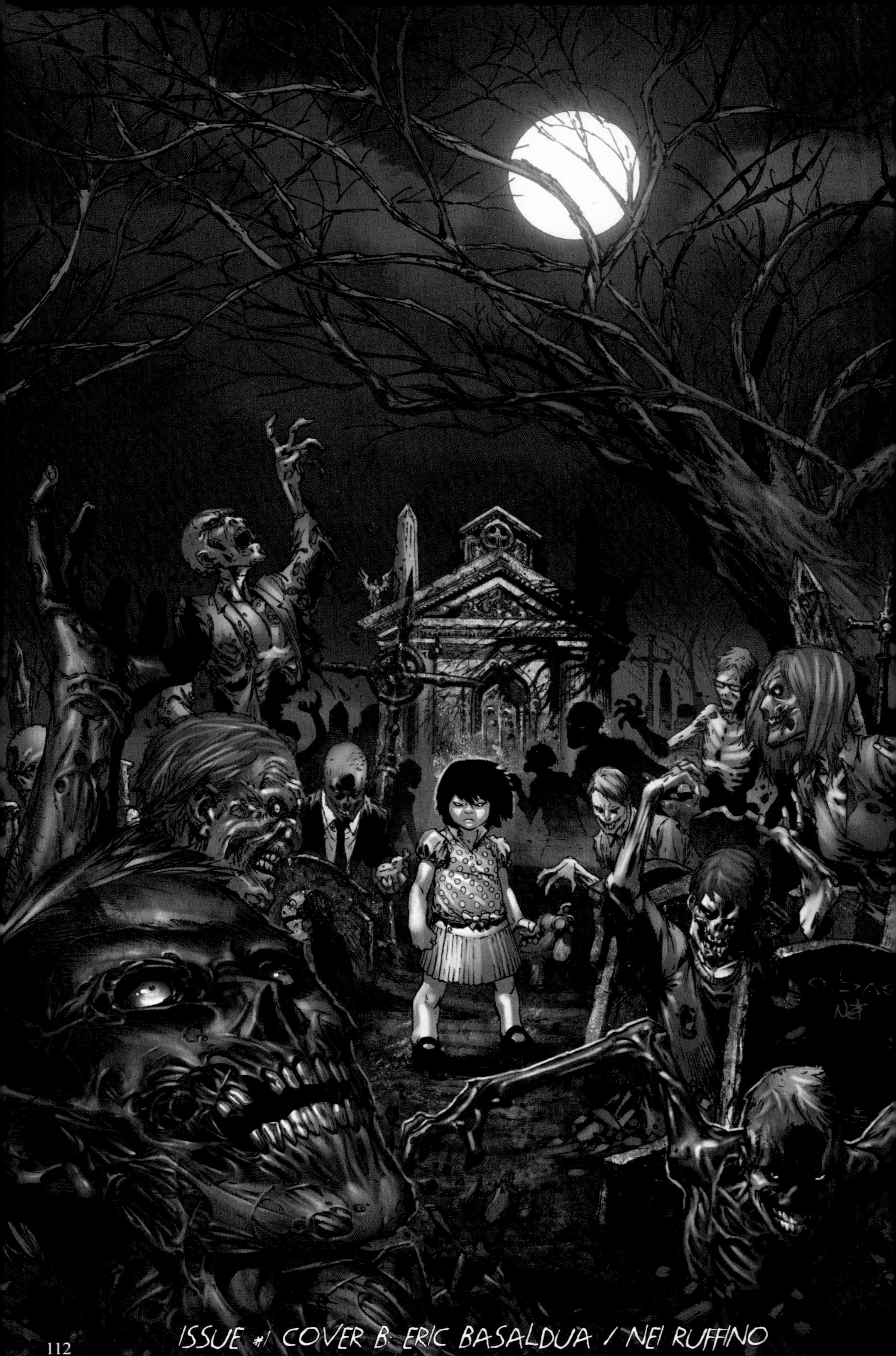

ISSUE #1 COVER B: ERIC BASALDUA / NEI RUFFINO

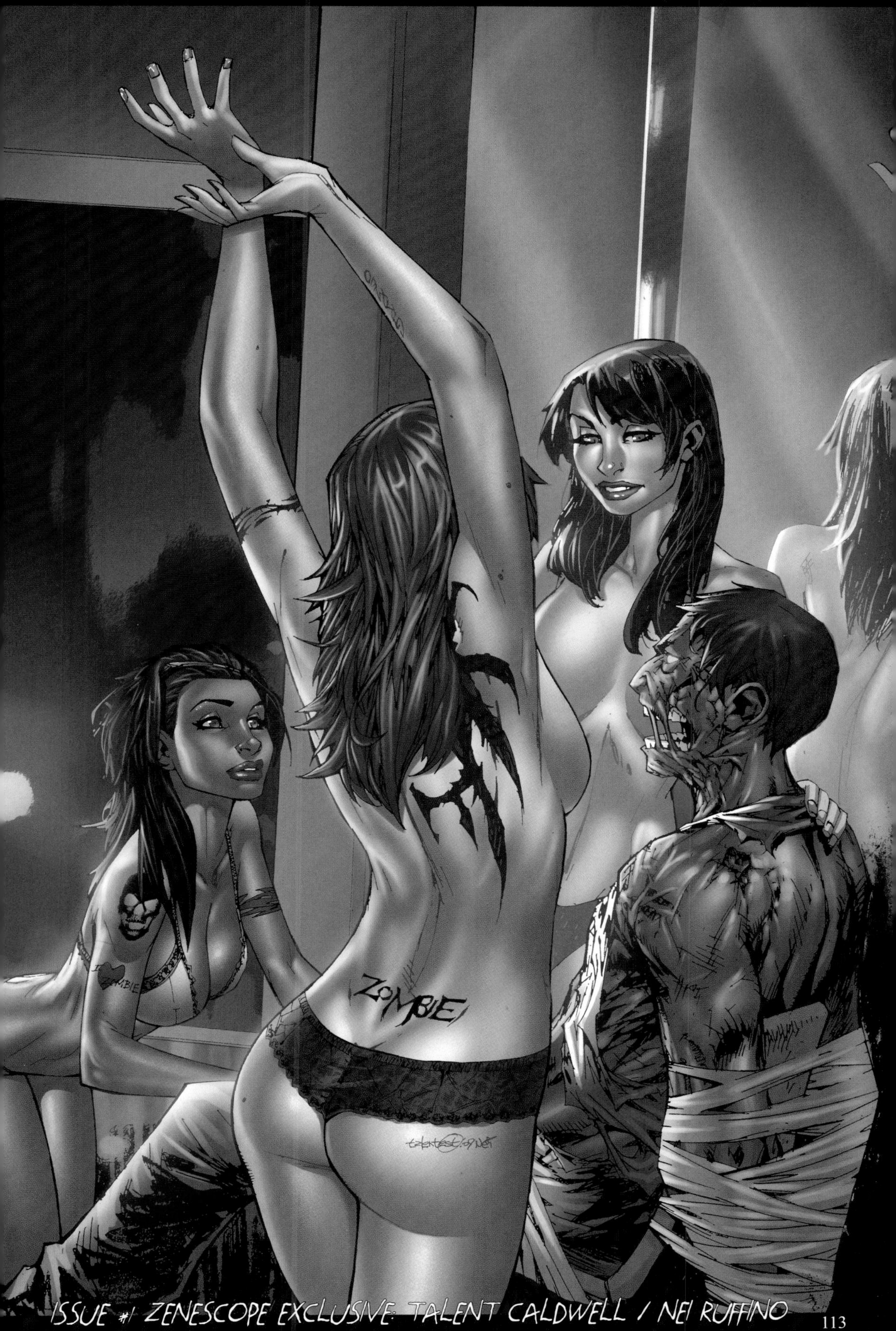
ZOMBIE

ISSUE #1 ZENESCOPE EXCLUSIVE: TALENT CALDWELL / NEI RUFFINO

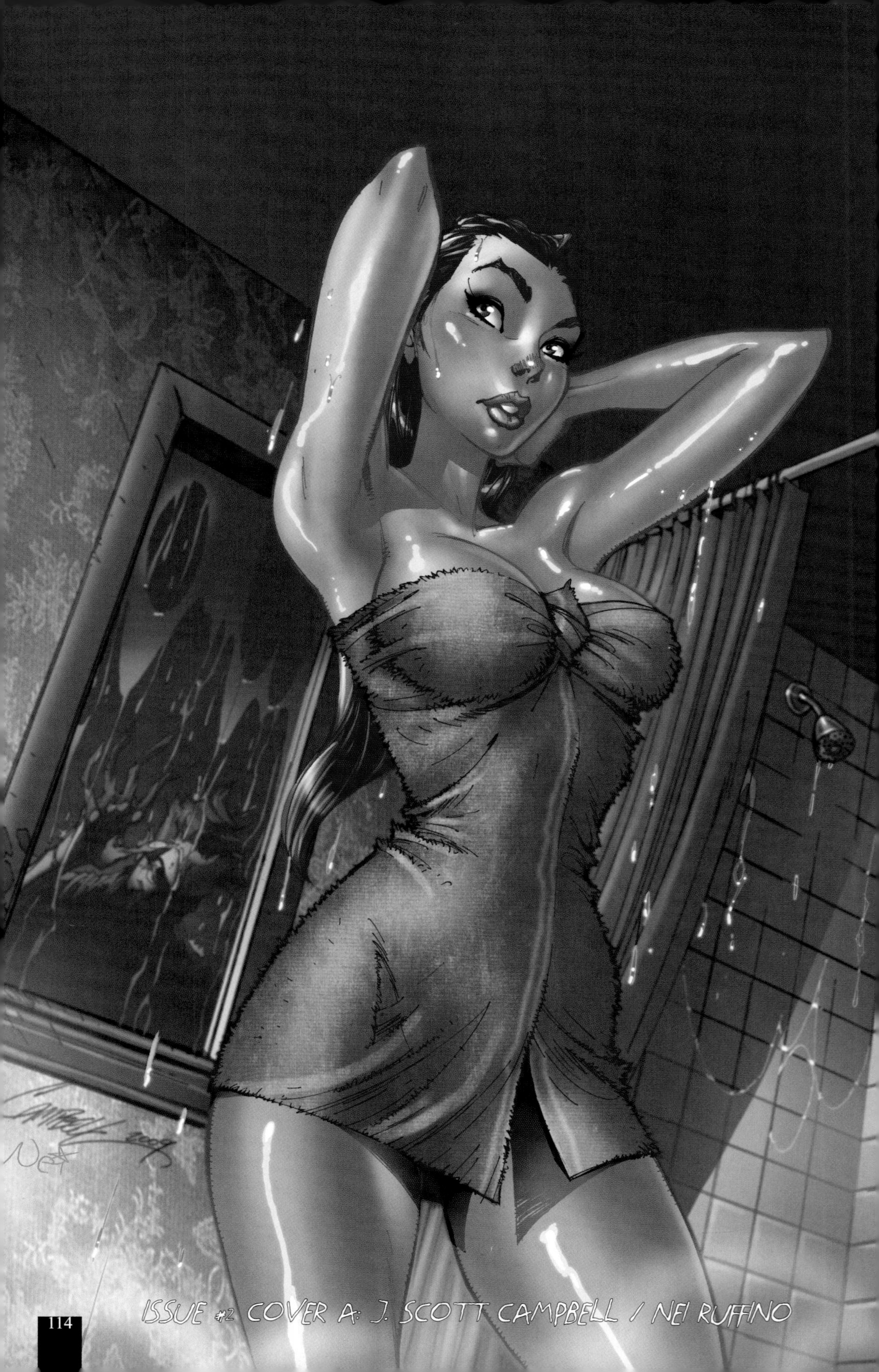

ISSUE #2 COVER A: J. SCOTT CAMPBELL / NEI RUFFINO

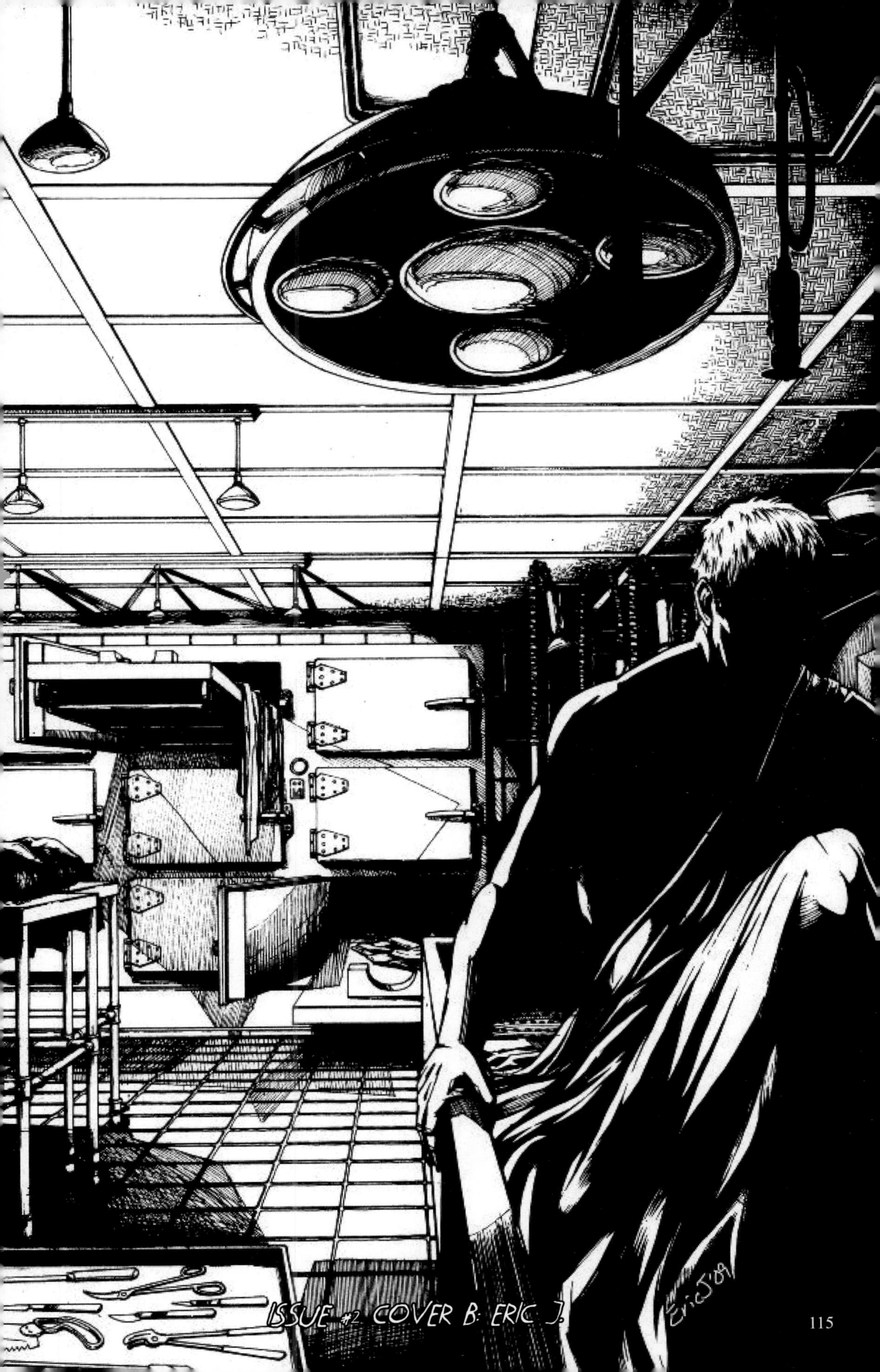
EricJ'09
ISSUE #2 COVER B: ERIC J.

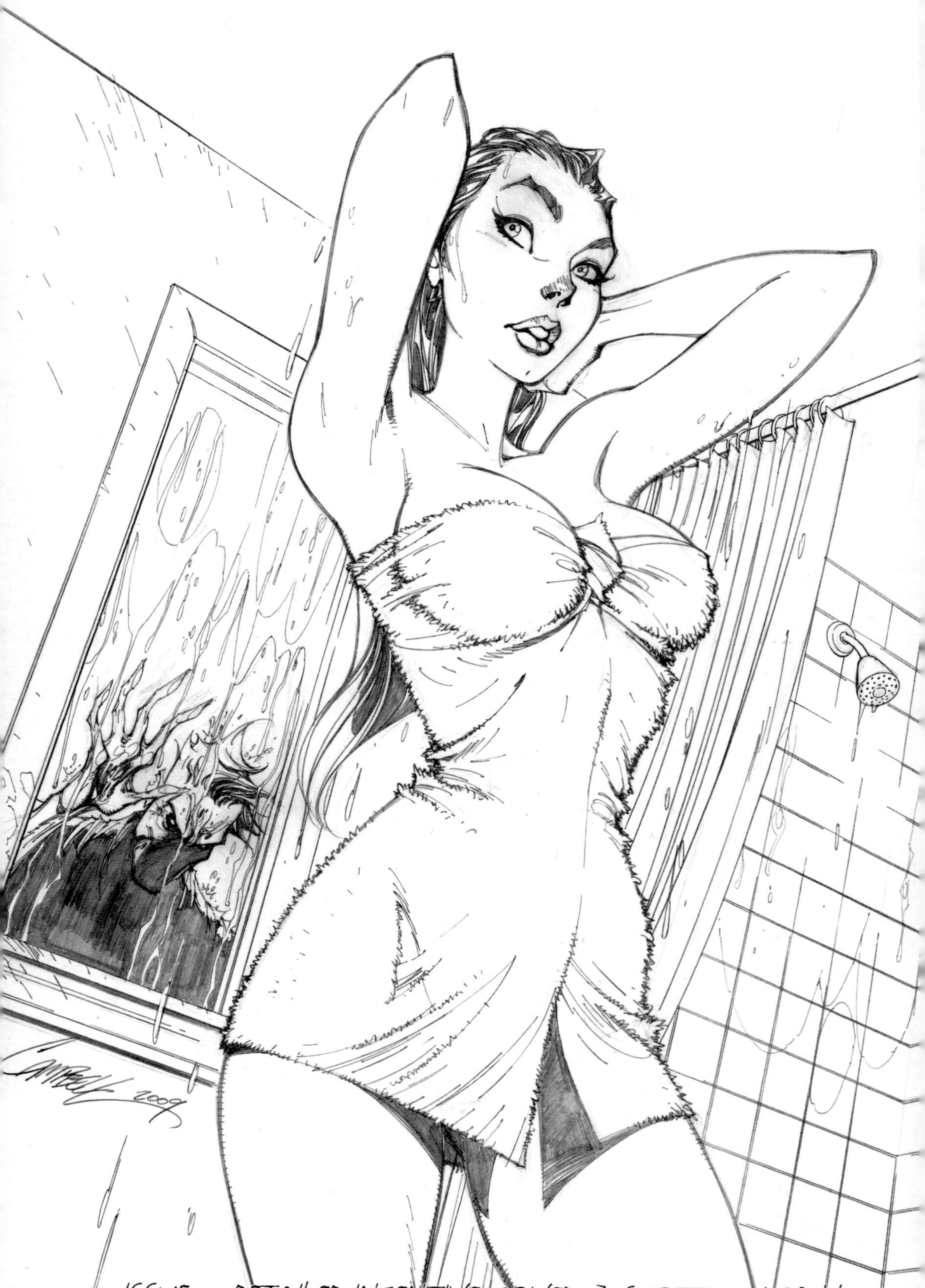

ISSUE #2 RETAILER INCENTIVE COVER: J. SCOTT CAMPBELL

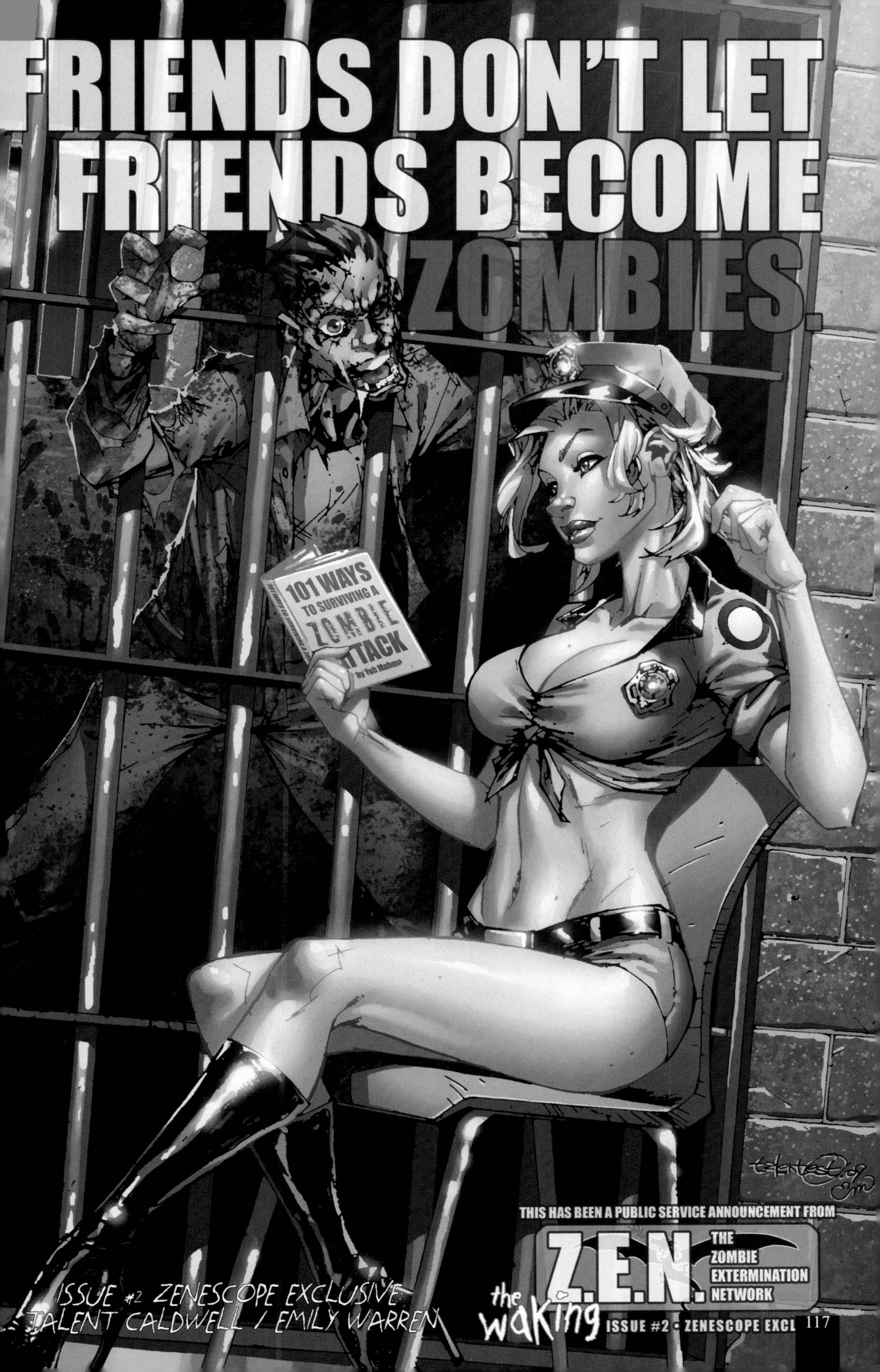
FRIENDS DON'T LET FRIENDS BECOME ZOMBIES.
101 WAYS TO SURVIVING A ZOMBIE ATTACK
by Yoh Mahma
THIS HAS BEEN A PUBLIC SERVICE ANNOUNCEMENT FROM
Z.E.N. THE ZOMBIE EXTERMINATION NETWORK
ISSUE #2 ZENESCOPE EXCLUSIVE:
TALENT CALDWELL / EMILY WARREN
the waking
ISSUE #2 • ZENESCOPE EXCL

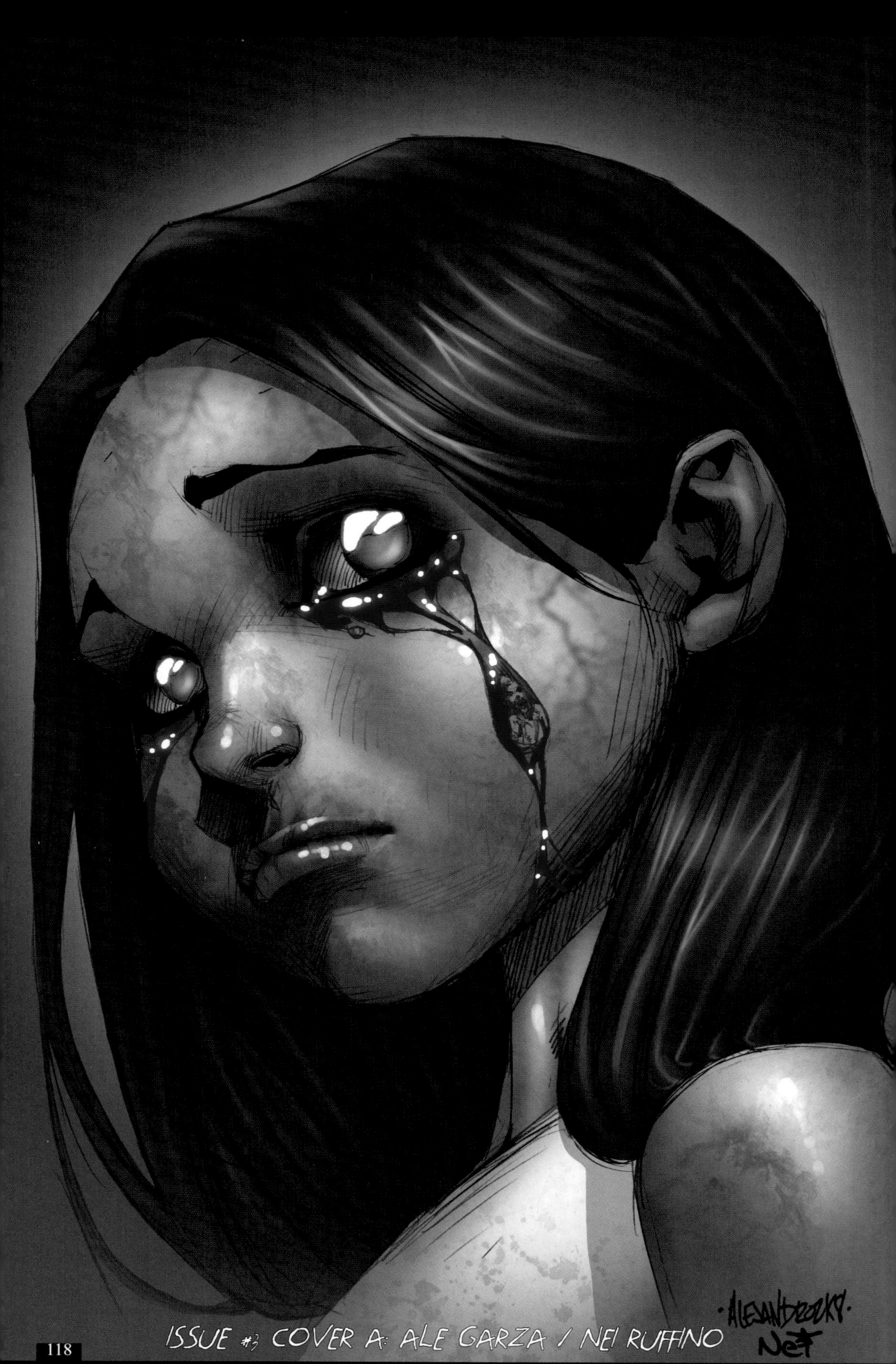

ISSUE #3 COVER A: ALE GARZA / NEI RUFFINO

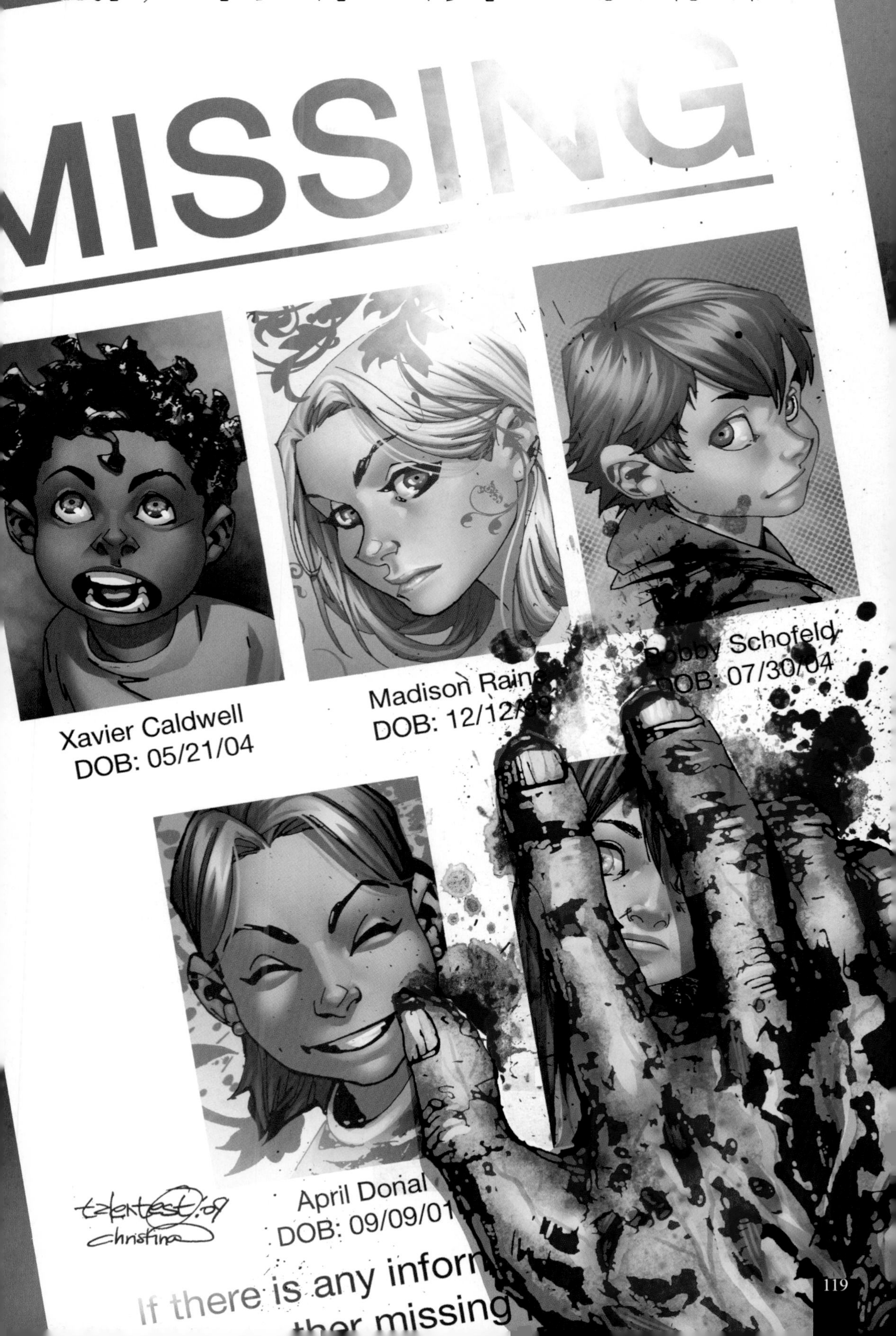
MISSING
Xavier Caldwell
DOB: 05/21/04
Madison Raine
DOB: 12/12/
Bobby Schofeld
DOB: 07/30/04
April Donal
DOB: 09/09/01
If there is any inform
ther missing

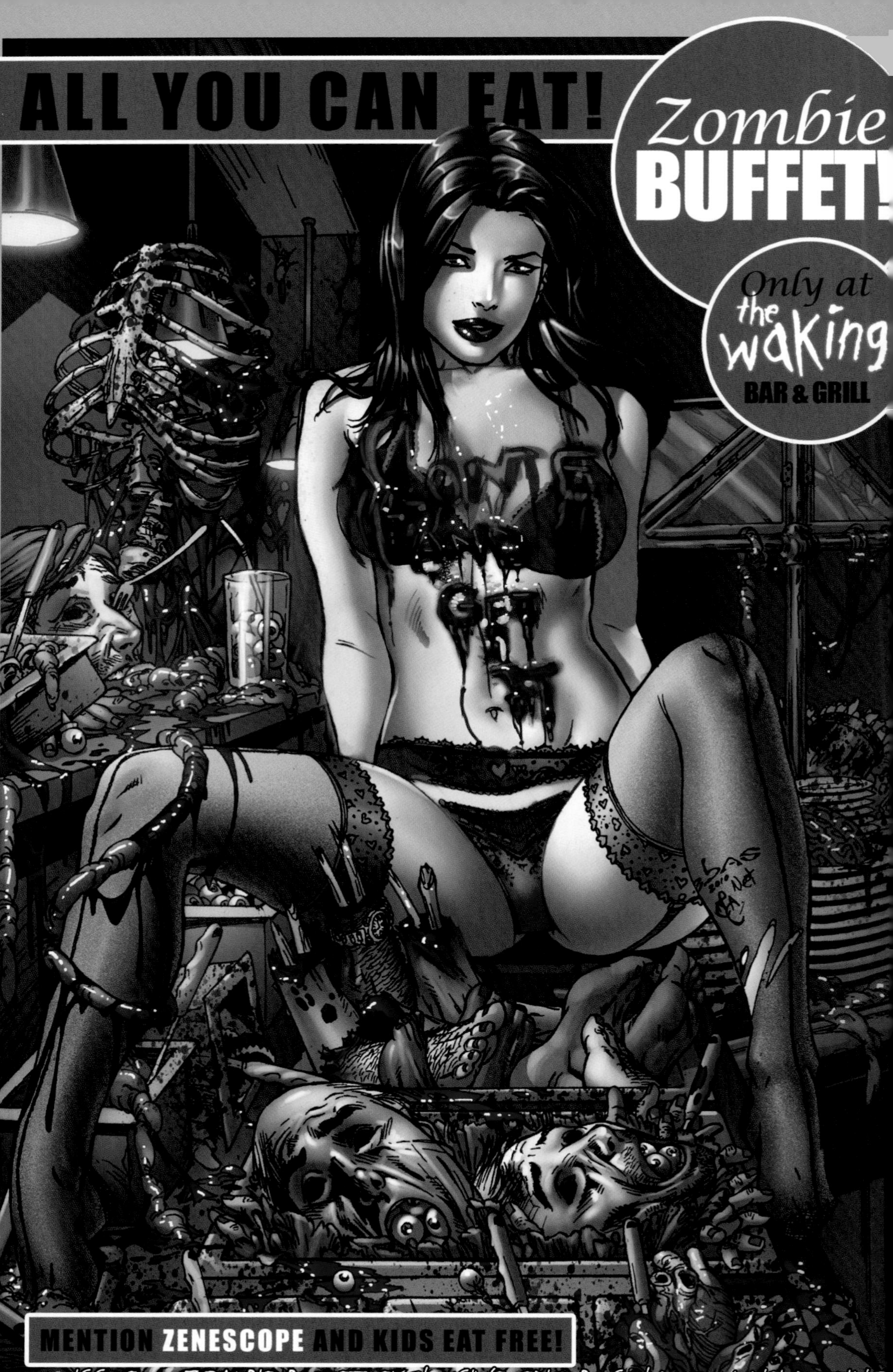
ALL YOU CAN EAT!
Zombie BUFFET!
Only at the waking BAR & GRILL
MENTION ZENESCOPE AND KIDS EAT FREE!

ISSUE #3 ZOMBIE BUFFET EXCLUSIVE: ERIC BASALDUA / NEI RUFFINO

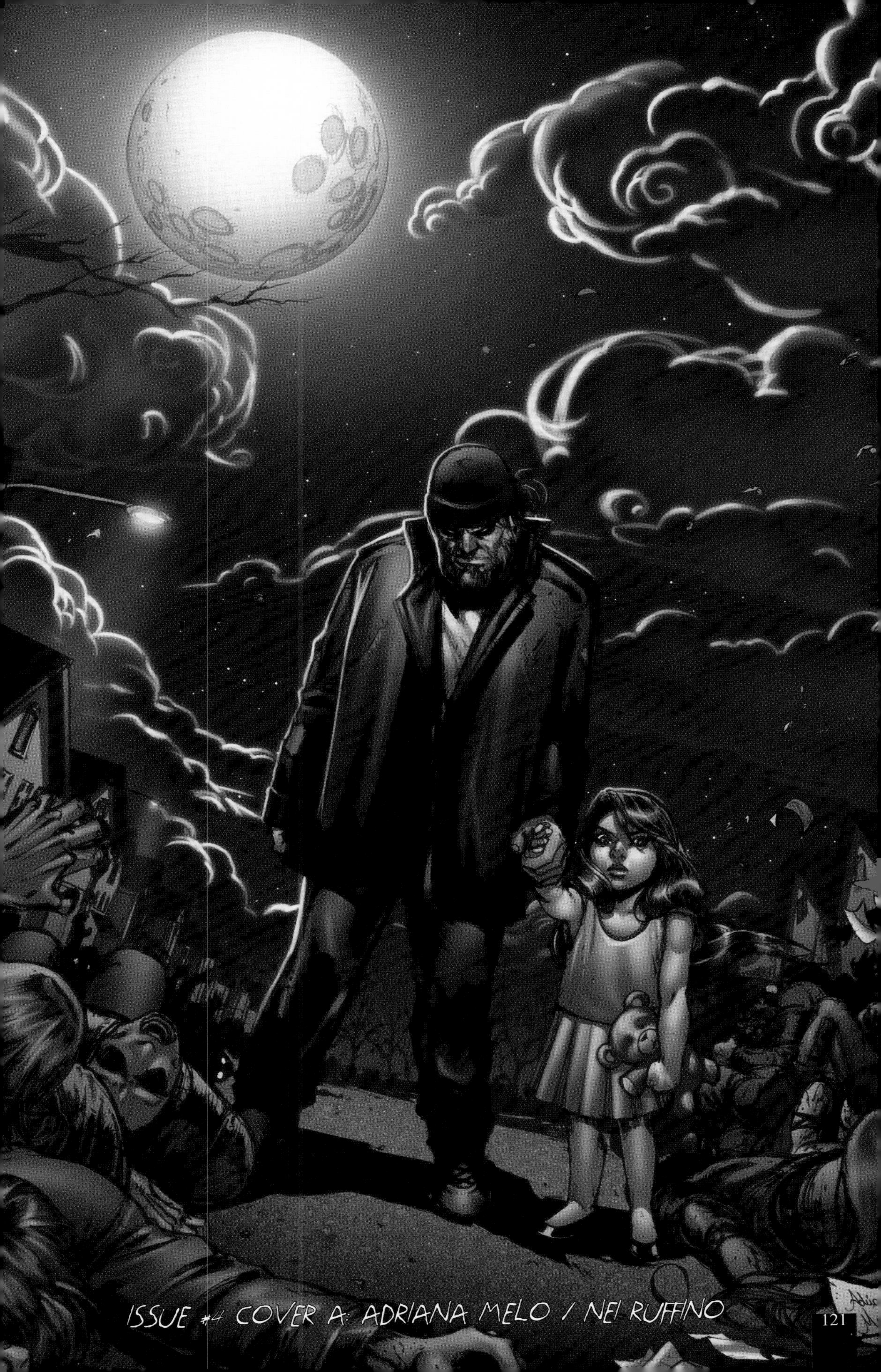

ISSUE #4 COVER A: ADRIANA MELO / NEI RUFFINO

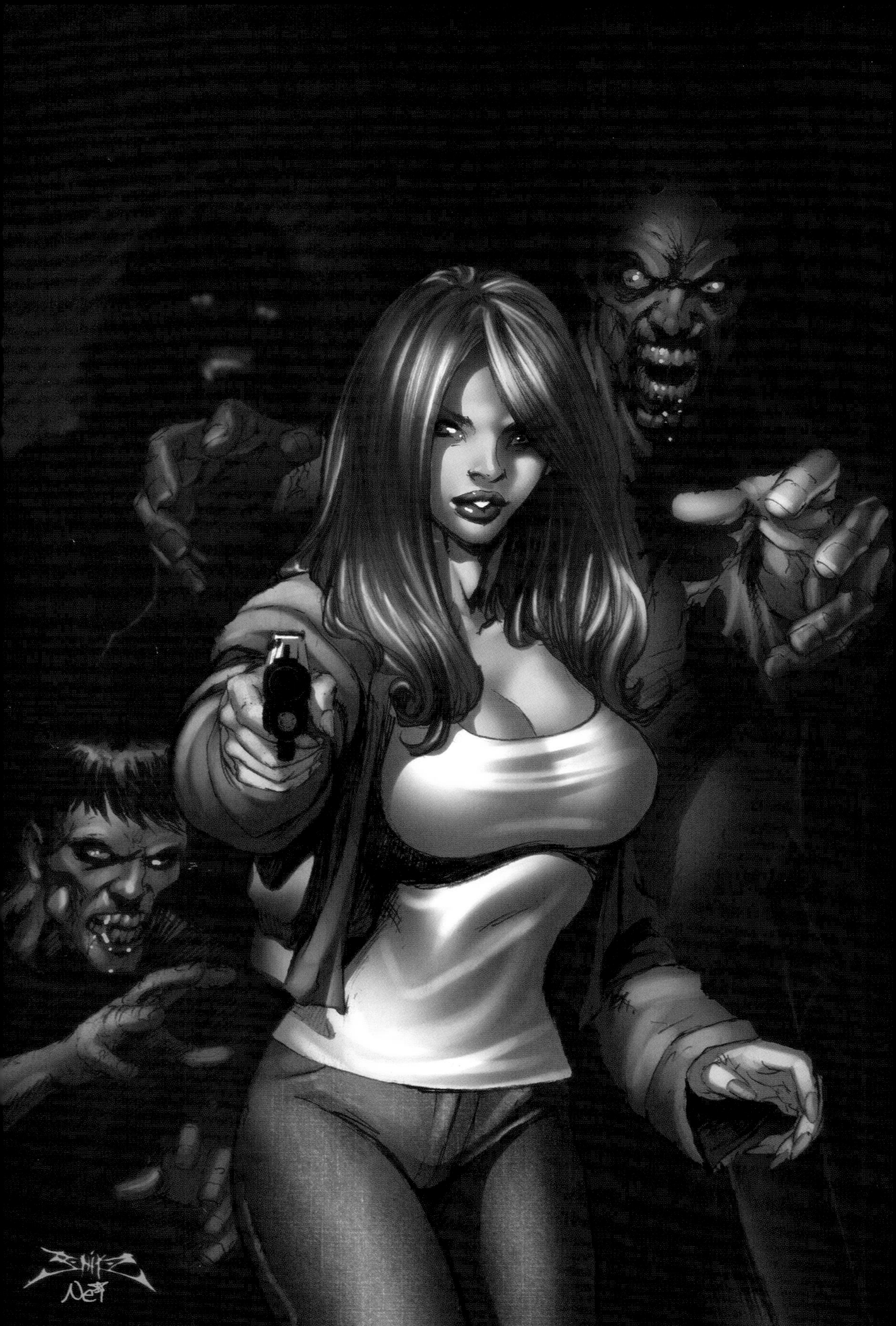

ISSUE #4 COVER B: JOE BENITEZ / NEI RUFFINO

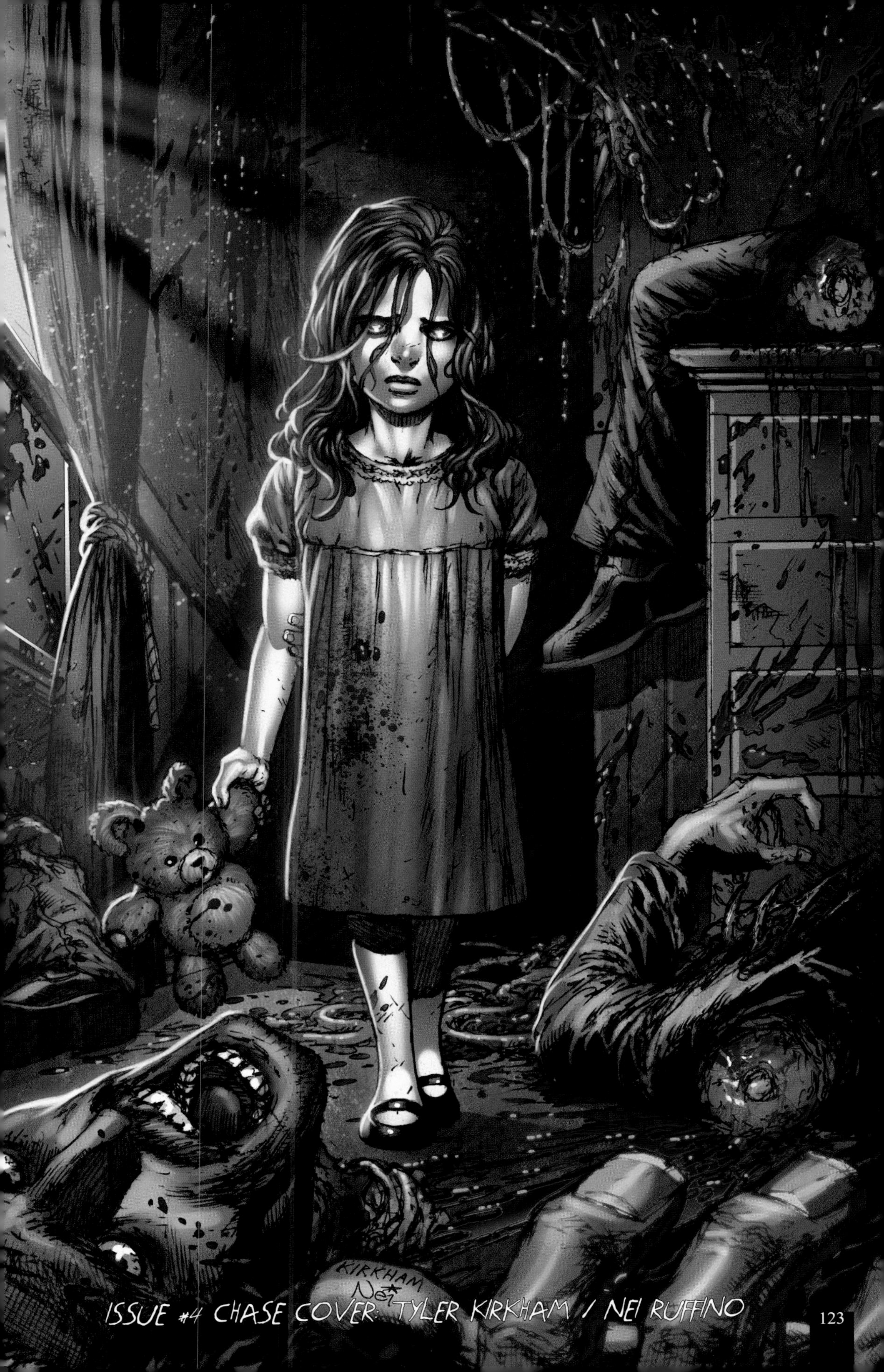
KIRKHAM
Nei

ISSUE #4 CHASE COVER: TYLER KIRKHAM / NEI RUFFINO

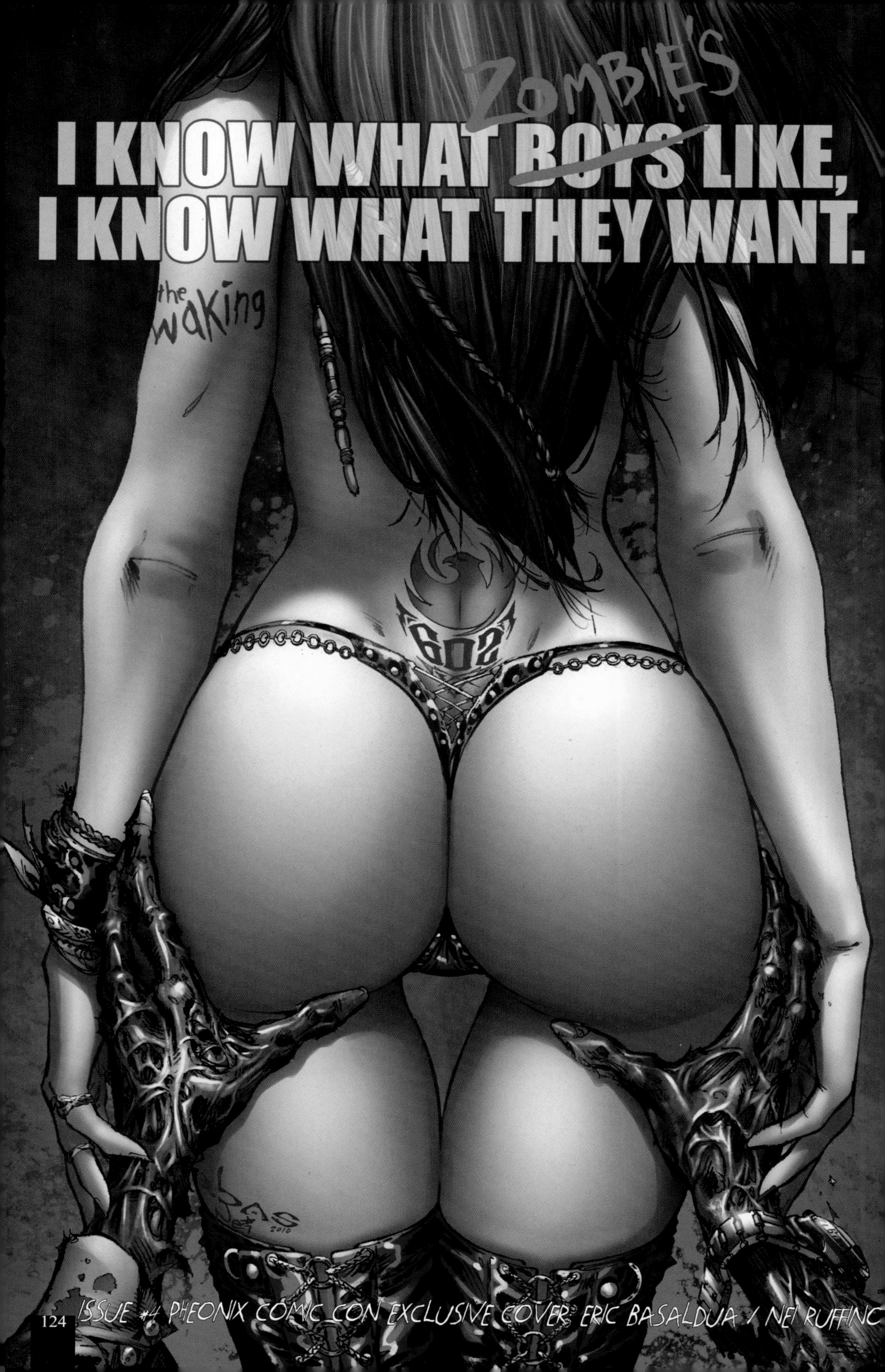
ZOMBIE'S
I KNOW WHAT BOYS LIKE,
I KNOW WHAT THEY WANT.
the waking
602

ISSUE #4 PHEONIX COMIC CON EXCLUSIVE COVER: ERIC BASALDUA / NEI RUFFINO

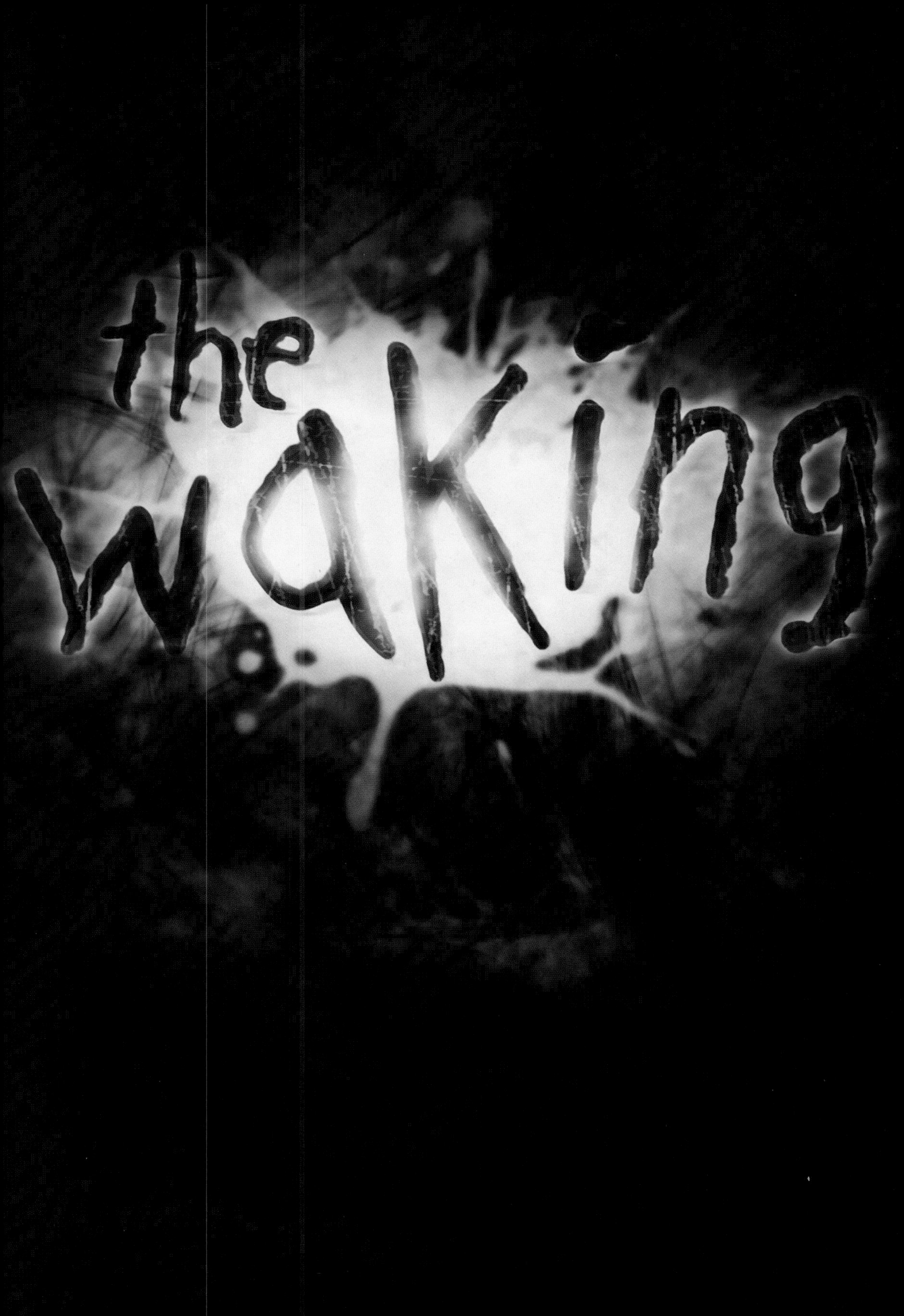
the waking

Zenescope Entertainment
Proudly Presents
Grimm Fairy Tales
NEVERLAND
NEW YORK.
THE CITY THAT
NEVER SLEEPS.
CHECK OUT THIS SPECIAL SNEAK PEEK PREVIEW OF NEVERLAND, ZENESCOPE'S DARK AND FRIGHTENING TWIST ON THE INFAMOUS PETER PAN MYTHOLOGY.

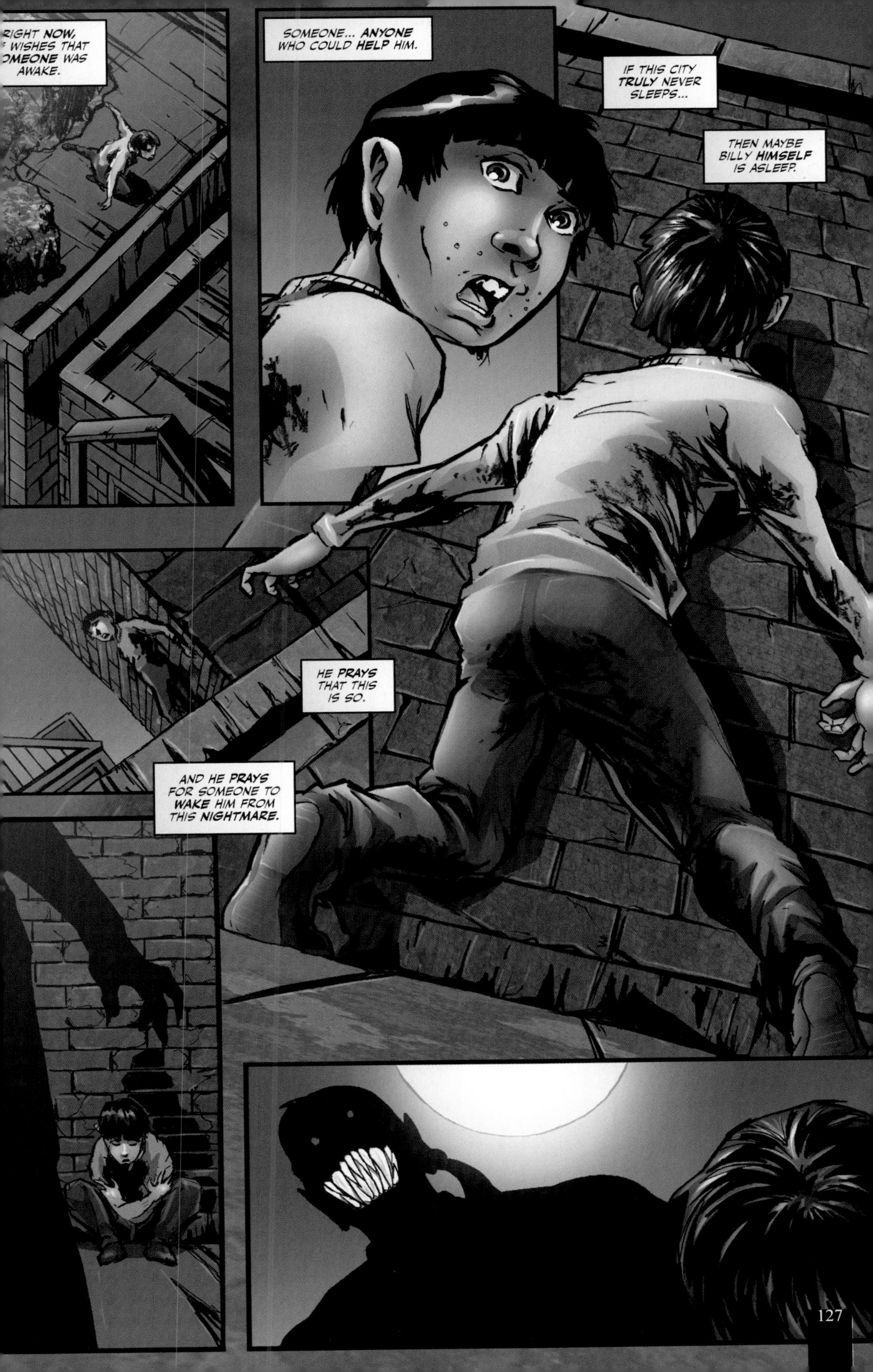
RIGHT NOW, [?] WISHES THAT [S]OMEONE WAS AWAKE.
SOMEONE... ANYONE WHO COULD HELP HIM.
IF THIS CITY TRULY NEVER SLEEPS...
THEN MAYBE BILLY HIMSELF IS ASLEEP.
HE PRAYS THAT THIS IS SO.
AND HE PRAYS FOR SOMEONE TO WAKE HIM FROM THIS NIGHTMARE.

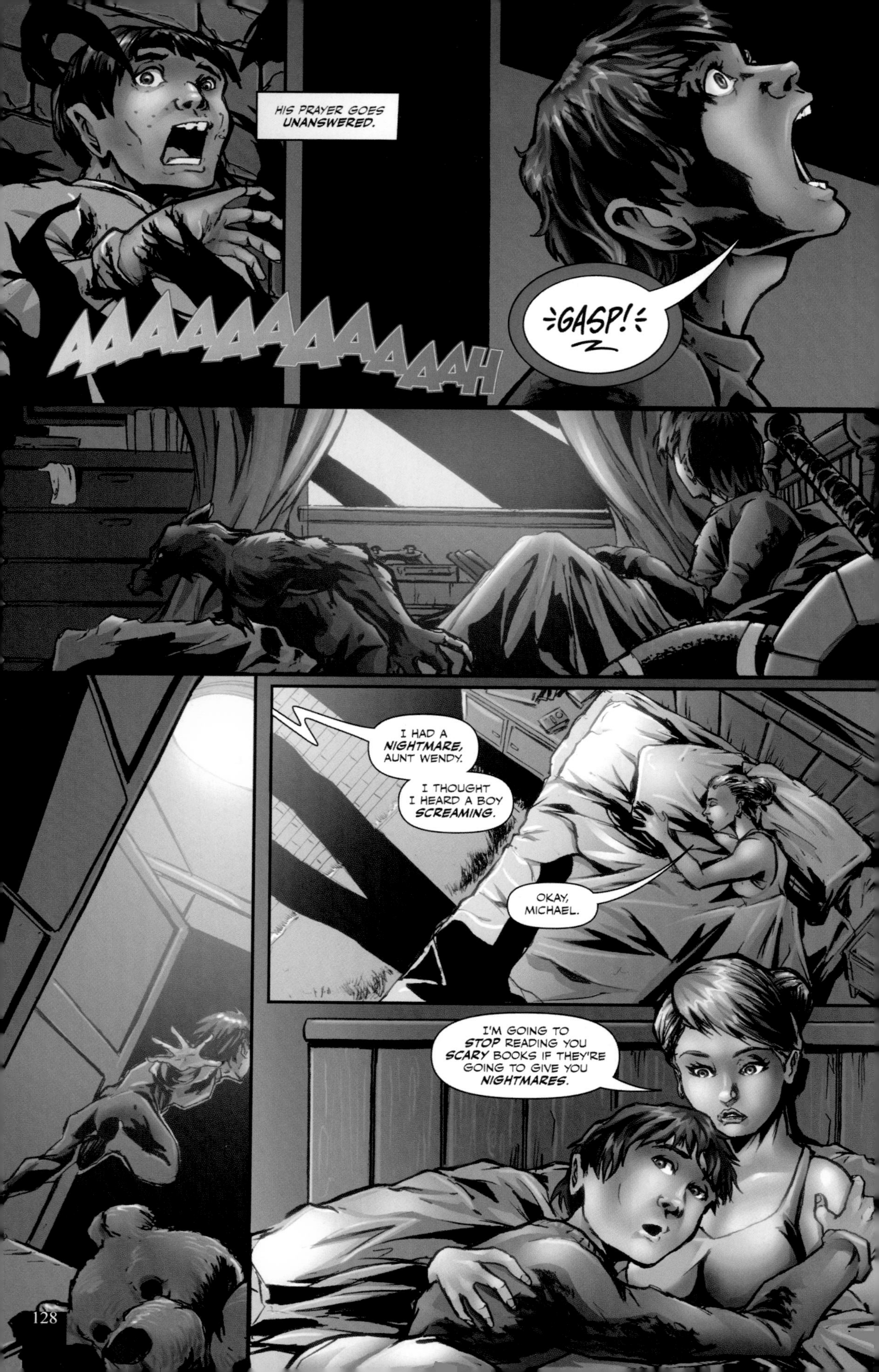
HIS PRAYER GOES UNANSWERED.
AAAAAAAAAAAAAAH
GASP!
I HAD A NIGHTMARE, AUNT WENDY.
I THOUGHT I HEARD A BOY SCREAMING.
OKAY, MICHAEL.
I'M GOING TO STOP READING YOU SCARY BOOKS IF THEY'RE GOING TO GIVE YOU NIGHTMARES.

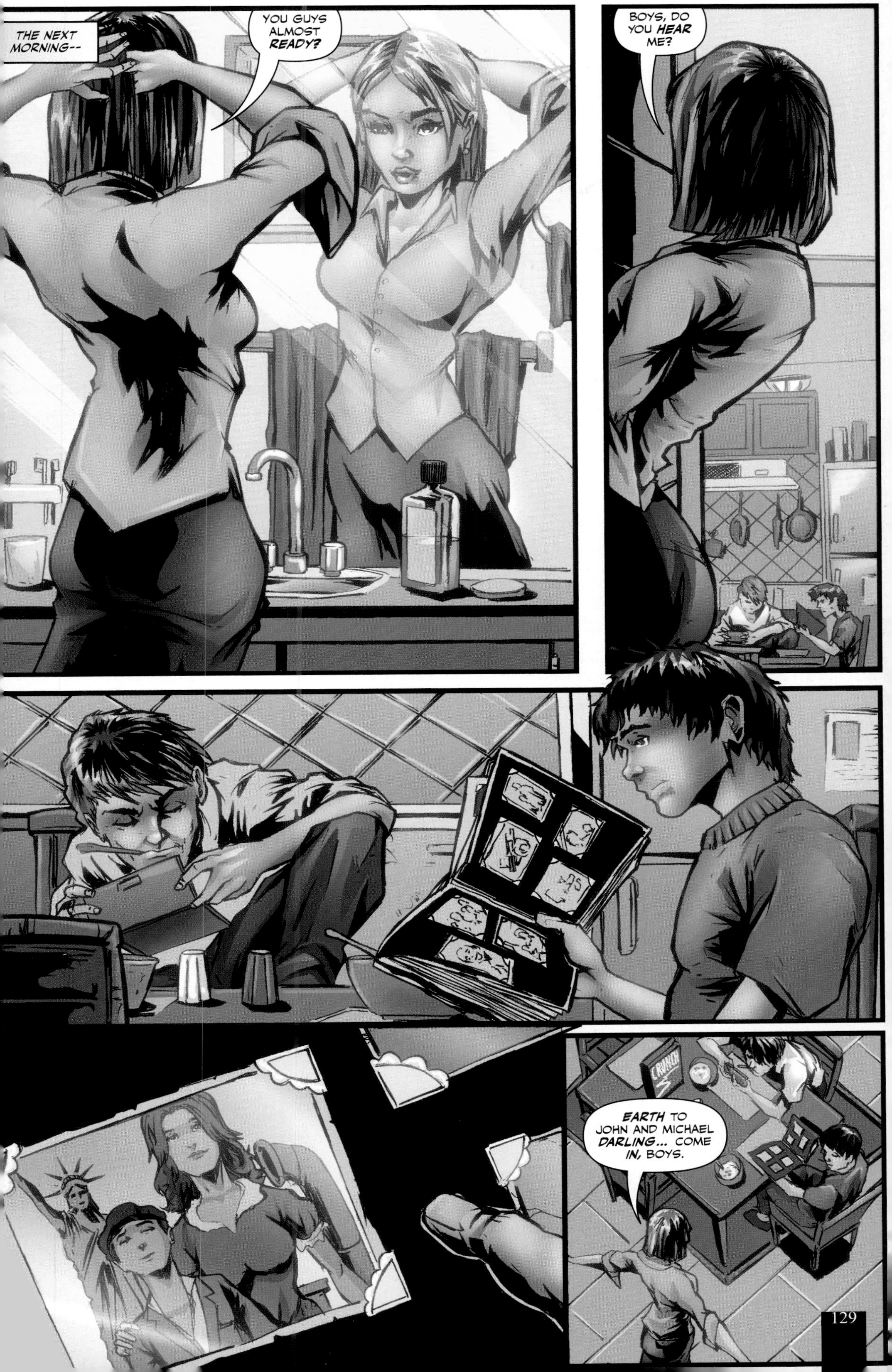
THE NEXT MORNING--
YOU GUYS ALMOST READY?
BOYS, DO YOU HEAR ME?
CRUNCH
EARTH TO JOHN AND MICHAEL DARLING... COME IN, BOYS.

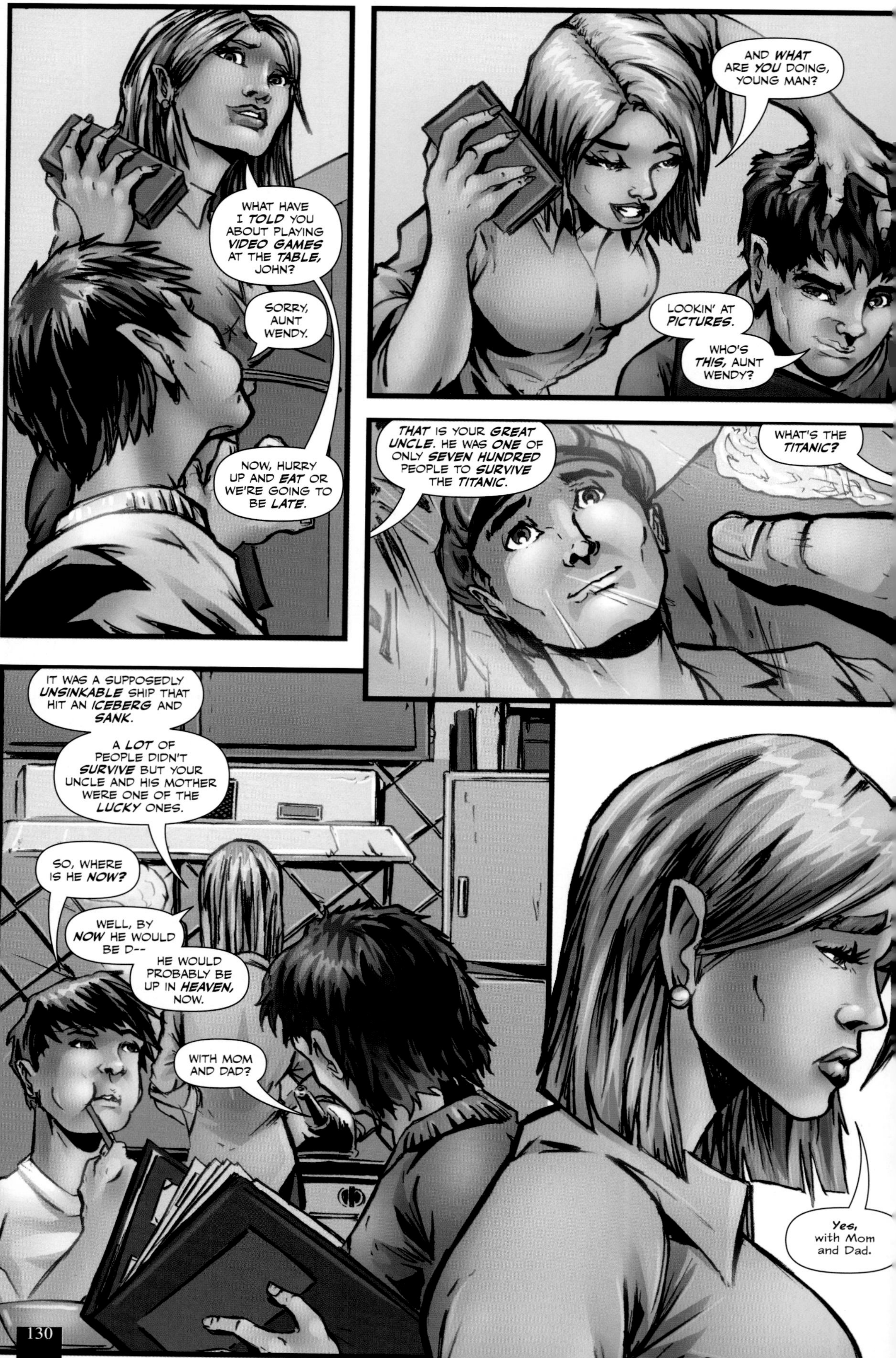

WHAT HAVE I TOLD YOU ABOUT PLAYING VIDEO GAMES AT THE TABLE, JOHN?
SORRY, AUNT WENDY.
NOW, HURRY UP AND EAT OR WE'RE GOING TO BE LATE.
AND WHAT ARE YOU DOING, YOUNG MAN?
LOOKIN' AT PICTURES.
WHO'S THIS, AUNT WENDY?
THAT IS YOUR GREAT UNCLE. HE WAS ONE OF ONLY SEVEN HUNDRED PEOPLE TO SURVIVE THE TITANIC.
WHAT'S THE TITANIC?
IT WAS A SUPPOSEDLY UNSINKABLE SHIP THAT HIT AN ICEBERG AND SANK.
A LOT OF PEOPLE DIDN'T SURVIVE BUT YOUR UNCLE AND HIS MOTHER WERE ONE OF THE LUCKY ONES.
SO, WHERE IS HE NOW?
WELL, BY NOW HE WOULD BE D--
HE WOULD PROBABLY BE UP IN HEAVEN, NOW.
WITH MOM AND DAD?
Yes, with Mom and Dad.

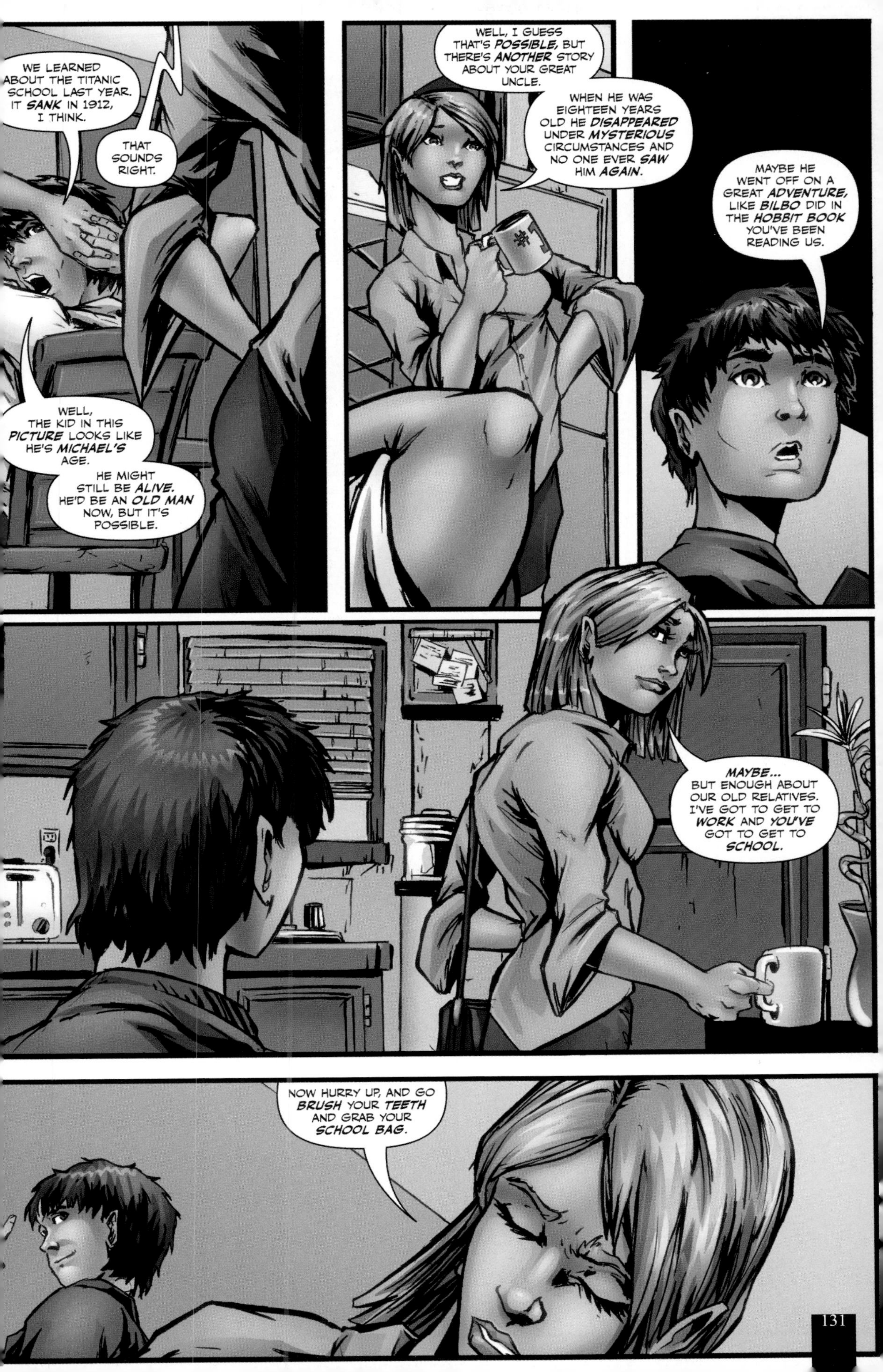
WE LEARNED ABOUT THE TITANIC SCHOOL LAST YEAR. IT SANK IN 1912, I THINK.
THAT SOUNDS RIGHT.
WELL, THE KID IN THIS PICTURE LOOKS LIKE HE'S MICHAEL'S AGE.
HE MIGHT STILL BE ALIVE. HE'D BE AN OLD MAN NOW, BUT IT'S POSSIBLE.
WELL, I GUESS THAT'S POSSIBLE, BUT THERE'S ANOTHER STORY ABOUT YOUR GREAT UNCLE.
WHEN HE WAS EIGHTEEN YEARS OLD HE DISAPPEARED UNDER MYSTERIOUS CIRCUMSTANCES AND NO ONE EVER SAW HIM AGAIN.
MAYBE HE WENT OFF ON A GREAT ADVENTURE, LIKE BILBO DID IN THE HOBBIT BOOK YOU'VE BEEN READING US.
MAYBE... BUT ENOUGH ABOUT OUR OLD RELATIVES. I'VE GOT TO GET TO WORK AND YOU'VE GOT TO GET TO SCHOOL.
NOW HURRY UP, AND GO BRUSH YOUR TEETH AND GRAB YOUR SCHOOL BAG.

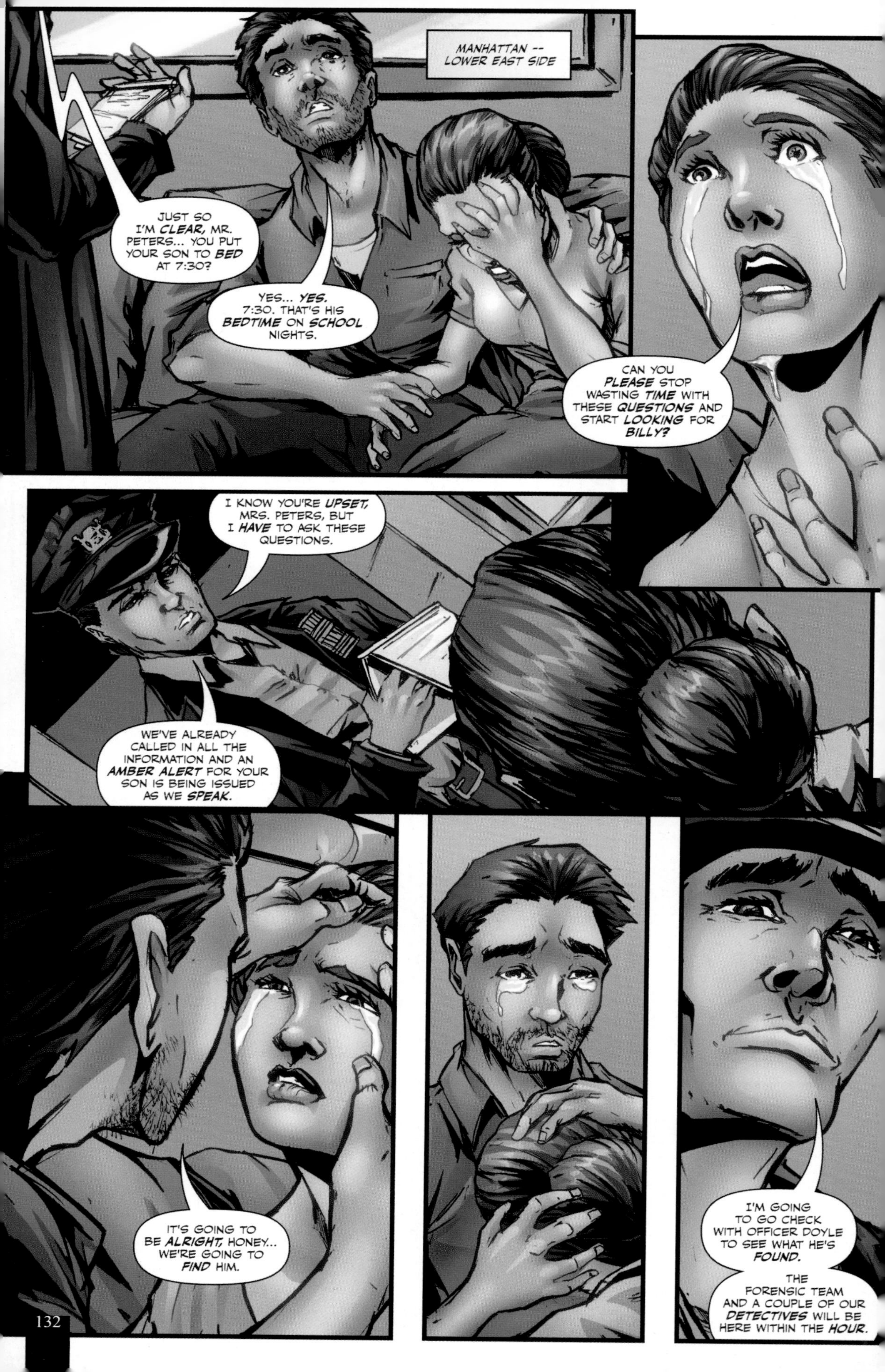
MANHATTAN -- LOWER EAST SIDE
JUST SO I'M CLEAR, MR. PETERS... YOU PUT YOUR SON TO BED AT 7:30?
YES... YES. 7:30. THAT'S HIS BEDTIME ON SCHOOL NIGHTS.
CAN YOU PLEASE STOP WASTING TIME WITH THESE QUESTIONS AND START LOOKING FOR BILLY?
I KNOW YOU'RE UPSET, MRS. PETERS, BUT I HAVE TO ASK THESE QUESTIONS.
WE'VE ALREADY CALLED IN ALL THE INFORMATION AND AN AMBER ALERT FOR YOUR SON IS BEING ISSUED AS WE SPEAK.
IT'S GOING TO BE ALRIGHT, HONEY... WE'RE GOING TO FIND HIM.
I'M GOING TO GO CHECK WITH OFFICER DOYLE TO SEE WHAT HE'S FOUND.
THE FORENSIC TEAM AND A COUPLE OF OUR DETECTIVES WILL BE HERE WITHIN THE HOUR.

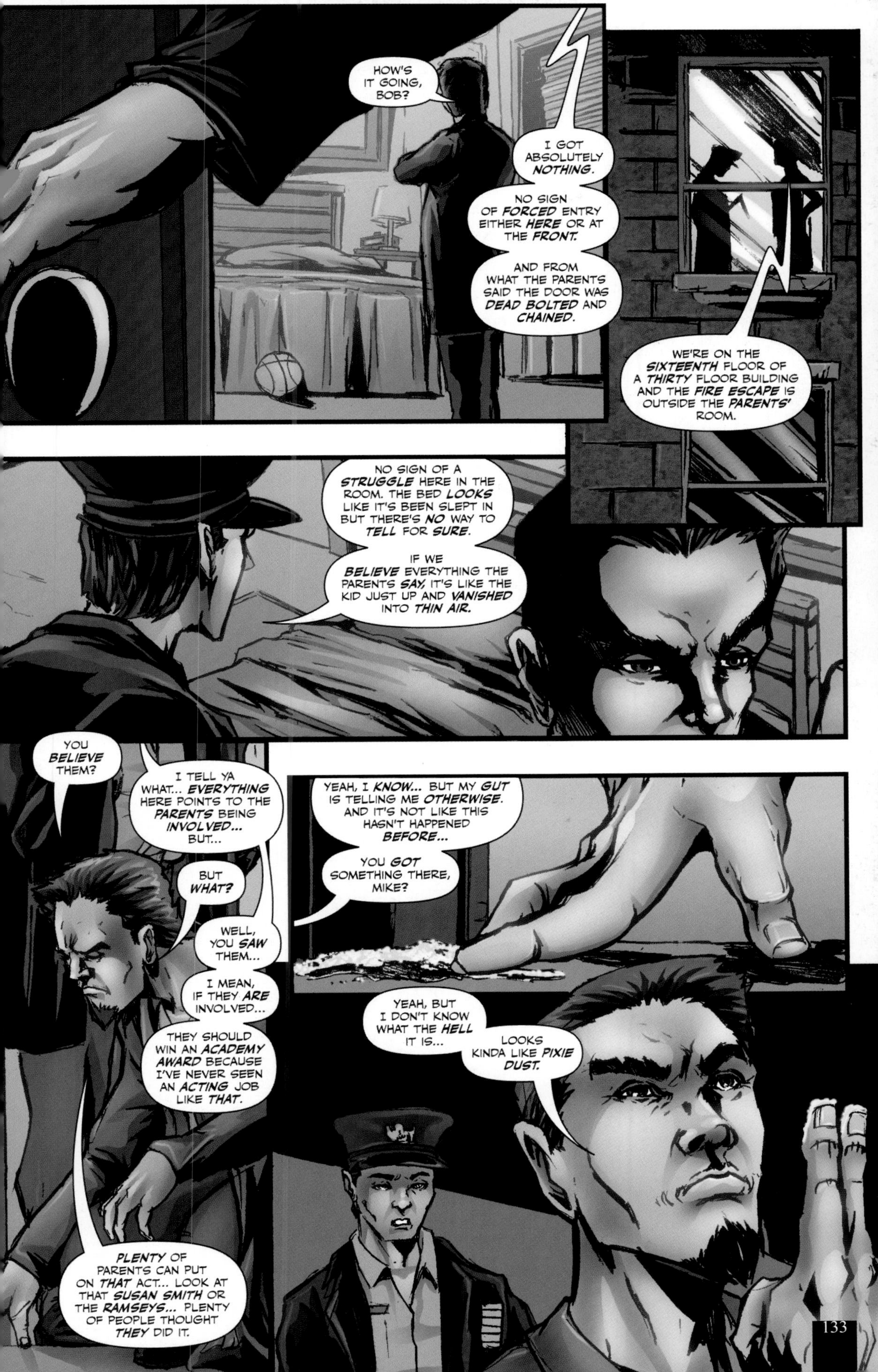
HOW'S IT GOING, BOB?
I GOT ABSOLUTELY NOTHING.
NO SIGN OF FORCED ENTRY EITHER HERE OR AT THE FRONT.
AND FROM WHAT THE PARENTS SAID THE DOOR WAS DEAD BOLTED AND CHAINED.
WE'RE ON THE SIXTEENTH FLOOR OF A THIRTY FLOOR BUILDING AND THE FIRE ESCAPE IS OUTSIDE THE PARENTS' ROOM.
NO SIGN OF A STRUGGLE HERE IN THE ROOM. THE BED LOOKS LIKE IT'S BEEN SLEPT IN BUT THERE'S NO WAY TO TELL FOR SURE.
IF WE BELIEVE EVERYTHING THE PARENTS SAY, IT'S LIKE THE KID JUST UP AND VANISHED INTO THIN AIR.
YOU BELIEVE THEM?
I TELL YA WHAT... EVERYTHING HERE POINTS TO THE PARENTS BEING INVOLVED... BUT...
BUT WHAT?
WELL, YOU SAW THEM...
I MEAN, IF THEY ARE INVOLVED...
THEY SHOULD WIN AN ACADEMY AWARD BECAUSE I'VE NEVER SEEN AN ACTING JOB LIKE THAT.
PLENTY OF PARENTS CAN PUT ON THAT ACT... LOOK AT THAT SUSAN SMITH OR THE RAMSEYS... PLENTY OF PEOPLE THOUGHT THEY DID IT.
YEAH, I KNOW... BUT MY GUT IS TELLING ME OTHERWISE. AND IT'S NOT LIKE THIS HASN'T HAPPENED BEFORE...
YOU GOT SOMETHING THERE, MIKE?
YEAH, BUT I DON'T KNOW WHAT THE HELL IT IS...
LOOKS KINDA LIKE PIXIE DUST.

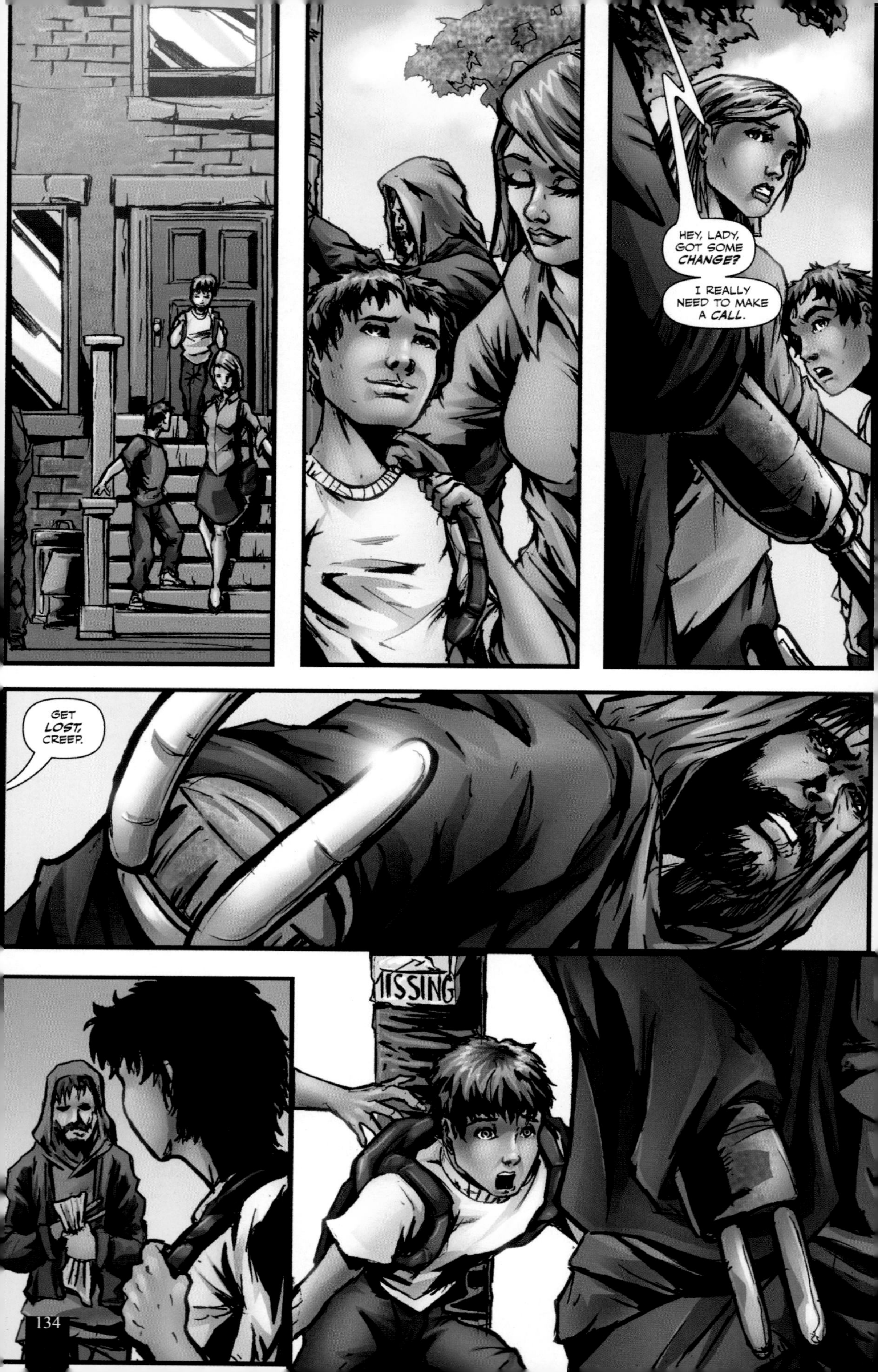
HEY, LADY, GOT SOME CHANGE?
I REALLY NEED TO MAKE A CALL.
GET LOST, CREEP.
MISSING

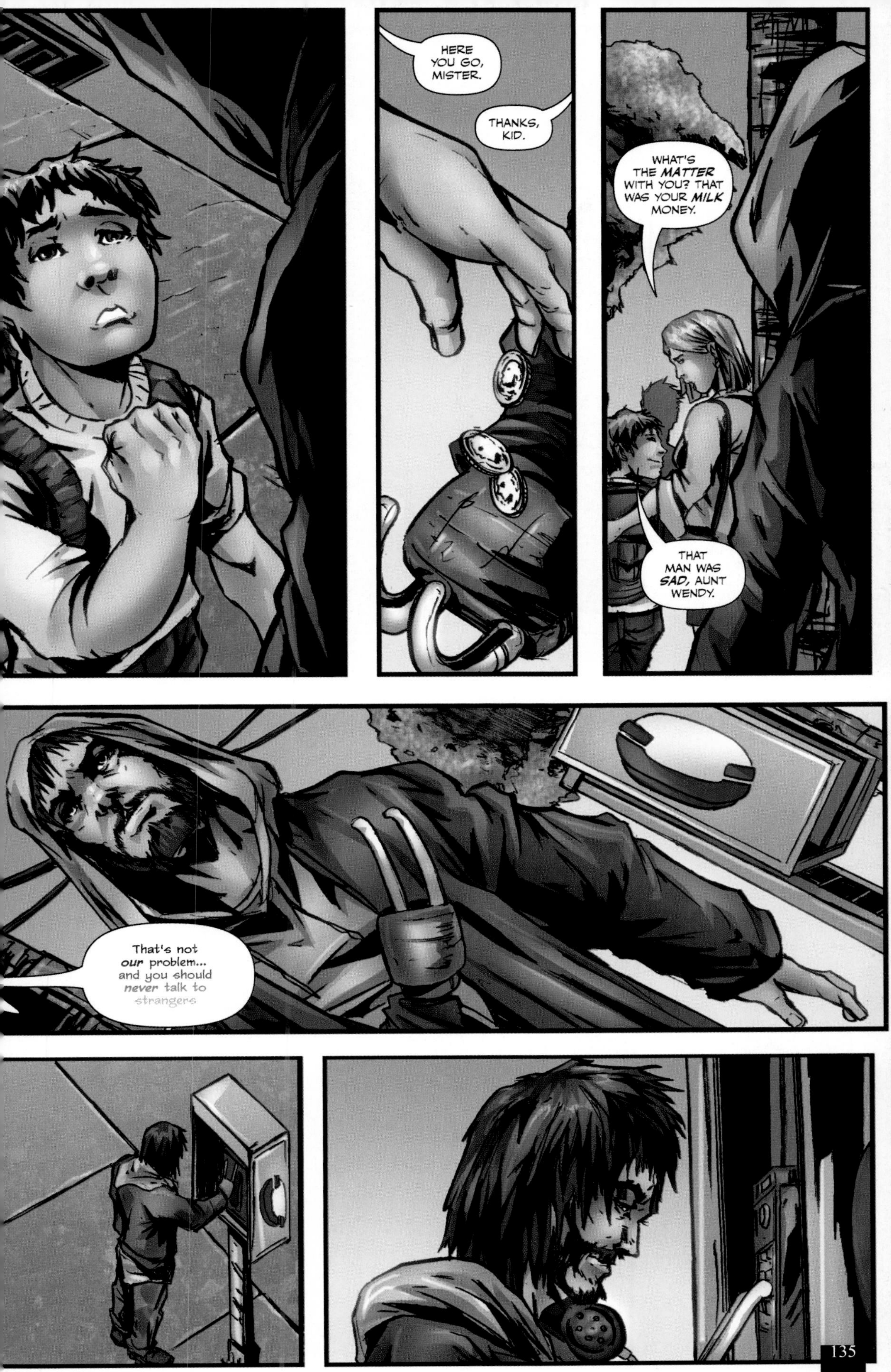
HERE YOU GO, MISTER.
THANKS, KID.
WHAT'S THE *MATTER* WITH YOU? THAT WAS YOUR *MILK* MONEY.
THAT MAN WAS *SAD,* AUNT WENDY.
That's not *our* problem... and you should *never* talk to strangers

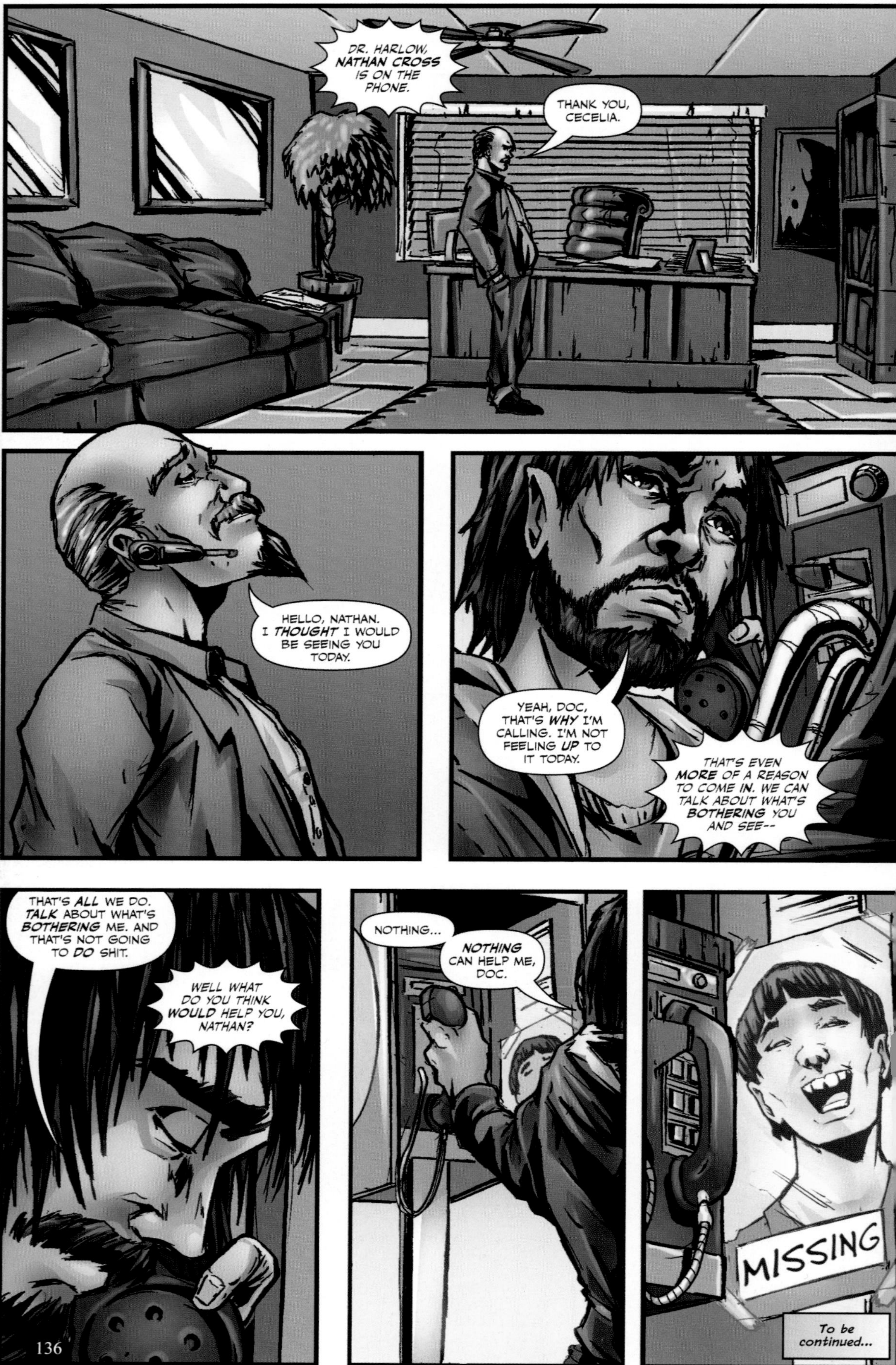
DR. HARLOW, NATHAN CROSS IS ON THE PHONE.
THANK YOU, CECELIA.
HELLO, NATHAN. I THOUGHT I WOULD BE SEEING YOU TODAY.
YEAH, DOC, THAT'S WHY I'M CALLING. I'M NOT FEELING UP TO IT TODAY.
THAT'S EVEN MORE OF A REASON TO COME IN. WE CAN TALK ABOUT WHAT'S BOTHERING YOU AND SEE--
THAT'S ALL WE DO. TALK ABOUT WHAT'S BOTHERING ME. AND THAT'S NOT GOING TO DO SHIT.
WELL WHAT DO YOU THINK WOULD HELP YOU, NATHAN?
NOTHING...
NOTHING CAN HELP ME, DOC.
MISSING
To be continued...

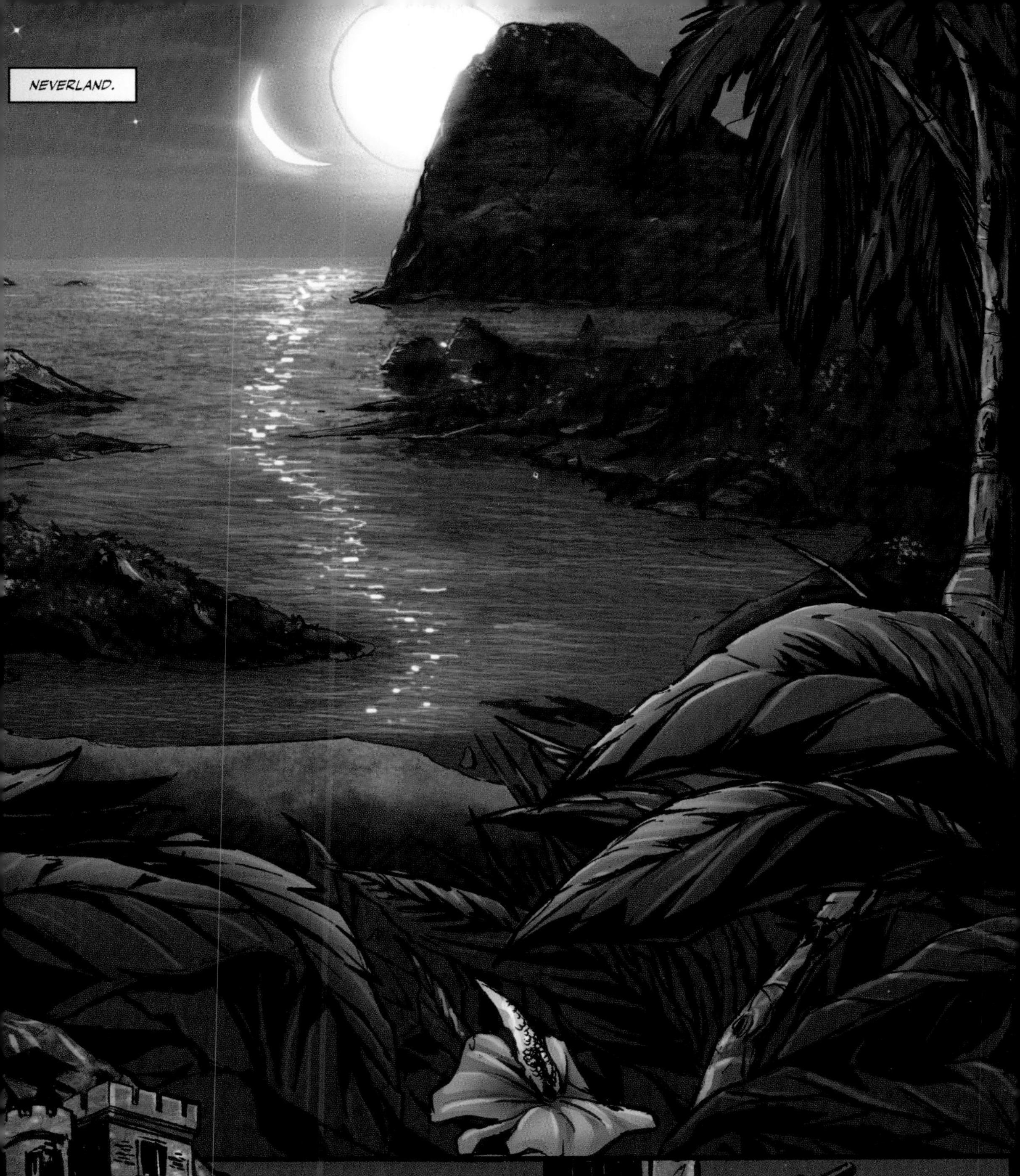
NEVERLAND.

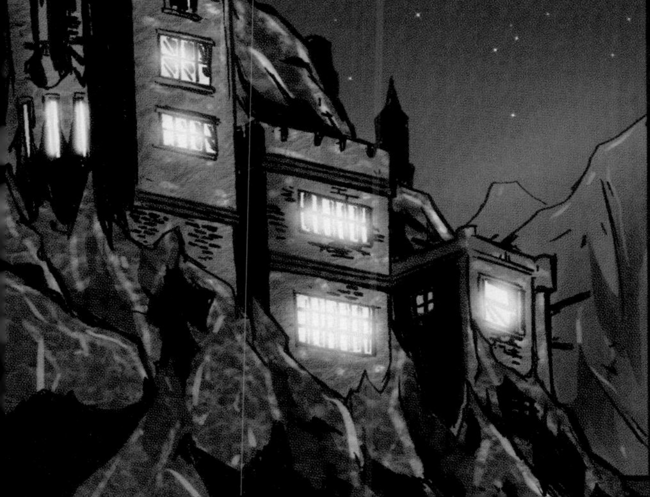

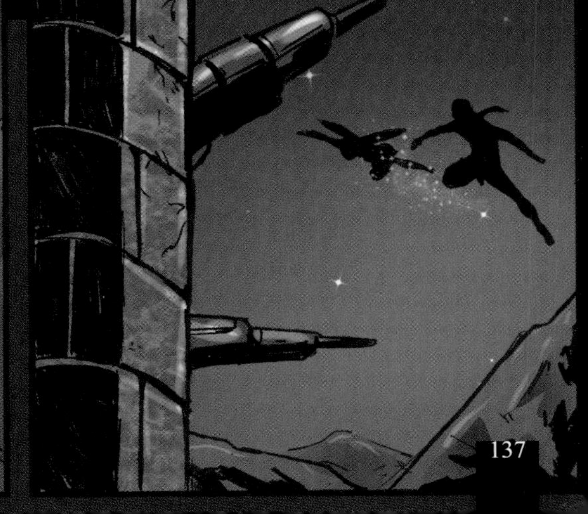

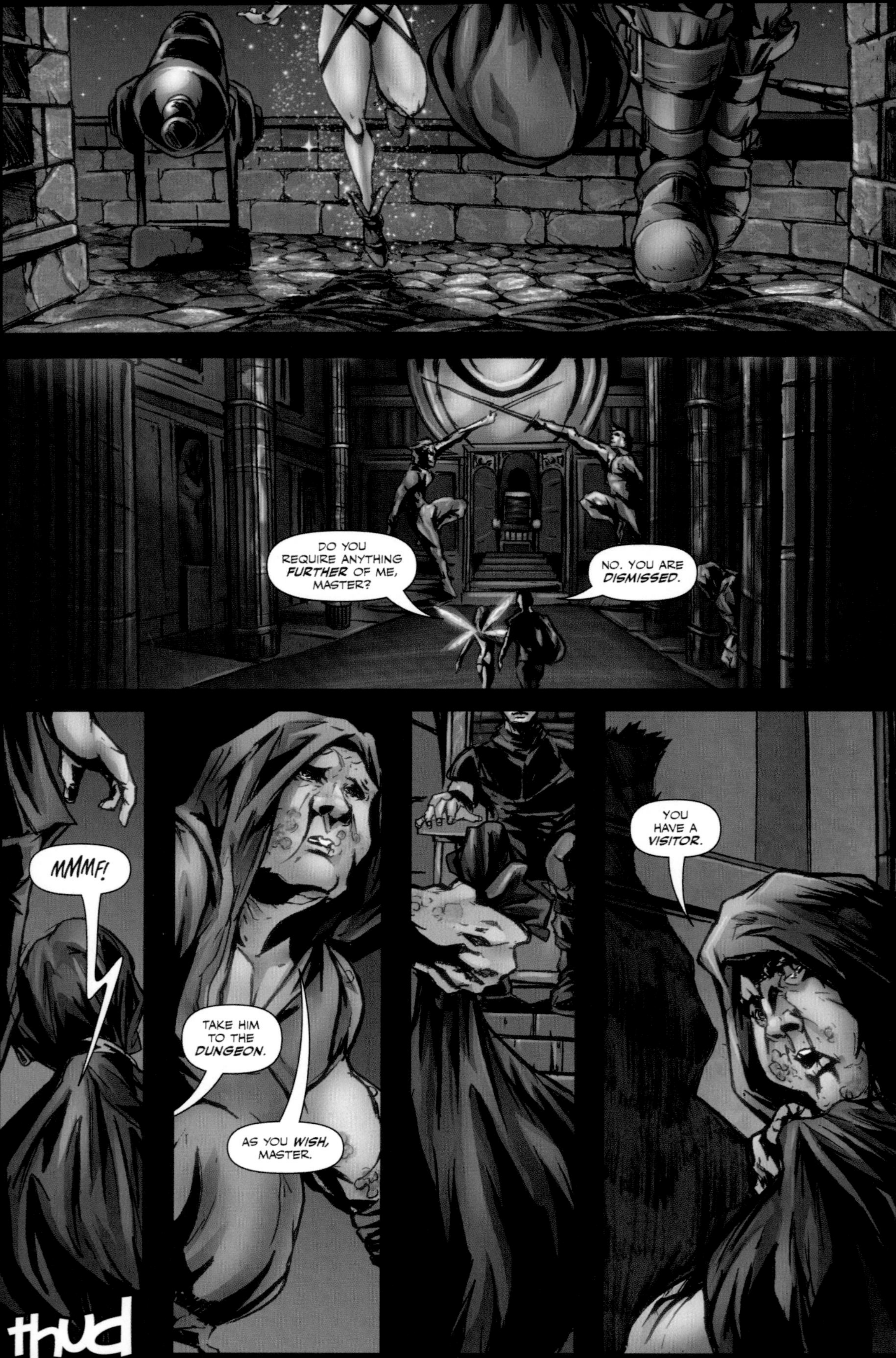
DO YOU REQUIRE ANYTHING FURTHER OF ME, MASTER?
NO. YOU ARE DISMISSED.
MMMF!
TAKE HIM TO THE DUNGEON.
AS YOU WISH, MASTER.
YOU HAVE A VISITOR.
thud

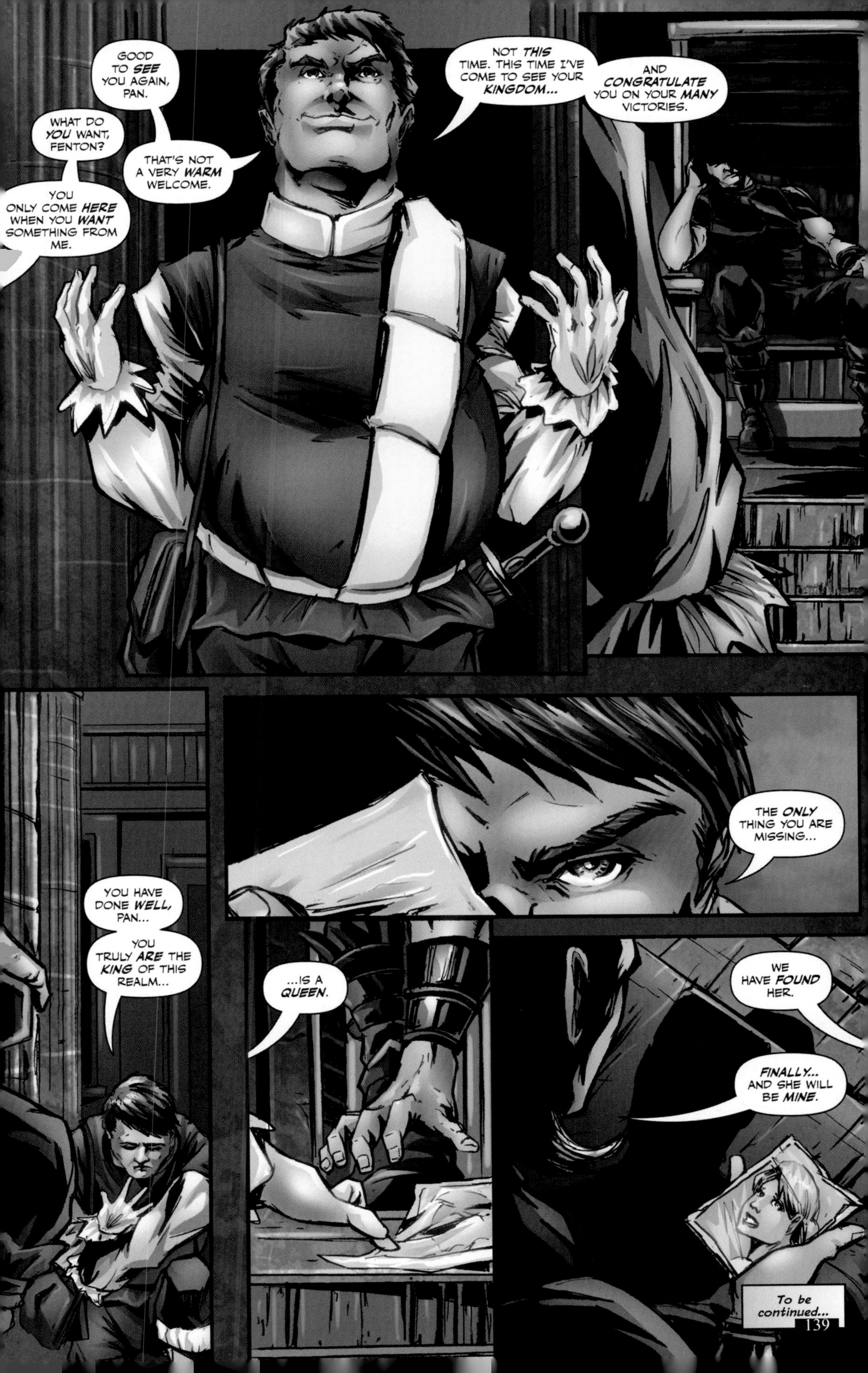

WHAT DO *YOU* WANT, FENTON?
YOU ONLY COME *HERE* WHEN YOU *WANT* SOMETHING FROM ME.
GOOD TO *SEE* YOU AGAIN, PAN.
THAT'S NOT A VERY *WARM* WELCOME.
NOT *THIS* TIME. THIS TIME I'VE COME TO SEE YOUR *KINGDOM...*
AND *CONGRATULATE* YOU ON YOUR *MANY* VICTORIES.
THE *ONLY* THING YOU ARE MISSING...
YOU HAVE DONE *WELL,* PAN...
YOU TRULY *ARE* THE *KING* OF THIS REALM...
...IS A *QUEEN*.
WE HAVE *FOUND* HER.
FINALLY... AND SHE WILL BE *MINE*.
To be continued...

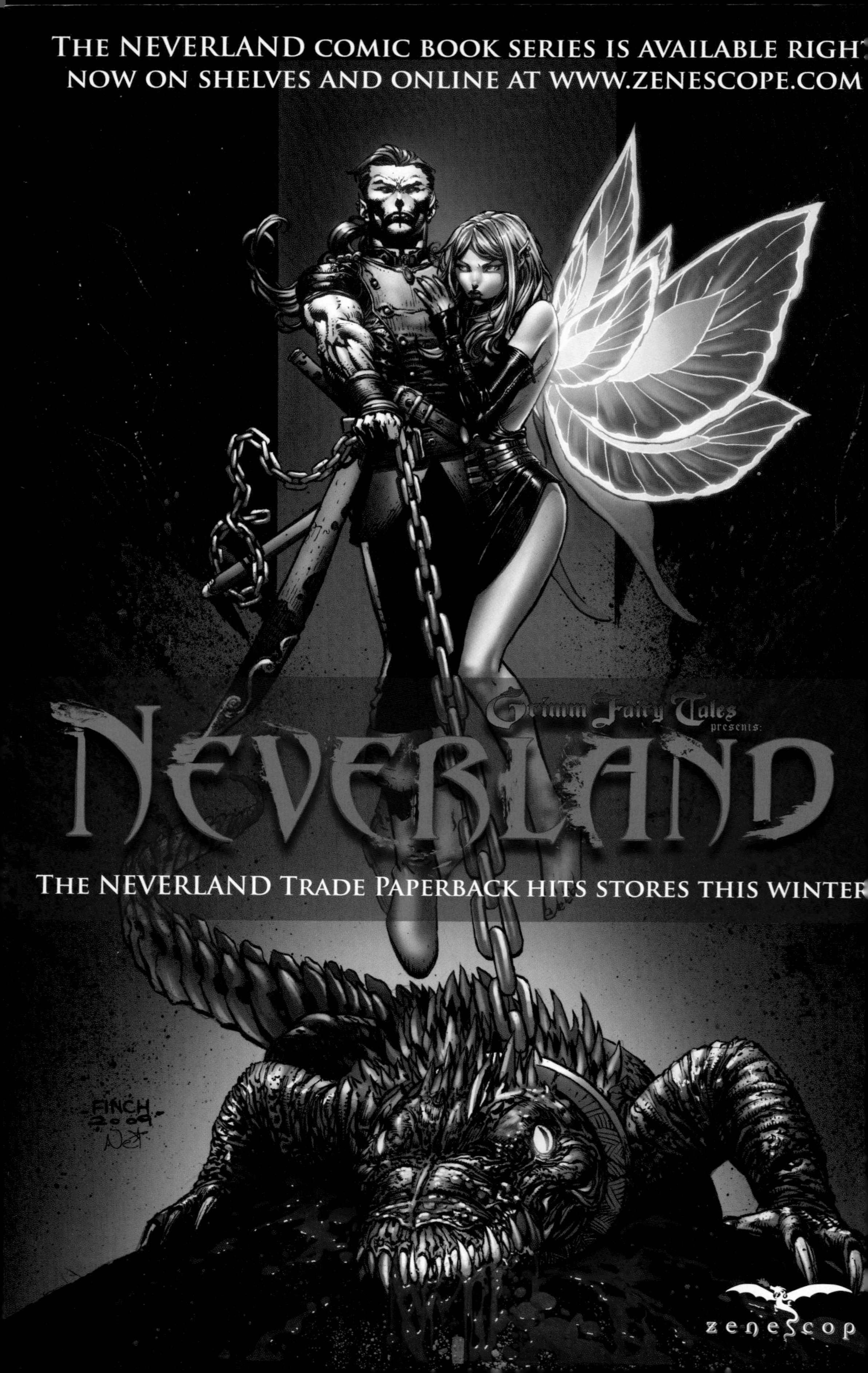
THE NEVERLAND COMIC BOOK SERIES IS AVAILABLE RIGH
NOW ON SHELVES AND ONLINE AT WWW.ZENESCOPE.COM
Grimm Fairy Tales presents:
NEVERLAND
THE NEVERLAND TRADE PAPERBACK HITS STORES THIS WINTER
FINCH 2009
zenescop

Grimm Fairy Tales
Myths & Legends

Our favorite heroes from Grimm Fairy Tales are back!
Brittany, Little Red Riding Hood from issue #1, is now
working in a treatment center for adolescents. Little does
she know that something from another realm has caught
her scent and will stop at nothing to find and destroy
her before her true destiny is revealed.

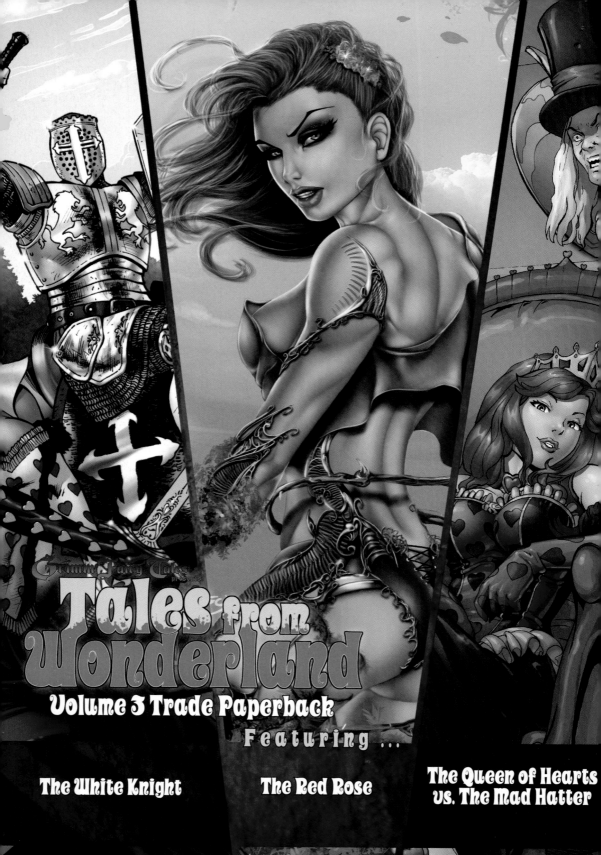

Grimm Fairy Tales presents

Tales from Wonderland

Volume 3 Trade Paperback

Featuring ...

The White Knight   **The Red Rose**   **The Queen of Hearts vs. The Mad Hatter**

On Sale Now!

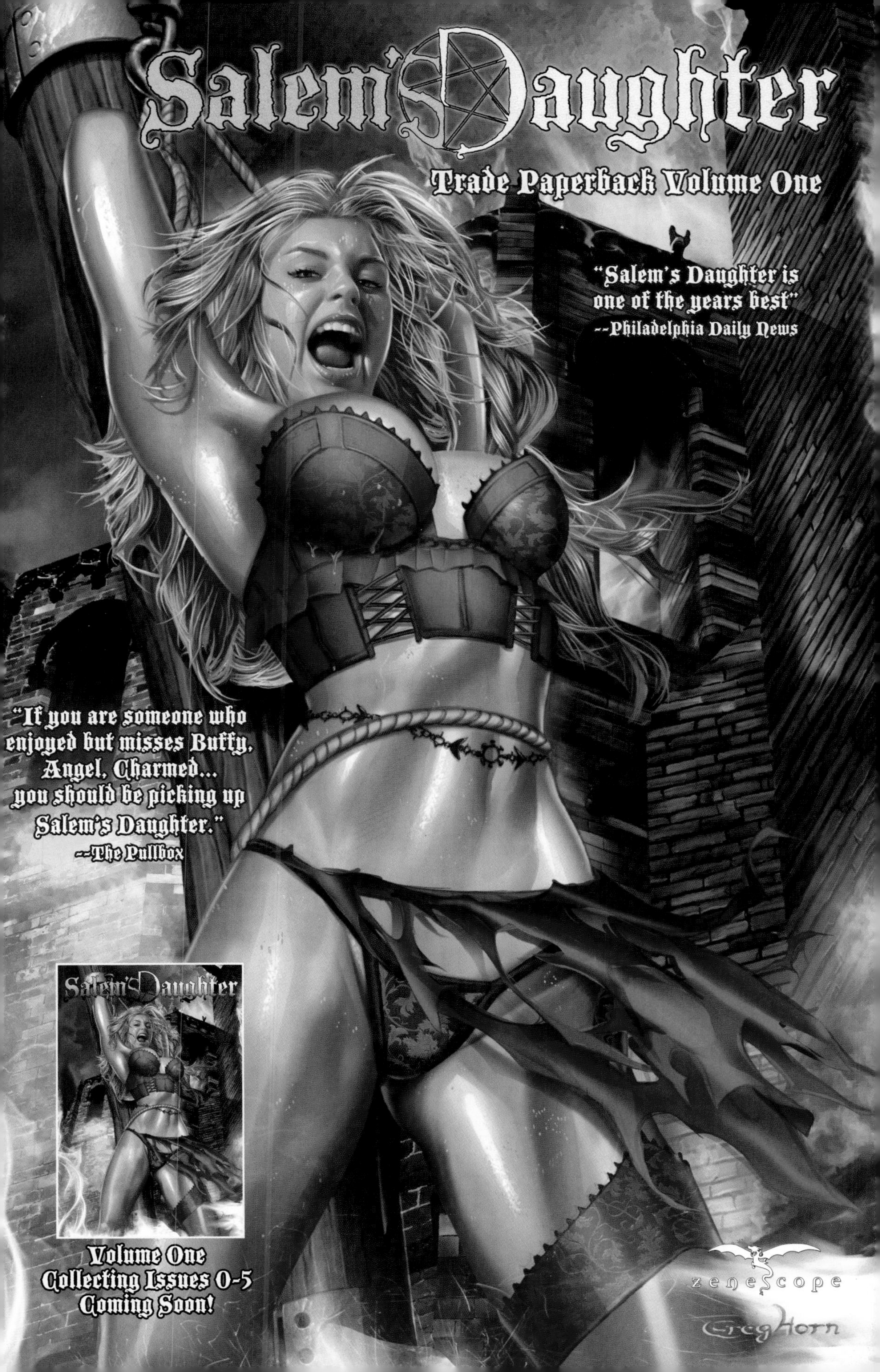
Salem's Daughter
Trade Paperback Volume One
"Salem's Daughter is one of the years best"
--Philadelphia Daily News
"If you are someone who enjoyed but misses Buffy, Angel, Charmed... you should be picking up Salem's Daughter."
--The Pullbox
Salem's Daughter
Volume One
Collecting Issues 0-5
Coming Soon!
zenescope
Greg Horn

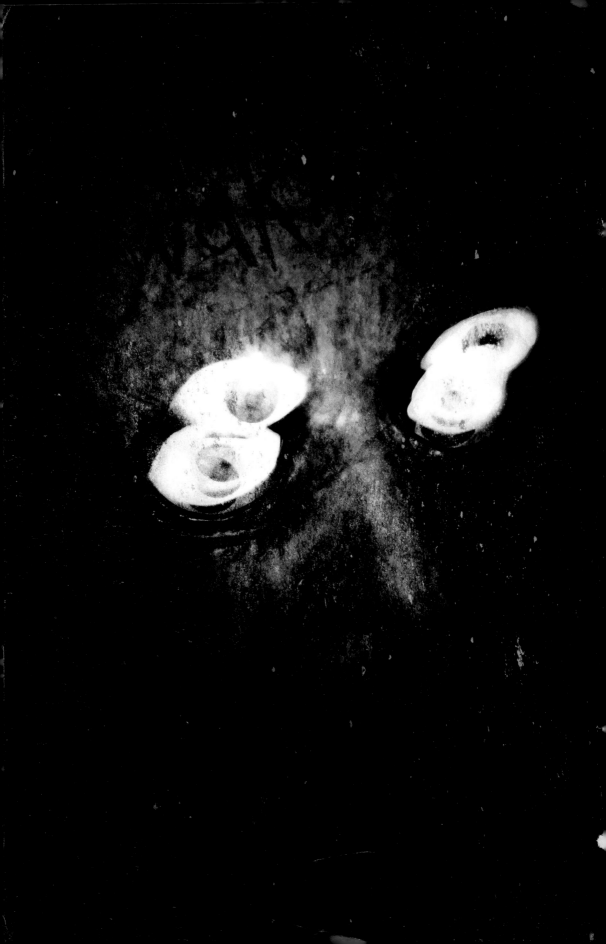